SOUTH PARK AND PHILOSOPHY

The Blackwell Philosophy and PopCulture Series
Series editor William Irwin

A spoonful of sugar helps the medicine go down, and a healthy help-ing of popular culture clears the cobwebs from Kant. Philosophy has had a public relations problem for a few centuries now. This series aims to change that, showing that philosophy is relevant to your life – and not just for answering the big questions like "To be or not to be?" but for answering the little questions: "To watch or not to watch *South Park*?" Thinking deeply about TV, movies, and music doesn't make you a "dummy" or a "complete idiot." In fact it might make you a philosopher, someone who believes the unexamined life is not worth living and the unexamined cartoon is not worth watching.

South Park and Philosophy
Edited by Robert Arp

Metallica and Philosophy
Edited by William Irwin

Family Guy and Philosophy
Edited by Jeremy Wisnewski

The Daily Show and Philosophy
Edited by Jason Holt

Lost and Philosophy
Edited by Sharon Kaye

24 and Philosophy
Edited by Richard Davis, Jennifer Hart Weed, and Ronald Weed

The Office and Philosophy
Edited by Jeremy Wisnewski

SOUTH PARK AND PHILOSOPHY

YOU KNOW, I LEARNED
SOMETHING TODAY

Edited by Robert Arp

Blackwell
Publishing

© 2007 by Blackwell Publishing Ltd

BLACKWELL PUBLISHING
350 Main Street, Malden, MA 02148-5020, USA
9600 Garsington Road, Oxford OX4 2DQ, UK
550 Swanston Street, Carlton, Victoria 3053, Australia

The right of Robert Arp to be identified as the Author of the Editorial Material in this Work has been asserted in accordance with the UK Copyright, Designs, and Patents Act 1988.

First published 2007 by Blackwell Publishing Ltd

1   2007

Library of Congress Cataloging-in-Publication Data

South Park and philosophy : you know, I learned something today / edited by
    Robert Arp.
        p. cm. — (The Blackwell philosophy and PopCulture series)
    Includes bibliographical references and index.
    ISBN-13: 978–1–4051–6160–2 (pbk. : alk. paper)
    ISBN-10: 1–4051–6160–4 (pbk. : alk. paper)
1. South Park (Television program)   I. Arp, Robert.

PN1992.77.S665S68 2006
791.45′72—dc22

                                                                    2006032843

A catalogue record for this title is available from the British Library.

Set in 10.5/13pt Sabon
by Graphicraft Limited, Hong Kong
Printed and bound in United States of America
by Sheridan Books, Inc., Chelsea, MI. USA

The publisher's policy is to use permanent paper from mills that operate a sustainable forestry policy, and which has been manufactured from pulp processed using acid-free and elementary chlorine-free practices. Furthermore, the publisher ensures that the text paper and cover board used have met acceptable environmental accreditation standards.

For further information on
Blackwell Publishing, visit our website:
www.blackwellpublishing.com

CONTENTS

CONTENTS

THE SUPER BEST CONTRIBUTORS

Robert Arp is an Assistant Professor of Philosophy at Southwest Minnesota State University, and has authored numerous articles in philosophy of mind, philosophy of biology, modern philosophy, and pop culture. His book *Scenario Visualization: An Evolutionary Account of Creative Problem Solving* is forthcoming. He is also working on another book, titled *An Integrated Approach to the Philosophy of Mind*. Besides editing this book, he is co-editing *Contemporary Debates in Philosophy of Biology* with Francisco Ayala (Blackwell Publishers) and *The Ashgate Companion to Contemporary Philosophy of Biology* with George Terzis. He thinks philosophy is good, but drugs are bad, m'kay.

Shai Biderman is a PhD candidate in Philosophy at Boston University. His primary research interests are contemporary continental philosophy, philosophy of literature and film, existentialism, and German philosophy. His recent publications include several papers on reasonability, revenge, and determinism, as well as writings on Kafka, Nietzsche, and Heidegger. He currently suffers from paranoia and insomnia, and is wary of the underpants gnomes.

Per F. Broman is an Assistant Professor of Music Theory at Bowling Green State University. He writes about twentieth-century music and aesthetics and is the author of *"Back to the Future": Towards an Aesthetic Theory of Bengt Hambræus*. Also, he has contributed to books and journals including *New Music in the Nordic Countries*, *Woody Allen and Philosophy*, *Perspectives of New Music*, *College*

Music Symposium, and *Journal of Popular Music Studies*. He can't be a non-conformist if he doesn't drink coffee.

Scott Calef is Associate Professor and Chair of the philosophy department at Ohio Wesleyan University. In addition to authoring articles on ancient philosophy, applied ethics, political philosophy, metaphysics, and the philosophy of religion, he has contributed to *The Beatles and Philosophy*, *Hitchcock and Philosophy* and *Metallica and Philosophy*. He met his wife at Raisins and knows what he wants to ask God in the year 4000.

Paul A. Cantor is Clifton Waller Barrett Professor of English at the University of Virginia. His award-winning essay on *The Simpsons*, "Atomistic Politics and the Nuclear Family," has been widely reprinted and translated into Russian, Spanish, and Australian. His book *Gilligan Unbound: Pop Culture in the Age of Globalization* was named one of the best non-fiction books of 2001 by the *LA Times*. Recently uncovered documents have shown, and DNA tests have confirmed, that he was switched at birth with Eric Cartman; he and his heirs are looking forward to all the residuals – and Cheesypoofs – they will now be collecting.

David Valleau Curtis is a Professor of Communications at Blackburn College and has authored a number of articles on the media and society. He is particularly interested in the Internet, new media, and e-commerce. He has completed a draft of a book on communications theorists Marshall McLuhan and Walter Ong called *The Priest and the Prophet* and is also working on a book about e-commerce profiling with Dr. Christian Vermehren, a European Internet entrepreneur. Dr. Curtis also enjoys biking, walking his dog, Penn State sports, and being exploited by ruthless Native Americans at the Three Feathers Indian Casino near South Park, Colorado.

William J. Devlin is a PhD candidate in Philosophy at Boston University, and a visiting instructor at Bridgewater State College and the University of Wyoming. His publications include papers on time travel, Friedrich Nietzsche, personal identity, and *Family Guy*. While his primary areas of research are philosophy of science, truth theories, Nietzsche, and existentialism, his life ambition is to join Tugger, makin' music, singin' songs, and fightin' round the world.

Jeffrey Dueck is a Lecturer at Buffalo State College and has written and spoken on numerous issues in American philosophy, epistemology, ethics, and religion. Every time he thinks of something clever, he finds out *The Simpsons* already did it.

Gerald J. Erion is an Assistant Professor of Philosophy at Medaille College, where his research includes work in ethics, philosophy of mind, and the teaching of philosophy. While traveling home from a recent academic conference he fell from a burning bridge, tumbled down a rocky cliff, and was impaled on a tree branch, then attacked by a mountain lion, shot by the Super Adventure Club, and mauled by a grizzly bear.

Karin Fry is an Assistant Professor of Philosophy at the University of Wisconsin, Stevens Point. She has published several articles in continental philosophy, aesthetics, and feminism. She hopes to have her own theme park some day so that she can ride the roller coaster all by herself.

John Scott Gray is an Assistant Professor of Humanities at Ferris State University in Big Rapids, Michigan. His main areas of research are political and social philosophy, philosophy of sex and gender, and applied ethics. He is the author of a number of articles, including articles related to same-sex marriage in the *South African Journal of Philosophy* and the *Review Journal of Political Philosophy*. He also does not tolerate intolerance.

Jacob M. Held is an Assistant Professor of Philosophy in the Department of Philosophy and Religion at the University of Central Arkansas. His research interests include political and social philosophy, Marx, and philosophy of law. He is co-editor of *James Bond and Philosophy*. He has published in several scholarly journals, including *Vera Lex* and the *Journal of the British Society for Phenomenology*, and has written on topics ranging from punishment to postmodernism. Although raised Catholic, his experiences aboard the Catholic Boat have led him to be wary of priests, religion, and cruises.

Henry Jacoby teaches philosophy at East Carolina University. He has published mostly in philosophy of mind. His current interests include Russell's solution to the mind-body problem and the nature of moral perception. He would never kill somebody – not unless they pissed him off.

Dale Jacquette is Professor of Philosophy at the Pennsylvania State University. He resides in the quiet, little, pissant, podunk, redneck mountain town of State College, PA (you bastards!), where he teaches logic, philosophy of mind, and a slate of mostly dead Greek, German, and Austrian thinkers. When he is not watching cartoons and wolfing down Cheesypoofs, he serves as spiritual advisor to La Resistance ('til only the righteous stand). He recently published "Zombie Gladiators" in *The Undead and Philosophy: Chicken Soup for the Soulless.*

Randall M. Jensen is an Associate Professor of Philosophy at Northwestern College in Orange City, Iowa. His philosophical interests include ethics, ancient Greek philosophy, and philosophy of religion. He is deathly afraid of wearing an orange parka.

David Kyle Johnson received his PhD in Philosophy from the University of Oklahoma and is currently a Visiting Assistant Professor of Philosophy at King's College in Wilkes-Barre PA. His philosophical specializations include religion, logic, and metaphysics. He teaches a course on Pop Culture and Philosophy (which incorporates a large amount of *South Park*) and will also have an article in the upcoming *Family Guy and Philosophy* volume. Kyle dedicates his chapter to the memory of Mitch Conner, the run of the mill con-man that cashed in his last chips impersonating Jennifer Lopez.

David R. Koepsell is a Research Assistant Professor at SUNY Buffalo and coordinates the Graduate Research Ethics program there. He is also on the Executive Committee of the Center for Inquiry and presently a Visiting Scholar at Yale University's Interdisciplinary Center for Bioethics. He is the author of *The Ontology of Cyberspace* and numerous scholarly articles in ethics, ontology, humanism, and law. Students who have seen his office know him and his dog, Buttercup (nicknamed Butters), as Professor Chaos and General Disarray.

Cynthia McWilliams is an Assistant Professor and Program Coordinator of Philosophy at the University of Texas – Pan American. She has published in the areas of healthcare ethics, professional ethics, and pedagogy and, oh my God, she killed Kenny! You bastard!

Ellen Miller is an Associate Professor of Philosophy at Rowan University. She has published articles on ethics, philosophy of art, and feminist philosophy. Her book *Releasing Philosophy, Thinking Art: A Bodily Hermeneutic of Sylvia Plath's Poetry* is forthcoming. She is also a faculty member in the Women's Studies and Honors programs. She loves teaching philosophy, and bakes a mean apple pie.

Kevin J. Murtagh is an Adjunct Lecturer in Philosophy at John Jay College of Criminal Justice and a PhD candidate at the Graduate Center of the City University of New York. He has written the entry on "Punishment" for *The Internet Encyclopedia of Philosophy*, and has published an article entitled "Disenfranchising Felons" with John Kleinig. His dissertation is on cruel, inhuman, and degrading punishment. He was briefly a member of Faith + 1, but he left the band because of "creative differences" with Eric Cartman.

Mark D. White is Associate Professor in the Department of Political Science, Economics, and Philosophy at the College of Staten Island in New York City, where he teaches courses combining economics, philosophy, and law. He co-edited the book *Economics and the Mind* and has written many articles and book chapters on economics and philosophy. He is currently circulating an online petition for a Mr. Hankey spin-off – starring Tom Cruise, of course.

William W. Young III is Assistant Professor of Humanities at Endicott College in Beverly, Massachusetts. He teaches religion and philosophy, and his research focuses primarily on the place of friendship in philosophical and religious thought. He has published articles in *Modern Theology*, *Journal of Religion*, and *Literature and Theology*, as well as his first book, *The Politics of Praise*. He has also contributed to *Baseball and Philosophy*, *Movies and the Meaning of Life*, and *Poker and Philosophy*. His favorite snack is Cheesypoofs, and in his spare time he helps Al Gore hunt for ManBearPig.

Catherine Yu is finishing her dissertation at the University of Washington. Her primary research interests are in ethics, social philosophy, and moral psychology. She will be collaborating with a team of manatees working with idea balls for her next paper.

SUCKING BALLS AND FUCKING OFF

An Introduction to the Bothersome *South Park and Philosophy*

Robert Arp

South Park bothers me. I question whether it's morally appropriate to laugh at the nurse with the dead fetus attached to her head, or the fact that Scott Tenorman has just been fed his own parents, or that Mr. Garrison's parents did *not* molest him when, apparently, they should have. And I wonder if cartoon characters telling each other to "suck my balls" or "fuck off" is something that should be censored for the simple fact that some impressionable kid might be watching.

Thankfully, *South Park* bothers other people even more. Unafraid to lampoon the extremist fanatics associated with *any* social, political, ethical, economic, and religious views, *South Park* is the most important series on TV. The fact of the matter is that people who think they have the "corner on truth" need to be taken down a peg. After all, people's perceptions of the truth are just that, people's perceptions, and it's OK to laugh at them. As Trey Parker said in an interview with Charlie Rose, "What we say with the show is not anything new, but I think it is something that is great to put out there. It is that the people screaming on this side and the people screaming on that side are the same people, and it's OK to be someone in the middle, laughing at both of them." Part of being a philosopher means never holding any belief as *so* sacred that we are never, ever willing to doubt it – or laugh at it. In other words, we need a healthy dose of skepticism about any belief, and this is one of the important lessons that *South Park*, along with philosophy, teaches us.

Are you bothered by *South Park*? More importantly, are you bothered by the *real life* crazy-assed people, events, and situations that *South Park* is courageous enough to talk about? I have to admit, I've been turned off by certain episodes because of the seeming insensitivity shown to a person or group. But I must also admit that there is value in shocking people in order to get them to start thinking.

You see *South Park*, just like philosophy, is misunderstood. People think that *South Park* is all about shock value for the sake of shock value in the same way they think philosophy is all about thinking about useless ideas for the sake of thinking about useless ideas! Nothing could be further from the truth. Believe it or not, the goal of both *South Park* and philosophy is to discover truth and make the world a better place in which to live. The difference is that philosophy usually takes a less shocking approach in getting people to think critically about themselves, their beliefs, and reality. Just like Stan, the philosophers in this book ask if Big Gay Al should be allowed to get married, whether there could be a god in the face of so much Cartmanland-type evil, and whether there really is a decent choice between a douche or a turd in a presidential election. And just like Kyle, the philosophers in this book question whether they exist as a dream in someone else's mind, if they have an obligation to obey unjust laws in a society, and whether certain forms of human expression should be censored.

The authors in this book are bothered by *South Park* in a good way. The show has caused them to philosophically reflect on various characters and events in that pissant white-bread mountain town. By the time you're through reading this book you should have a deeper appreciation for both *South Park* and for philosophy. Our hope is that you will have indeed "learned something today." If not, suck my balls! Hey, at least I didn't tell you to fuck off. So, let's go on down to the bothersome *South Park and Philosophy* and meet some philosophical friends of mine.

PART ONE

TAKING *SOUTH PARK* SERIOUSLY . . . M'KAY

1

FLATULENCE AND PHILOSOPHY

A Lot of Hot Air, or the Corruption of Youth?

William W. Young III

The "Danger" of *South Park*

In the episode "Death," Kyle's mother leads a boycott of the boys' favorite cartoon show – *Terrance and Philip* – because of its continuous farting, name-calling, and general "potty humor." While the parents are up in arms over this "moral" issue, the boys wrestle with the problem of euthanasia for Stan's grandfather, something none of the parents will discuss with them. "Death" brings together many of the central issues that have made *South Park* successful and controversial: vulgarity, the misplaced moral concerns of American culture, the discussion of controversial moral topics, and the criticism that *South Park* itself is a "disgusting" show. Since "Death" the criticism of the show has only grown – getting even bigger than Cartman's fat ass – drawing fire for its obscene language, criticisms of religion, and emphasis upon freedom of speech.

Like the parents protesting *The Terrance and Philip Show*, critics of *South Park* make claims that are strikingly similar to those that have been leveled against Western philosophy since its beginnings. It mocks religious beliefs, leads younger folks to question accepted authority and values, and corrupts our children and culture. The "it" in the previous sentence refers to *South Park*, but in fact, the same criticisms formed the basis for Socrates' (470–399 BCE) trial and

5

execution in Athens, Greece in 399 BCE.[1] So in this chapter we'll explore the heretical possibility that people perceive *South Park* as dangerous precisely because it is a form of philosophy. The "danger" that *South Park* poses has to do with its depiction of dialogue and free thinking. In the end we will have learned something: like Socrates, *South Park* harms no one. Philosophy and *South Park* actually instruct people and provide them with the intellectual tools they need to become wise, free, and good.

Oh My God! They Killed Socrates! You Bastards!

In Plato's (427–327 BCE) *Apology*, Socrates defends himself against two charges: (1) impiety (false teachings about the gods, possibly that they don't exist) and (2) corrupting the youth of Athens. In reality, Socrates probably had as much chance of winning his case as Chef did against Johnny Cochran's "Chewbacca" defense! What is most important about Socrates' defense, however, is not so much what he says as *how* he says it. He defends himself by questioning his accuser, Meletus, leading him through a process of reasoning. For example, Socrates refutes the charge of corrupting the youth as follows:

Socrates: You say you have discovered the one who corrupts them, namely me, and you bring me here and accuse me to the jury . . . All the Athenians, it seems, make the young into fine good men, except me, and I alone corrupt them. Is that what you mean?
Meletus: That is most definitely what I mean.
Socrates: You condemn me to a great misfortune. Tell me: does this also apply to horses do you think? That all men improve them and one individual corrupts them? Or is quite the contrary true, one individual is able to improve them, or very few, namely the horse

---

[1] Plato, *Apology*, in *Five Dialogues: Euthyphro, Apology, Crito, Meno, Phaedo*, trans. by G.M.A. Grube (Indianapolis: Hackett Publishing, 1981). Hereafter noted as (*Apology*, p. "x") in the text. Also see Xenophon, *Recollections of Socrates, and Socrates' Defense Before the Jury*, trans. by Anna Benjamin (Indianapolis: Bobbs-Merrill, 1965).

breeders, whereas the majority, if they have horses and use them, corrupt them? Is that not the case, Meletus, both with horses and all other animals? . . . It would be a happy state of affairs if only one person corrupted our youth, while the others improved them. You have made it sufficiently obvious, Meletus, that you have never had any concern for our youth; you show your indifference clearly; that you have given no thought to the subjects about which you bring me to trial. (*Apology*, p. 30)

Through the analogy with horse training, Socrates shows how illogical the accusations against him really are. Just as a majority of people would injure horses by training them, and only a few good trainers improve them, so too it is likely that a few teachers improve the virtue of the youth, while many others corrupt them. Socrates argues, further, that he is in fact the one who is teaching Athens' youth what virtue involves, while many others – including the idiots sitting before him – corrupt them. (As you can imagine, this did not go over well with the jury.)

While showing that the accusations are groundless, this "apology" – a word that also can mean *defense* – demonstrates why Socrates got a death sentence of hemlock. Socrates is famous for saying "I know that I don't know" and, actually, this is a wise insight. For Socrates, philosophy was the love and pursuit of wisdom, and this required questioning others to find out what they do or don't know. Unfortunately, people often believe they are wiser than they are. By questioning them, Socrates would show them that they don't know what they believe they know: "I go around seeking out anyone, citizen or stranger, whom I think wise. Then if I do not think he is, I come to the assistance of the god and show him that he is not wise" (*Apology*, pp. 28–9). What makes Socrates wise is his recognition of his own ignorance, through continuous questioning of himself and others. Many powerful people in Athens saw him as dangerous because his questioning and debate would undermine their bases for power.

In the town of South Park, people in positions of power believe they are teaching the children wisdom and virtue. However, as in Athens, the many people of South Park seem to make the children worse, not better. For example, Mr. Garrison "teaches" the children life lessons from re-runs of *Barnaby Jones*, Mrs. Broflovski always goes to crazy extremes with her "moral" outrage, Uncle Jim and Ned teach the boys to kill harmless bunnies and squirrels in "self-defense," and the mayor panders shamelessly to voters. None of the townsfolk really *talk* to the children, except Chef, who teaches the art of making sweet, sweet love to a woman. Blindly following the crowd, from protesting *The Terrance and Philip Show* to boycotting Harbucks, to – yes – burying their heads in the sand to avoid watching *Family Guy*, the parents of South Park corrupt the children far more than a television show ever could. Like the Athenians, the adults don't know as much as they believe they know. Ultimately, if television does corrupt them, it does so because they are left to it by their parents, with no one to educate them about what they are seeing. Of course, there are also cases where parents and people in powerful positions *do* try to discuss issues and ideas with the children. These discussions, though, support the same point, as the adult usually sounds like a bumbling idiot.

Cartman Gets a Banal Probe

One of the most significant philosophical reflections on evil in the twentieth century is Hannah Arendt's *Eichmann in Jerusalem: A Report on the Banality of Evil*, a study of the trial of Adolf Eichmann for his role in the deportations of millions of European Jews to concentration camps during the Jewish Holocaust. Eichmann just followed the law of the land, whatever it happened to be, and when Hitler was making the laws, Eichmann simply carried them out.[2] In the words of Arendt, Eichmann was an unreflective person, unable to think for himself and *definitely* unable "to think from the standpoint of somebody else" (Arendt, p. 49). What was really monstrous about Eichmann was not his vicious cruelty, but rather the way that he was not that different from so many Germans who, under Hitler, accepted and supported laws that were obviously evil and believed that they were doing what was right. Eichmann's banality – the fact that there is nothing distinctive or exceptional about him – is *precisely* what makes him evil. He was one of the "crowd" who *didn't* walk to the

---

[2] Hannah Arendt, *Eichmann in Jerusalem: A Report on the Banality of Evil* (New York: Viking Press, 1964), pp. 135–50. Hereafter cited as (Arendt, p. "x") in the text.

beat of a different drummer and *didn't* rock the boat. He embodied complicit citizenship under a dictatorship, which speaks *for* its subjects and, thus, cuts off their reflective and critical thought.

Thoughtlessness leads to evil, as Arendt says, because it doesn't let us see things from others' perspectives. By blindly following orders, Eichmann didn't think about what his actions were doing to others, or even what they were doing to himself. By saying he was "following the law" and "doing his duty," he ignored how his actions sent millions to their deaths and, despite his protests, made him a murderer. Thinking, according to Arendt, requires taking another's standpoint, reflecting on how you might be harming others, and asking if you can live with what you are doing.

While the adults in South Park blindly follow the latest fad, or what they are told, it is the children who bring out the absurdity and potential harm that lurks in such thoughtlessness. To be more accurate, it's usually Kyle or Stan who are the reflective ones, while Cartman's mind is as empty as the Cheesypoofs he devours daily. He is often sadistic, cruel, and evil. Like Eichmann, Cartman is probably evil because, when it comes to "authorita," he lacks reflection and critical analysis. (And like Eichmann, he has a Nazi uniform that he has sported on occasion.) Cartman sings the Cheesypoofs song so well because all he can do is imitate what he hears on television. His evil is an imitation of the evil characters of our culture, as prepackaged as his afternoon snacks. Cartman consumes evil and imitates it as blindly and thoughtlessly as Eichmann. Most importantly, because of this thoughtlessness, Cartman is unable to see things from anyone else's viewpoint (as illustrated most clearly in his manipulation of his mother). As Arendt says, such thoughtlessness is precisely what allows evil to emerge in modern society, and Cartman's mindless consumption is as thoughtless as it gets.

Friendship Kicks Ass!
The Dialogues of Kyle and Stan

Part of what makes *South Park* philosophically interesting is the contrast between Cartman's evil stupidity and the non-conformist, reflective virtue of Kyle and Stan. Philosophers like Plato and

Aristotle (384–322 BCE) have noted the importance of how critical reflection leads to harmony or balance and helps us to avoid extremes. After all, the "extremes" of thinking and acting often lead to mistaken beliefs and harmful behavior. In fact, following Plato's lead, Aristotle put forward the idea that *virtue* is concerned with striking a balance or hitting the mark between two extreme viewpoints, ideas, beliefs, emotions, or actions.[3] *South Park* addresses moral issues through a discussion and criticism of established "moral" positions, both conservative and liberal, which are found to be inadequate. Kyle and Stan come to a virtuous position, in part, by negotiating and listening to these views before reaching their own conclusion through questioning and reason. Frequently, their conclusion recognizes that there is some truth to each position, but that its limited perspective is still dangerous. For example, it's true that hybrid cars are more environmentally responsible than gas-guzzling SUVs. But when an air of moral superiority clouds one's judgment, this "smug cloud" creates hostility and pollutes society in other ways.

How Stan and Kyle reach their conclusions is more significant than the conclusions themselves. Think of how they discuss whether it's wrong to kill Stan's grandpa, who wants to die. They, like Socrates, question those around them, seeking to know if the people are as wise as they believe. Their parents, Mr. Garrison, and Jesus won't discuss or touch this issue "with a 60-foot pole." What Kyle and Stan ultimately realize – with the help of Stan's great-great-grandfather's ghost – is that they shouldn't kill his grandfather because the action would change and harm them. As it turns out, Stan's grandfather is wrong in asking them to do this vicious action. Note that the boys reach this conclusion through living with each other, recognizing their differences, and engaging in debate. Stan and Kyle – unlike Eichmann and Cartman – learn to see things from others' perspectives, through their ongoing conversation.

In the *Apology* Socrates makes the claim that a good person cannot be harmed by the actions of others. This seems false. After all, aside from being a cartoon character, what could prevent Cartman from punching out the Dalai Lama? But what Socrates means by "good" is

---

[3] See Plato, *The Republic of Plato*, trans. by David Bloom (New York: Basic Books, 1991); Aristotle, *Nicomachean Ethics*, trans. by Terence Irwin (Indianapolis: Hackett Publishing, 1999).

something different than we often realize. Goodness means reflectively thinking about one's actions and *being able to live with what one has done*. Despite any *physical* harm – torture, imprisonment, exile, or death – that may come that person's way, no one could "hurt" a virtuous person by making them *do* something bad. Cartman, for example, couldn't make the Dalai Lama punch *him*. Socrates, for his part, refused to execute an innocent person, or to try generals for "crimes" beyond the laws of the city. And, significantly, Socrates would rather die than give up the thinking and questioning that he sees as central to philosophy:

> Perhaps someone might say: But Socrates, if you leave us will you not be able to live quietly, without talking? Now this is the most difficult point on which to convince some of you. If I say that it is impossible for me to keep quiet because that means disobeying the god, you will not believe me . . . On the other hand, if I say that it is the greatest good for a man to discuss virtue every day and those other things about which you hear me conversing and testing myself and others, for the unexamined life is not worth living for man, you will believe me even less. (*Apology*, p. 41)

Arendt has a similar conception of goodness. Ethics, for those (unlike Eichmann) who resisted the Nazis, was being able to look back on one's life without shame, rather than adhering to a set of rules. Her description deserves quoting:

> Their criterion [for goodness], I think, was a different one; they asked themselves to what extent they would still be able to live in peace with themselves after having committed certain deeds; and they decided that it would be better to do nothing, not because the world would then be changed for the better, but simply because only on this condition could they go on living with themselves at all. Hence, they also chose to die when they were forced to participate. To put it crudely, they refused to murder . . . because they were unwilling to live together with a murderer – themselves. The precondition for this kind of judging is not a highly developed intelligence or sophistication in moral matters, but rather the disposition to live together explicitly with oneself, to have intercourse with oneself, that is, to be engaged in that silent dialogue between me and myself which, since Socrates and Plato, we usually call thinking.[4]

---

[4] Hannah Arendt, "Personal Responsibility Under Dictatorship," in *Responsibility and Judgment* (New York: Schocken, 2003), pp. 40–1.

Thinking, for Arendt, is a twofold process: it involves seeing things through another's eyes, in dialogue and reflection, as well as asking what you can live with for yourself. It is, then, both an internal and an external dialogue, and it is only through this dialogue that critical reflection and goodness become possible. Whereas Eichmann and Cartman do not critically reflect upon the consequences of actions, nor put themselves in another's shoes, thoughtful dialogue makes us attentive to others around us, lets us live with them, and helps us attend to our own goodness. Such dialogue allows us to live with ourselves – even when, like Socrates or those who resisted the Nazis, this means we must die.

Of course, in *South Park* there is no Socrates to teach philosophy or help us engage in dialogue. Surrounded by ignorance and violence, the boys are on their own. While the four are friends, *South Park* makes a compelling point about philosophy and ethics through the particulars of the friendship of Kyle and Stan. For instance, in "Spooky Fish," where the "evil" Cartman (who is good) arrives from a parallel universe, an evil Kyle and Stan arrive *together*. Their friendship – thinking from one another's perspective – is what helps them to be good, both for themselves and for others. In Arendt's words, to live well is to "be plural," so that the good life is never simply one's own.[5] This probably is why Plato wrote about important philosophical issues in a dialogue format, so that it becomes clear that debate and discussion of ideas are essential to any intellectual and moral growth.

For all their faults, Kyle and Stan still debate and discuss whether certain actions are wrong. On his own, Stan will sometimes just go along with the crowd (an important exception is his refusal to kill). Through their conversations they learn goodness and engage in the "thinking" Arendt describes. Friendship, then, helps us to examine our lives. In the episode "Prehistoric Ice Man" Larry says that "living is about sharing our ups and downs with our friends," and when we fail to do this we aren't really living at all. If thinking and goodness only arise through real dialogue with others – through critically questioning and examining *our own* views – then we need more friendships like the one Kyle and Stan share.

[5] Arendt, "Some Questions of Moral Philosophy," in *Responsibility and Judgment*, pp. 96–7.

An Apology for *South Park*:
Getting in Touch with Your Inner Cartman

If friendships help us to critically examine the lives that we lead, then perhaps it's no accident that the critical voice of *South Park* has been created by two friends – Trey Parker and Matt Stone. In the *Apology* Socrates likens himself to a gadfly, an annoying pest that goes around "stinging" people with his challenging questions and critical reflections so as to keep them intellectually awake and on their toes. *South Park*, too, serves as a gadfly, trying to wake American culture from its thoughtlessness and ignorance. The show generates discussion and debate and leads many people into discussions of ethical issues that would otherwise be passed over in silence. For a show that supposedly corrupts, it has far more of a focus on religion, ethics, and democracy than its critics would like to admit. But of course we could still ask if the *way* that *South Park* presents these issues is really necessary. For example, is it philosophically wise and necessary to use the word *shit* 163 times in one show? Or have so much farting, vomiting, and violence? What philosophical goal can such vulgarity serve?

The vulgarity and crudeness of *South Park* are often defended on the grounds of free speech. However, a different issue is also in play. *South Park* often says what is not socially or morally acceptable to say – what, in Freudian terms, must be repressed. According to Freud, our thoughts and actions are shaped by what he calls "drives," examples of which include emotions, desires, and energy that can be aggressive, hostile, and consumptive. (Freud would have a field day with Cartman's twisted little mind, on this score.) These drives are part of our embodied being, yet, since they are dangerous and often violent, we try to control or even silence them. This control is a form of repression, but it can often have unintended consequences. Repression of a drive can lead to other sorts of unconscious, violent behavior, and such suppressed wishes form the content of dreams, our "unconscious" life.[6] Repression, as a form of internal censorship, redirects but does not diminish our aggression. In spite of our intentions, this

---

[6] See Sigmund Freud, *The Interpretation of Dreams* (New York: Avon Books, 1965), pp. 156–66.

unconscious aggression often shapes who we are, how we think, and what we do.

What Freud discovered with psychoanalysis was that talking out and interpreting our dreams may serve as a way to address this repression and its associated violence. When we talk these ideas and feelings out, the repression is broken and, through the realization, we can come to terms with the desire and shape it through thinking. Representing desires lets them be *ex*pressed, and this helps us to integrate them into the structure of our lives.[7] By bringing to light what had been unconscious, dream-interpretation lets us think through these aspects of ourselves.

Freud thought that jokes work much like dreams. When one person tells a joke, its spontaneous and unexpected word-form breaks through another person's repression. Laughter is a "release of energy" that has been blocked, because we have tried to repress the wish or drive; this is why many jokes have a vulgar or obscene dimension. As Freud points out, the one who supplies it has to deny it – jokes only really work when the person telling them doesn't laugh, so that the surprise can make others laugh.[8] There is pleasure in laughing at the joke, and in telling it, as well as pleasure in freeing others from their repression.

Through its vulgarity, *South Park* verbalizes the drives and desires that we often repress; and, it allows us to laugh so as to reveal these inhibitions. This is what makes the show's crudeness essential. By showing us "Token" or the conjoined fetus nurse, or saying *shit* over and over, it brings out the aggression and desire that we feel we cannot express. And, for things that really *shouldn't* be said, Kenny says them in a muffled way, and the other boys comment on it. By verbalizing these drives, the show lets us begin to think these through – it makes it possible to analyze them, and thereby distance ourselves from them. For instance, many episodes address how outsiders are berated and subjected to racist or xenophobic slander. However, by working through these statements, the show argues that in many cases, such slander is used among friends as well – and that such

---

[7] For more on this issue, see Jonathan Lear, *Love and Its Place in Nature: A Philosophical Interpretation of Freudian Psychoanalysis* (New York: Farrar, Strauss, and Giroux, 1990).

[8] Freud, *Wit and Its Relation to the Unconscious*, trans. by A.A. Brill (New York: Dover, 1993), pp. 261–73.

verbal sparring, when so understood, need not lead to violence or exclusion. It doesn't justify such speech, but it does create a space in which the hostility can be interpreted and analyzed.

Likewise, one can analyze all of the farting on *Terrance and Philip*. At least two interpretations of this show-within-the-show are possible. First, there is the issue of why the boys love such a stupid show so much. It's not that they wish they could fart all the time. Rather, when they fart, Terrance and Philip do what is forbidden: they transgress the parents' social prohibition. This appeals to the boys, because they wish they too could be free from parental control and regulation.

Second, regular viewers (mostly my students) have noted that *Terrance and Philip* is self-referential, a way for *South Park* to comment on itself. The opening of *South Park* tells us that, like *Terrance and Philip*, the show has no redeeming value and should be watched by no one. The stupidity and vulgarity of the cartoon is better understood, however, if we look beyond *South Park*. Is *Terrance and Philip* really more vapid, crude, and pointless than *Jerry Springer* or *Wife Swap*? Is it more mindless than *Fox News*, *The 700 Club*, or *Law and Order*? The answer is no. When we see Kyle, Cartman, Kenny, and Stan watching *The Terrance and Philip Show*, it shows us that television fulfills our wish for mindlessness. What offends the parents in South Park, and the critics of *South Park*, is not that the show is vulgar and pointless, but that it highlights the mindlessness of television in general.

What both of these interpretations show is that there are multiple levels of censorship that need to be questioned. On the one hand, there is the censorship that simply looks at vulgarity, and decides what can and cannot be seen, based upon social norms. *South Park* clearly questions this sort of censorship, saying so often what cannot be said and challenging social forms of repression. But, if part of *South Park*'s message is the need for thinking, then it also questions how television, by fulfilling our wish for mindlessness, supposedly represses thinking. Of course, such mindlessness can't simply be blamed on one's parents, or television corporations, or two doofusses from Colorado who can't draw straight. Like the mindless Athenians who were to blame for their own ignorance, or Eichmann's responsibility when he thought he was just obeying the law, the mindlessness that prevents thinking is ultimately our own doing. Like Socrates, perhaps *South Park* – and Kyle and Stan more specifically – presents us with a way to think about what *we think* we really know, and through reflection move beyond our mindlessness.

The Talking Cure for Our Culture

By ceaselessly testing the limits of our culture's tolerance, *South Park* asks us to examine the things we think we know, why certain words and actions are prohibited, what we desire, and what we are teaching our children. Through its provocation, it asks us to think about what is truly harmful, and what issues we really should be outraged about. Breaking the silence of our culture's repressions could be the starting point for a Socratic dialogue that helps us to think, analyze our desires and aggression, and become good. If we take the opportunity to discuss the show, why it is funny, and what it tells us about our culture and our own desires, then the show need not be mindless, vulgar, or corrupting, but rather a path to thinking that helps us to live with one another, and with ourselves.

2

IS IT OKAY TO LAUGH
AT *SOUTH PARK*?

Catherine Yu

Recall That It Is Cartman's Ten-Year-Old Hand That Ben Has Sex With After All

In the episode "Fatbutt and Pancake Head," Eric Cartman wins $20 from the Latino Endowment Council for his presentation on the role of Latinos in the arts. Far from giving a thoughtful, insightful presentation, Cartman simply performs a ventriloquist act, using his hand as a puppet of Jennifer Lopez. The "Hennifer Lopez" puppet sings about running for the border, burritos, and taco-flavored kisses. Soon after, the real Jennifer Lopez – Ben Affleck in tow – shows up in South Park and has a showdown with the puppet Jennifer. Ben falls in love with Cartman's puppet Jennifer, and the adventure ends with Lopez's arrest, an identity thief's confession, and a puppet's suicide.

"Fatbutt and Pancake Head" may be one of the more ethically objectionable *South Park* episodes. Puppet Jennifer's distorted accent and seemingly insatiable appetite for tacos is racially insensitive, if not downright racist. The context in which Cartman increasingly loses control of his hand's alter ego makes light of a psychotic disorder that should be no laughing matter. And Ben and puppet Jennifer's love affair takes a truly disturbing turn when one recalls that it is Cartman's ten-year-old hand that Ben has sex with after all. Even so, one can barely suppress a grin as one thinks of all of these shenanigans.

And so it is with much of *South Park*, as we laugh and snicker at everything that is wrong and twisted in South Park, Colorado. But could it be morally wrong to laugh? Is there something wrong with finding amusement in the way that puppet Jennifer says her own name or in the many ways that poor Kenny gets maimed and killed? Might there be something morally perverse about laughing at cripple fights and Starvin' Marvin's starving family? Or, is it all just moral prudishness to even suggest that it might be so?

This chapter will take a brief look at the ethics of amusement and will provide an answer to the question: Is it okay to laugh at *South Park*?

Child Abduction Is Not Funny, You Dick!

There are two issues that make up the ethics of amusement: one is the aesthetic question, which has to do with when it is *fitting* to laugh at something, while the other is the ethical question, which has to do with when it is *morally wrong* to laugh at something. These are independent evaluations, but the distinction gets muddled very quickly because we use phrases like "Don't laugh, it's not funny!" or "How can you think that's funny?" When we say such things we typically run the two questions together, confusing and conflating the distinction. So, the first task is to separate these two types of evaluation.

Consider the title of this section, "Child Abduction Is Not Funny, You Dick!", which is also the title of a *South Park* episode. This title can mean that child abduction doesn't have the features that something must have in order to be funny. In which case, we would be talking about the aesthetic question of whether it's correct or warranted or fitting to laugh at it. On this interpretation, the claim that child abduction is not funny would be similar to Cartman's criticism of *Family Guy* in "Cartoon Wars, Part I." Cartman claims that *Family Guy* isn't funny because it uses absurd cutaways that have nothing to do with the plot. So, if someone is amused by *Family Guy*, they are laughing when they shouldn't be in the aesthetic sense. It's not that they have done anything immoral, it's just that there has been an error in judgment in identifying *Family Guy*'s aesthetic qualities and, to that extent only, they have done something "unfitting." On this interpretation, "Child abduction is not funny" just means that child abduction fails as a comedy. But there is nothing morally wrong – or right, for that matter – with this failure as such; it's just incorrect.

This talk about fittingness may appear to be downright ludicrous since it seems to presume that there is an objective notion of something's really being funny. Philosophers sometimes say that something is objective insofar as it is mind-independent; that is, insofar as its existence and qualities are independent of a mind or minds.[1] In this sense, something's being funny is clearly not objective because something's being funny is intimately tied to the human emotion of amusement. Thus, if there were no minds around to be amused, then there could be nothing that is funny.

However, philosophers also say that a *judgment* or *claim* is objective insofar as it is independent of the thoughts and impulses of a particular mind. This is sometimes called epistemic objectivity, intersubjectivity, or objectivity by agreement. Take the claim that child abduction is morally wrong. Mind-independent or not, the claim is not subject to the caprices of any particular mind. The claim is subject to correction – that is, we can honestly say that someone who thinks child abduction is okay has got it all wrong, whereas we cannot do the same with someone who thinks, for example, that chocolate is better than vanilla. Whatever they are and however we get them, there are standards by which we can legitimately assess moral claims. In the same way, whether something is funny isn't only a matter of personal taste. We think that people who don't laugh at Cartman's mom's sluttiness are getting something wrong; we wouldn't try to talk them out of their opinions or explain the jokes if we didn't think so. Fittingness does presuppose that something's being funny is an objective evaluation. But the sort of objectivity required here is a modest sort: the sort that says just because you *think* something is (or isn't) funny, doesn't mean that it necessarily is (or isn't) funny.

The aesthetic question is not, however, the only question that can be raised. And, it's probably not what someone who says "Child abduction is not funny!" is trying to point out. Sometimes, when we say that something isn't funny we actually mean that it's morally

---

[1] For more on objectivity and its different senses, see, for example, Ronald Dworkin, "Objectivity and Truth" *Philosophy and Public Affairs* 25 (1996), pp. 87–139; Thomas Nagel, *The View From Nowhere* (New York: Oxford University Press, 1986); Richard Rorty, *Objectivity, Relativism, and Truth: Philosophical Papers Volume I* (Cambridge: Cambridge University Press, 1991); and John Searle, *The Construction of Social Reality* (New York: Free Press, 1995).

wrong to laugh at it. This is the ethical question. In this sense, child abduction isn't funny because we'd be morally awful people to laugh at something so tragic and ghastly. The same thing is happening when an audience member at the *Timmy and the Lords of the Underworld* concert says, "Boys! You shouldn't laugh at Timmy! He's handicapped! How would you like to be handicapped? Do you think that would be funny?" That is, it's mean to laugh at someone who's handicapped so you shouldn't do it, morally (the ethical question). It's not just that you shouldn't laugh because it is unfitting to do so (the aesthetic question).

These are, then, the two ways in which amusement can be evaluated. The trouble begins when we try to identify the relationship between these two aspects of the ethics of amusement. Consider the following commonsense ethics of amusement suggested by Ronald de Sousa: "Laugh when it's funny, grow up and stop snickering at dirty jokes, don't laugh at cripples (unless you are one yourself), and show respect. To show respect means not to laugh . . . when something is too sad, when it would be unkind, when it would offend a sacred memory, and when it might be taken to insult a mother, a country, or a religion."[2] If de Sousa's right, then little of *South Park* would escape moral censure. More to the point, however, is that de Sousa tells us to "laugh when it's funny," while the rest of what he says has to do with when it's morally wrong to laugh. Subscribing to de Sousa's commonsense ethics of amusement fails to make the distinction between the two senses in which we should not laugh at something, either because it isn't fitting to laugh or because it would be morally bad to laugh.

This muddling doesn't just occur in the everyday world. According to the philosophical position known as *aesthetic moralism*, the aesthetic quality of an object is dependent on its moral quality. In its most extreme form, the aesthetic quality of an artwork is wholly determined by its moral quality; an immoral artwork simply cannot be aesthetically pleasing, while a morally meritorious artwork is aesthetically pleasing. In its moderate form, the moral quality of an artwork contributes in some way to the artwork's aesthetic merit

---

[2] Ronald de Sousa, *The Rationality of Emotions* (Cambridge, MA: MIT Press, 1990), p. 278. Hereafter cited as (de Sousa, p. "x") in the text.

or demerit.[3] In both cases, aesthetic moralists deny that judgments about the ethical and aesthetic qualities of an artwork have a separate, independent evaluative base.

Even though it differs drastically from what one may normally think of as art, *South Park* is a creative work consciously put forward by Stone and Parker for our aesthetic enjoyment. In this case, the aesthetic enjoyment takes the particular form of comedy. If aesthetic moralism were true, then *South Park* would be less funny or, not funny at all, when it was morally bad. Of course, aesthetic moralism deliberately tries to make aesthetic judgments dependent on judgments about the moral quality of an artwork, simply claiming that whether something is objectively funny is dependent, at least in part, on whether it is morally good as well.

Now, according to most accounts of emotions, to have an emotion is to see an aspect of the world in a certain value-laden way.[4] For example, to fear a spider is to see a spider as threatening or even sinister, and not just as a spider. In this way, to feel an emotion is to key into some norm about the way things are supposed to be (that spiders are to be feared). Emotions can thus be assessed for how accurately they present their objects – unless spiders are actually threatening or sinister, fearing them is inappropriate even if understandable (they really aren't to be feared even though the arachnophobe would say otherwise).[5]

---

[3] See, for example, the articles in Anthony O'Hear (ed.), *Philosophy, the Good, the True and the Beautiful* (Cambridge: Cambridge University Press, 2000); Noel Carroll, *Beyond Aesthetics: Philosophical Essays* (Cambridge: Cambridge University Press, 2001); Berys Gaut, "Just Joking: The Ethics and Aesthetics of Humor," *Philosophy and Literature* 22 (1998), pp. 51–68; also, Virginia Postrel, *The Substance of Style: How the Rise of Aesthetic Value is Remaking Commerce, Culture, and Consciousness* (New York: Harper Collins, 2003).

[4] See, for example, Paul Ekman and Richard Davidson (eds.), *The Nature of Emotion: Fundamental Questions* (New York: Oxford University Press, 1994); Robert Nozick, "Emotions" in *The Examined Life* (New York: Touchstone, 1989), pp. 87–98; Robert Solomon (ed.), *What is an Emotion? Classic and Contemporary Readings* (New York: Oxford University Press, 2003), pp. 236–47; Kenneth Strongman, *The Psychology of Emotion: From Everyday Life to Theory* (Hoboken, NJ: John Wiley, 2003).

[5] See, for example, Justin D'Arms and Daniel Jacobson, "The Moralistic Fallacy: On the 'Appropriateness' of Emotions," *Philosophy and Phenomenological Research* 61 (2000), pp. 65–88; Gabriele Taylor, "Justifying the Emotions," *Mind* 84 (1975), pp. 390–402.

Likewise, to feel amused about something is to key into a norm about what is to be laughed about. It may be tempting to conclude that since all such norms prescribe responses and actions that we're automatically talking about ethical norms. But not all norms are ethical norms. Aesthetic norms and ethical norms have different aims. Aesthetic norms aim at what is beautiful or, in this case, the peculiar space of aesthetic enjoyment that humor occupies. They prescribe what is to be done when someone wants to make something beautiful or even what is to be done if someone wants to appreciate the beautiful. Ethical norms aim at what is right or good for human flourishing. They prescribe what is to be done on pain of moral censure. One can see how these aims constitute independent and sometimes wildly divergent ends when we consider whether it is even possible for something to be beautiful but not a part of human flourishing.[6] So long as it is even coherent to claim that something could be funny but harmful or morally meritorious but ugly, then, contra the aesthetic moralists, the aesthetic and moral aims are independent of each other.

So, why is all this important? First, it's useful to be clear on what kind of evaluation is being pursued in this chapter (the moral kind). It's also useful to be clear on what the limits of moral evaluation are (what is right or good, not what is correct or fitting). But most importantly, so long as aesthetic moralism is false, the fact that *South Park* is funny doesn't settle the question of whether it's okay for us to be amused by it. Recall that according to aesthetic moralism, only those artworks that are morally praiseworthy or permissible can be aesthetically pleasing or, at the least, that morally corrupt artwork is less aesthetically pleasing than it would have been otherwise. David Hume (1711–1776), a classical moralist, writes that when a work of art is morally objectionable, we could never "relish the composition," nor would it be proper to do so even if we could.[7] *South Park* is funny, really funny – we wouldn't be here reading this if we all didn't think so. We "relish" it, in Hume's words. There is no quarrel over *South Park*'s funniness. M'kay. But since the aesthetic and the moral

---

6 The Nazi propaganda film *Triumph of the Will* is often pointed to as the premier example of an aesthetically brilliant film that is morally objectionable.
7 David Hume, "Of the Standard of Taste," in *Essays, Political and Literary* (Indianapolis: Liberty Classics, 1987). See, especially, p. 246.

questions are independent of each other, that doesn't necessarily make it okay to laugh at Hennifer's love of burritos.

What Would Susan Wolf and Aristotle Do (Besides Act Like Goody-Friggin'-Two-Shoes)?

So how can we decide whether it's morally wrong to laugh at *South Park*? How do we determine whether laughing at *South Park* is part of the morally good life? Philosophers sometimes use the idea of a *moral saint* as a device to tease out the right way to act or be. A moral saint is a person who is as good as possible. By imagining and reflecting on what a moral saint would be like, we can draw out answers about how we should act and be. So, would a moral saint laugh at *South Park*?

To answer the question, we must first imagine what a moral saint would be like. Moral philosopher Susan Wolf presents two character-izations of the moral saint that are useful here, the *loving saint* and the *rational saint*. The loving saint is someone who cares only for the interests of others. The rational saint cares for her own interests while recognizing that her duties to others outweigh or override the pursuit of her own interests.[8] For both, the welfare and happiness of others is paramount. The difference lies in the sense of sacrifice that only the rational saint will feel. Would either saint laugh at Terrance and Philip's farting or the image of Nurse Gollum with a dead fetus attached to her head?

Wolf would probably say no, suggesting that "although a moral saint might well enjoy a good episode of *Father Knows Best*, he may not in good conscience be able to laugh at a Marx Brothers movie or enjoy a play by George Bernard Shaw" (Wolf, p. 422). Why? Because the humor in the Marx Brothers and Shaw typically occurs at some-one else's expense. People are made out to be idiots, or are insulted, or find themselves in some awkward or nasty situation and, because of these misfortunes, we laugh at them. Being considered an idiot, being insulted, or finding oneself in an unfortunate situation can

---

[8] Susan Wolf, "Moral Saints," *Journal of Philosophy* 79 (1982), pp. 419–39. Hereafter cited as (Wolf, p. "x") in the text.

cause emotional and psychological harm to the "victim" and, consequently, the saint should not take joy in these harms through laughter. But even more than the potential for harm, the saint's attention to the interests of others makes it doubtful that she would ever feel enjoyment when others are feeling pain or are otherwise facing adversity. If nothing else, the saint's efforts and energy will be so dominated by trying to help the "victim" or feeling sympathy and compassion for the person that it wouldn't occur to the saint to react with ridicule, glee, or pleasure.

If a Marx Brothers movie is too sordid for these saints, Nurse Gollum's fantastic disfigurement is surely beyond the pale. As silly as Mrs. Broflovski's reaction to Nurse Gollum is to us, it more closely approximates the saintly reaction than our laughter. Even though Conjoined Twin Myslexia is a fictional condition, the saint who observes someone with a major disfigurement like Nurse Gollum's would surely not find it entertaining. The fart gags, on the other hand, are not as clearly excluded because they don't require the dark sense of humor that is inconsistent with the saints' personas. Nevertheless, laughing at fart gags is probably unbecoming of a saint, as there is still more "laughing at" in a snicker than a saint's compassion can bear. In short, it seems that the loving and rational saints would be incapable of laughing at *South Park*. Even if they could laugh, they certainly *shouldn't* laugh and, so, we shouldn't be laughing either.

But Wolf's two saints are not the only characterizations of the ideal moral person. Aristotle (384–322 BCE) puts forward a conception of the ideal moral person who is courageous, generous, self-controlled, just, reflective, and able to associate with members of society in a friendly manner.[9] Unlike Wolf's saints, it's likely that such a person could laugh at *South Park*, as there is nothing in this saint's character that rules out a slightly wicked sense of humor. Because humans have rational capacities that distinguish them from all other kinds of animals, Aristotle thinks that the life of intellectual contemplation and moral virtue are what humans really should be striving for (Aristotle, pp. 11, 163). Such rational qualities would also include understanding the relevance of the rhetoric, innuendo, analogy, and incongruity associated with humor, even more "wicked" forms of humor that

---

[9] Aristotle, *Nicomachean Ethics*, trans. by Terence Irwin (Indianapolis: Hackett, 1999), p. 54 (1122a28). Hereafter cited as (Aristotle, p. "x") in the text.

result from the misfortunes of others. So in the end, the Aristotelian saint probably would sit around and laugh at *South Park* once in a while. But, in the attempt to tap into her contemplative side, she would probably also go further and read a book like this one to get a deeper sense of what the show means!

So, who's right, Wolf or Aristotle? There seems to be something true in what they both have to say. So, at this point, we're still not sure if it is morally appropriate to laugh at *South Park*. We need to know more about *how* a morally good character can or can't accommodate this salty sense of humor. This holds for *any* characterization of the moral saint, regardless of the particular moral theory from which we draw the characterization. What we need, in short, is an account of how amusement works.

If You Think "She Sells Seashells by the Seashore" is Hard, Try To Say *Phthonic Humor* Ten Times Quickly

Ronald de Sousa may help us here, as he presents an explanation of how amusement works. To clarify, de Sousa is not trying to explain what makes something funny. Instead, he provides a description of what takes place *psychologically* when we are amused by something. In this way, if de Sousa's account is true, it will provide us with the necessary information to complete our analysis.

De Sousa claims that in order to be amused by something, we have to endorse the attitudes and assumptions that are represented in the thing we find humorous as well as the background context for the humorous thing. Merely having knowledge of these attitudes and assumptions is inadequate. De Sousa offers the following joke as an illustration: "M. visits the hockey team. When she emerges she complains that she has been gang-raped. Wishful thinking" (de Sousa, p. 290). Some of us may find this joke funny, while others will not. The difference is in whether one *endorses* the attitudes and assumptions attached to the joke. Only those who are sexist can laugh at the joke because they have the attitudes and make the assumptions necessary to get the joke. Merely *knowing* that the joke assumes that women secretly want to be raped or that rape is just sex, is not enough to find the joke funny. One has to actually *endorse* the sexist assumptions that the joke trades on to find it funny. (Who's laughing now, you sexist jerk?)

In this way, to be amused by this joke "marks" someone as a sexist (de Sousa, p. 290). Thus, it would be immoral to be amused by this joke since to find it amusing is to be sexist. Indeed, to enjoy *phthonic humor* – humor that endorses an element of malice directed toward the target, or butt, of a joke – in general is morally wrong. For, in order to find phthonic humor funny, one must actually share in the nasty attitudes and assumptions that are necessary for the uptake of the phthonic humor. Importantly, the sin lies in the amusement itself. That is, de Sousa does not use the fact that someone is amused by a sexist joke as evidence for that person being sexist, though it would probably also serve that purpose. Rather, since to find the joke funny requires the hearer to endorse the sexist assumptions that are essential to the joke, the condition of being amused by the joke is itself what is immoral.

The moral saint is, recall, the ideal moral person. If de Sousa's account is correct, then the saint cannot find amusement in phthonic humor because the very condition of being phthonically amused is what is morally problematic. In this way, we have an even stronger prohibition against certain kinds of amusement than Wolf has suggested. It's no mere matter of being unable "in good conscience" to laugh at something phthonic or having one's attention otherwise engaged; it's a kind of psychological dysfunction. The Aristotelian saint is equally out of luck. So long as appreciation of phthonic humor requires actual endorsement of nefarious attitudes, then the Aristotelian saint cannot participate. The Aristotelian saint would probably have a richer sense of humor than either the rational saint or the loving saint and would enjoy some of the wittier and more satirical aspects of *South Park*. Nonetheless, the Aristotelian saint cannot be sexist, racist, ageist, intolerant, xenophobic, insensitive, flippant, or have otherwise morally dubious qualities. According to de Sousa, though, that is just how someone has to be in order to grasp phthonic humor.

And since phthonic humor is, for the most part, just what we grasp when we follow the misadventures of Cartman and the boys, it turns out that we're being quite horrid people when we enjoy *South Park*. Though *South Park* is rarely as witless as de Sousa's hockey joke, there is something mean-spirited or base about the amusement it provides. We like watching Kenny die and Cartman's monstrous selfishness wreak havoc on everyone around him. We relish the way that Butters' or Pip's mild dispositions are abused and taken advantage of by the other children. We savor the way that *South Park* takes shots at Scientology, Christianity, cultural diversity, Alcoholics Anonymous, and practically everything else. The humor is edgy, which is really just a nice way of saying that it's a little wicked. And so we really shouldn't be laughing at *South Park*.

This would be bleak news indeed for those of us who enjoy *South Park*. Luckily, de Sousa's account is not justified. He's right to claim that merely knowing what assumptions are at play in a joke isn't enough for the joke to be funny. That is, comprehending the joke isn't enough to enable one to laugh at the joke. The problem with the account is that de Sousa claims that someone must actually endorse the attitudes and assumptions essential to a joke. However, one need not *actually endorse* these attitudes in order to adopt them so as to see the humor associated with them. To illustrate, recall that in "Bigbutt and Pancake Face" the hand-puppet version of Jennifer Lopez loves to eat tacos and burritos. In itself, there really isn't anything funny about someone, even a Hispanic person, who loves to eat tacos and burritos. There is, however, something potentially funny about imagining a person as a fast-talking, r-rolling taco and burrito loving chola. *South Park* similarly plays on racist attitudes and assumptions for many of its other characters. To find these portrayals funny, one need only be aware of what stereotypes and caricatures are in attendance and use this information to imaginatively adopt the relevant attitudes. One only has to be able to imagine what it's like to see a person as a fast-talking, r-rolling, taco and burrito loving chola, for instance.

There is, in short, a middle ground between endorsing pernicious attitudes and merely knowing about them. In the simplest case, we can imagine what it's like to be a racist and how such a person would picture a young Hispanic woman. In doing so, we adopt, for a moment, the morally objectionable attitudes the racist holds towards young Hispanic women. But this imaginative adoption hardly "marks" someone as a racist. That it is imagined disqualifies it from being a genuine attribute: no more is a person who imagines being a superhero actually a superhero than a person who imagines being racist is actually racist. The transitory nature of the imagined adoption further belies any claim to endorsement. And an imaginative adoption of attitudes is, contra de Sousa, all that we need to do in order to laugh at "Hennifer Lopez."

Laugh Away, All of You Fast-Talking, R-Rolling Taco and Burrito Loving Cholas!

So where does this leave us concerning the ethics of amusement? If it's correct that we can imagine hypothetical scenarios without endorsing them, then the moral saint could be saintly and still enjoy *South Park*'s humor. Imagining doesn't necessarily have to do with what a person *actually* believes, thinks, wants, endorses, or even secretly wishes. In fact, a person might even be considered a defective moral saint if she *didn't* have a good imagination. Creative ability is probably a good quality for a saint to have – if not in its own right, then at least to the extent that it plays a role in empathy and understanding.

None of this is to say that one can't be immoral when laughing at *South Park*. If one were to endorse malicious attitudes or hurtful intentions for the sake of being hurtful, for example, phthonic amusement would be immoral. We wonder, perhaps, how someone who *really* is a racist would respond to *South Park*. When we imaginatively adopt pernicious attitudes, the malicious portrayal doesn't completely encompass the attitudes we have towards the target of the joke. Can the person who is really racist see past their maliciousness in this way? Would they grin and chuckle out of delight at the "Hennifer Lopez" caricature or would their laughter instead be what psychologist Boris Sidis called the snarl of the brute?[10] Such laughter is the product of ridicule and scorn. Though amusement can contain ridicule, the point remains that the laughter of the real racist has a different tone than the laughter of the person who merely imaginatively adopts the racist attitudes. Snarling like a brute, then, is something that the moral saint could not do, and to be amused in this fashion is correspondingly wrong. But, as we have seen, a little imagination is all we need. Thus, even Wolf's saints could laugh at *South Park*. So, laugh away all of you fast-talking, r-rolling taco and burrito loving cholas!

10 Boris Sidis, *The Psychology of Laughter* (New York: Appleton, 1913).

3

BLASPHEMOUS HUMOR IN SOUTH PARK

Kevin J. Murtagh

A Chick Bleeding Out Her Vagina is No Miracle

In "Bloody Mary," a statue of the Virgin Mary is depicted as bleeding, apparently, "out its ass." People come from all over to witness this supposed miracle, and a Cardinal is sent by the Vatican to inspect the statue. He looks closely at the blood mark, and the statue seemingly farts and sprays blood all over his face. "It's a miracle!" he decrees. Shortly thereafter, Pope Benedict XVI shows up to inspect the statue himself. After the statue "farts" blood into his face, he declares that the statue is not bleeding out its ass, but out its vagina, and that a "chick bleeding out her vagina is no miracle. Chicks bleed out their vaginas all the time."

A statue of the Virgin Mary *bleeding out its ass?* The thought alone is disgusting, and finding out later that the statue was just having its period does nothing to lessen the disgust. And menstrual blood being sprayed *on the Pope's face?* This all struck me as over the line, and something about it seemed *wrong*. Have I "gone soft" as I've gotten older? Perhaps I've become a bit of a prude, the kind of person that younger people like to mock for being too stuffy and serious. But I doubt that. After all, "Bloody Mary" made me laugh, even as I cringed.

Are Parker and Stone doing something morally wrong by using blasphemy for comic effect? There seemed to me something morally wrong about the "Bloody Mary" episode. I had, you might say, an *intuition* that some moral boundary was crossed. But, while moral philosophy (the branch of philosophy concerned with what one ought to do and how one ought to live) can sometimes begin with intuitions, it cannot end with them. A philosophical position that proclaims an action moral or immoral must be grounded in good reasons and solid evidence, along with intuitions. Perhaps examining this question through the lens of *utilitarianism* – a very influential moral theory popularized by John Stuart Mill (1806–1873) – will help us to answer it. Utilitarians attempt to calculate the potential positive and negative consequences of acting in a situation. They believe that the morally right decision is the one that promotes the greatest balance of positive over negative consequences, taking all people affected into consideration.[1] So, from a utilitarian perspective, it may be that blasphemous humor is morally acceptable on grounds that it makes a lot of people happy; or, it may be immoral on grounds that it causes a lot of shock, anger, and displeasure. But before we discuss this ethical issue, it will be helpful to get a better idea of what blasphemy is.

What In God's Name is Blasphemy?

Blasphemy is difficult to define. Like many words, we have a general idea of what it means, but giving a precise definition of it proves to be difficult. Blasphemy is characterized by irreverence or disrespect for something deemed sacred, such as a god, gods, or "people of God" like the Pope, priests, and nuns. Blasphemy also often involves showing contempt for or hatred of God.[2] Consider The Mole in the *South Park* movie, who calls God many names, including "cocksucking asshole," "bitch," "faggot," and "fucking rat." If there are any clear instances of blasphemy, these certainly are.

Playing on or making statements that contain religious stereotypes is not necessarily blasphemy. In the episode "Christian Rock Hard" Kyle's father refuses to give him money to buy CDs and Kyle says,

---

[1] See J.S. Mill, *Utilitarianism* (Indianapolis: Hackett Publishing, 2003). Hereafter cited as (*Utilitarianism*, p. "x") in the text.

[2] See, for example, the entry for *blasphemy* in *Shorter Oxford English Dictionary*, ed. by William Trumble and Lesley Brown (Oxford: Oxford University Press, 2002).

"Aw, come on Dad, don't be such a Jew!" This statement, of course, plays on the stereotype that Jews are cheap. As such, it may involve prejudice, but not blasphemy. It's important to point this out, since *South Park* is full of humor that trades on religious stereotypes. This sort of humor, provided it does not also show disrespect for the sacred, is not blasphemous. Of course, that doesn't mean that it's morally unproblematic. It just means that it's not blasphemous.

It may also be helpful to offer a definition of blasphemous humor. This proves difficult for the same reason that defining blasphemy is difficult: we have a general idea of what *humor* means, but how to formulate a precise definition? Whatever humor is, it seems to have something to do with amusement or funniness.[3] So, for our purposes, we can define *blasphemous humor* as some sort of presentation that is intended to be amusing or funny, in which something deemed sacred is portrayed in a disrespectful or irreverent manner. By "some sort of presentation" I mean, for example, a joke, a skit, or a television episode. This definition is far from perfect, but it will suit us just fine. Given this definition, it's clear that *South Park* contains a great deal of blasphemous humor.

Do You Care At All About People's Feelings?
A Utilitarian Perspective

Now that we've clarified some concepts, we can return to our question. Are Parker and Stone doing something morally wrong by using blasphemous humor? Let's attempt to answer this question with a utilitarian theory.

In chapter two of *Utilitarianism*, Mill explains his theory in the following way: "The creed which accepts as the foundation of morals 'utility' or the 'greatest happiness principle' holds that actions are right in proportion as they tend to promote happiness; wrong as they tend to produce the reverse of happiness. By happiness is intended pleasure and the absence of pain; by unhappiness, pain and the privation of pleasure" (p. 7). Mill believes that there is a single, basic

---

[3] See, for example, the entry for *humor* in *Shorter Oxford English Dictionary*.

moral principle, which he refers to as the *principle of utility* or *greatest happiness principle*. This principle demands that we focus on the consequences of our actions and, in particular, on the happiness and unhappiness produced by them. The moral action will be the one that produces the greatest balance of happiness over unhappiness, everyone considered.

Now, we can't just take into consideration the happiness and unhappiness of those we care about, or those in our community; we must take into consideration everyone who is affected, directly or indirectly, by the action. Furthermore, we must weigh the happiness and unhappiness of each individual equally. On Mill's theory, I cannot take my own happiness to be more important than yours because I am me, and I cannot take the happiness of my friends to be more important than the happiness of strangers because I happen to have a close bond with my friends. The happiness of every individual that is affected by the action must be given equal weight.

A utilitarian needs to consider alternative courses of action and, for each course of action, must attempt to determine the balance of happiness over unhappiness that is, or would be, brought about by taking it. Here are two alternatives: (a) Parker and Stone making *South Park* with the blasphemous humor, the way they do in fact make it, or (b) Parker and Stone making it without the blasphemous humor. Which course of action would have better consequences? Or, to pose the question in a way that's closer to the language of Mill's theory, which course of action would produce the greater balance of happiness over unhappiness? To answer this question, we need to look at the ways in which the blasphemous humor in *South Park* leads to happiness and the ways in which it leads to unhappiness.

First, let's look at the negative consequences. Quite obviously, blasphemous humor is offensive to many people, and offending people tends to promote unhappiness. Returning to "Bloody Mary," it's clear why Christians were offended by that episode. According to Christian teachings, Mary was the mother of Jesus Christ, the son of God. As the mother of Jesus, Mary is considered to be a sacred figure in the Christian faith. Many Christians pray to Mary, and Catholics especially view her as an individual of immense spiritual importance. So, it's not terribly surprising that many Christians were offended by an episode that depicted a statue of Mary spraying blood out of a bodily orifice onto people's faces (whether it's her "ass" or her vagina seems to matter little). This offense was presumably compounded by the fact that she sprayed blood onto the face of a Cardinal and, later, the Pope.

In "Cartoon Wars, Part I" we actually find Cartman (of all characters!) objecting to blasphemous humor. A little set-up is required here. In this episode, the adults in South Park are terrified because an episode of *Family Guy* that will be aired shortly is supposed to contain an animated depiction of Mohammed, the Islamic prophet and a sacred figure in the Muslim faith. Muslims consider any sort of depiction of their prophet to be blasphemous, and the adults in South Park are worried that Muslims will be upset by the *Family Guy* episode and will react violently.[4] The episode airs, with the image of Mohammed blocked-out, and Cartman, Stan, and Kyle discuss whether or not it was wrong for the people behind *Family Guy* to attempt to show an image of Mohammed:

Stan: What? What's the big deal?

Cartman: What's the big deal? You guys, they just made fun of the religion of an entire group of people. What, you guys think that's okay? Do you care at all about people's feelings?

Kyle: Since when do you care about being sensitive to people's religion, Cartman?

Stan: Yeah, you rip on people's religion all the time!

Cartman: That's different! I'm just a little boy! That's a cartoon! Millions of people watch it! How would you feel, Kyle, if there was a cartoon on television that made fun of Jews all the time? Huh?

Kyle: Uhhh . . .

Cartman: I'm telling you guys, it's wrong!

According to Cartman, it's wrong for the creators of *Family Guy* to use blasphemous humor in this instance because doing so will offend many people and, thereby, hurt their feelings. What compounds the wrong is that "millions of people watch it," so the offended Muslims will know that millions of people are seeing this depiction of their

---

[4] In case you spent a portion of 2006 under a rock, after the republication in European newspapers of Danish cartoons that depicted Mohammed as a terrorist, violence erupted in, among other places, Afghanistan.

prophet, which they find disrespectful. The fact that the show is so popular intensifies the insult and increases the unhappiness of the Muslims. Here, Cartman is arguing like a utilitarian, or at least he's backing up his view with reasons that a utilitarian would recognize as relevant. (Of course, Cartman doesn't really care about Muslims. He just hates *Family Guy* and wants it off the air, but that doesn't change the argument.)

The unhappiness that results from offending people is a direct consequence of blasphemous humor, but there may also be negative *indirect* consequences of such humor. Utilitarianism demands that we take all consequences (insofar as they are reasonably foreseeable) into account, both direct and indirect. So, what negative consequences might indirectly result from blasphemous humor? In her article " 'Just Joking!' The Ethics Of Humor," Robin Tapley writes that joking is "another way of putting a belief out into the community. Whether one personally holds a belief to be true is really not the point. It is that beliefs put out into the community, especially in the disarming guise of humor, have the power to challenge, desensitize, confirm, or reinforce our own beliefs and the beliefs that are prevalent in the society."[5] Here, Tapley is writing specifically about jokes, but what she says would hold true for humor in general.

So, if Tapley is right, the importance for our discussion is clear. Blasphemous humor could lead people to be less tolerant and sensitive in their dealings with certain religious groups, or religious people in general. I defy any atheist fan of *South Park* to deny that he has had at least one self-satisfied moment while watching the show with the thought, "Silly religious people and their superstitious beliefs." Of course, if I am right about this, it doesn't prove that the blasphemous episodes have any lasting desensitizing effects, and I don't know of any research that specifically investigates the relationship between exposure to blasphemy and religious sensitivity and tolerance. But there is good reason to believe that what people watch on television and in the movies can have an effect on their attitudes and emotions. Consider the research that supports the claim that exposure to media violence often has the effect of desensitizing people to violence and

[5] Robin Tapley, " 'Just Joking!' The Ethics of Humor," *Yeditepe'de Felsefe* 4 (2005), p. 175.

increasing violent and aggressive behavior.[6] Of course, exposure to violence and exposure to blasphemy are different, but it seems reasonable to suppose that exposure to blasphemous humor could have a desensitizing effect. It's clear how all of this relates to happiness and unhappiness. A lack of sensitivity and tolerance leads to ridicule, conflict, and a lack of respect for others, and, thereby, unhappiness.

South Park Has the Potential to Make People Think

Thus far, we have focused on the negative consequences of Parker and Stone's blasphemous humor, looking at ways that it leads, or could lead, to unhappiness. But there seem to be positive consequences as well, and no utilitarian evaluation is complete without looking at both sides of the coin. Again, we need to look at both direct and indirect consequences. Quite clearly, there is at least one positive direct consequence: many people find the blasphemous humor funny. They are entertained by it, and when people are entertained, they tend to be happy. There's really no need to offer extensive support for that claim.

What positive indirect consequences result from the blasphemous humor in *South Park*? Let's return to "Bloody Mary." There was much more going on in that episode than the images of a statue of Mary spraying . . . well, you know. Here's a bit more about the plot. Stan's dad, Randy, is convinced that he is an alcoholic and that he is powerless to control his addiction. When Randy finds out about the bleeding statue, he believes that if he is touched by Mary's "divine ass

---

[6] For a discussion of this claim, see the research and discussion in Steven Kirsh, *Children, Adolescents, and Media Violence: A Critical Look at the Research* (Thousand Oaks, CA: Sage, 2006); also, Dave Grossman and Gloria DeGaetano, *Stop Teaching Our Kids to Kill: A Call to Action Against TV, Movie, and Video Game Violence* (New York: Crown Books, 1999); the papers in Ulla Carlsson (ed.), *Children and Media Violence* (Philadelphia: Coronet Books, 1998); and Henry Nardone and Gregory Bassham, "Pissin' Metal: Columbine, Malvo, and the Matrix of Violence," in William Irwin (ed.), *More Matrix and Philosophy: Revolutions and Reloaded Decoded* (Chicago: Open Court, 2005), pp. 187–90.

blood" he will be cured, so he goes to visit the statue, gets sprayed by the blood, and believes that he is cured by this "miracle." He is sober for five days, but then finds out that the bleeding statue is not a miracle (recall the Pope's words: "A chick bleeding out her vagina is no miracle"), so he decides that he has not been cured and begins drinking heavily. Stan is upset and they have the following exchange:

Stan: Dad, you don't have to do this! You have the power. You haven't drank since seeing the statue.
Randy: But the statue wasn't a miracle!
Stan: Yeah. The statue wasn't a miracle, Dad. So that means you did it. That means you didn't have a drink for five days all on your own.

The message here is clear. According to what Stan says, rather than looking to a divine power for help with our problems, we should recognize that we have considerable willpower and that we can help ourselves.

Now, we're not concerned here with examining the value of that particular message, and Alcoholics Anonymous – which is being satirized in this episode – has helped a great many people. What we're concerned with (and this will not come as a surprise to *South Park* fans) is showing that this episode has a message. It has content and presents ideas and, in its own way, makes an argument. Sometimes the message is good, and other times it's bad. But, because there is a message, *South Park* has the potential to make people think. It can, and often does, promote reflection and discussion about important issues. The other chapters in this book are testament to that.

You Have to Hit Them with a Sledgehammer

But why the blasphemy? Is it really necessary for the good conse-quences? Yes. People are too complacent. Unless they are somehow shocked, many people neglect discussing important moral and social issues. To quote the character John Doe from the movie *Seven*, "Wanting people to listen, you can't just tap them on the shoulder anymore. You have to hit them with a sledgehammer. And then you'll notice you have their strict attention."[7] (I'm aware that the character is a serial killer, but I like the quotation.) It would be wonderful if people were more inclined to engage in reflection and discussion about important issues; however, for whatever reason, they seem not to be so inclined. Blasphemous humor can shock, unsettle, prod, and provoke people into thinking and talking.

And now – to make the tie into utilitarianism explicit – reflection and discussion are beneficial to individuals and society as a whole. A society in which there is more discourse and exchange of ideas is, on balance, happier than a society with less social discourse and dialogue.[8] In *On Liberty*, Mill details the benefits of open dialogue. Discussing ideas, he says, can help to bring us closer to the truth, and even when it doesn't, discussion of someone's false opinion can help to prevent the contrary true opinion from becoming "a dead dogma," as opposed to "a living truth."[9]

So, we've explored the negative and positive consequences, both direct and indirect, of blasphemous humor in *South Park*. Now we need to consider the two main alternatives and their consequences. The first alternative is *South Park* as is, with the blasphemous humor. The second alternative is *South Park* without the blasphemous humor. If Parker and Stone took this second alternative, many of the negative consequences would be avoided, but many of the positive consequences would be lost. Sure, the people who were offended would be spared the offense, and the risk of desensitization and promotion of intolerance would be avoided. But the show wouldn't have been as funny or as shocking and controversial and, probably, it would have a much smaller audience. And if watching *South Park* can be a valuable experience, as I have been arguing, then many people would have gone without that experience.

Comparing these two alternatives through a utilitarian lens involves attempting to figure out which course of action would produce a greater balance of happiness over unhappiness. Figuring this out is,

---

[7] *Seven*, dir. David Fincher, 127 min., New Line Cinema, 1995, DVD.

[8] Consider the general misery and injustices of various kinds of totalitarian regimes, both past and present, where there is limited freedom of speech and expression. See, for example, Michael Halberstam, *Totalitarianism and the Modern Conception of Politics* (New Haven, CT: Yale University Press, 2000).

[9] J.S. Mill, *On Liberty* (London: Penguin, 1974), p. 97.

predictably, difficult. First of all, we aren't even close to having all of the relevant information about the actual consequences of the blasphemous humor in *South Park*. Throughout this discussion, I've been using generalizations, analogies, and intuitions. This is often unavoidable when examining a moral issue through a utilitarian lens. Secondly, there is no precise way to measure happiness and unhappiness, so our judgments are imprecise and, to a large extent, intuitive.

All that said, it seems that a greater balance of happiness over unhappiness is brought about by making *South Park* with the blasphemous humor. Of course, people are offended by it, and this fact must not be ignored. But I wonder how many people are actually directly caused significant pain by the blasphemy in *South Park*. Certain media watchdog groups have spoken out against the show, and the Catholic League for Religious and Civil Rights kicked up a lot of dust over "Bloody Mary." But most people who find the blasphemous humor offensive probably don't watch the show, and if they hear about the blasphemous episodes, they may be somewhat distressed, but they probably don't get too terribly upset about the latest *South Park* episode. In short, we need to remember that interest groups aren't necessarily expressing the widespread outrage of the groups they (claim to) represent.

Regarding the potential for negative indirect consequences, I am skeptical as to the extent to which the blasphemous humor in the context of most *South Park* episodes promotes insensitivity and intolerance, especially given that there are aspects of the show that may counteract whatever negative influences there are. Consider the fact that Uncle Jimbo, an intolerant, closed-minded character, is often portrayed as a complete idiot. Also, the messages in some of the blasphemous episodes are messages of tolerance. In "Super Best Friends" Stan makes the following statement, voicing one of the "lessons" of the episode: "See, all religions have something valuable to teach, but, just like the Super Best Friends learned, it requires a little bit of them all." Whether or not that statement is true, it is certainly an expression of tolerance.

The blasphemy operates within the context of an episode and a series of episodes, making the evaluation of its use a complex matter. But all in all, the blasphemy draws a lot of attention to a show that can be very rewarding. *South Park* is indeed a rare show. It is massively successful *and* it tackles important issues. Furthermore, it often does so explicitly. The characters make arguments all the time. They state their views clearly, and you don't have to be a careful viewer constantly searching for subtext to get the message and the food for thought.

A Final Point

In my discussion, I've argued that a public presentation containing blasphemous humor can have negative consequences that are undeniably morally relevant and that it is morally justifiable to use blasphemous humor *if it is an important part of a presentation that has significant social value.* In other words, there must be positive consequences to offset the negative ones. This view has the implication that blasphemous humor "just to piss people off" is morally wrong. If there are no, or minimal, foreseeable positive consequences to offset the negative ones, the blasphemous humor is morally unjustifiable. This implication seems right. Whatever else morality is concerned with, an important part of morality involves being concerned with the consequences of actions and refraining from hurting others pointlessly or merely for profit. So, when people use blasphemous humor gratuitously or merely for financial gain, they are indeed acting wrongly and deserve our moral condemnation, God damn it.

4

THE CHEWBACCA DEFENSE

A *South Park* Logic Lesson

Robert Arp

It Does Not Make Sense!

The episode "Chef Aid" is classic *South Park* with its cartoon Johnnie Cochran's "Chewbacca Defense," a satire of Cochran's actual closing arguments in the O.J. Simpson case. In the episode, Alanis Morissette comes out with a hit song "Stinky Britches," which, it turns out, Chef had written some twenty years ago. Chef produces a tape of himself performing the song, and takes the record company to court, asking only that he be credited for writing the hit. The record company executives then hire Cochran. In his defense of the record company, Cochran shows the jury a picture of Chewbacca and claims that, because Chewbacca is from Kashyyyk and lives on Endor with the Ewoks, "It does not make sense." Cochran continues: "Why would a Wookie, an eight-foot tall Wookie, want to live on Endor with a bunch of two-foot tall Ewoks? That does not make sense. If Chewbacca lives on Endor, you must acquit! The defense rests." The jury is so convinced by Cochran's "argument," that not only do they apparently deny Chef's request for credit recognition, but they also find Chef guilty of harassing a major record label, fining him two million dollars to be paid within twenty-four hours. Friends of Chef then organize "Chef Aid" to pay his fine.

We laugh at Cochran's defense because it has absolutely nothing to do with the actual case. We laugh all the more at the absurdity when the Chewbacca Defense is also used to find Chef guilty of harassing the very record company that had produced a stolen song. The issue of Chewbacca living on Endor has absolutely nothing to do with, and is in no way logically related to, the issues of whether Chef should receive credit for the song, or whether he has harassed the record company. As rational thinkers, we recognize this, laugh at the absurdities, and wonder why anyone in their right mind would be convinced that the Chewbacca Defense and the other issues are related. In fact, logicians (people who study the principles of correct reasoning) have a term for the kind of bad thinking involved in the Chewbacca Defense. They call it a *fallacy*. A fallacy is faulty reasoning that inappropriately or incorrectly draws a conclusion from evidence that does not support the conclusion. To draw the conclusions that the record company is not liable for crediting Chef with writing the song *and* that Chef has harassed the record company based upon reasons that have to do with the Chewbacca Defense is fallacious reasoning.

Fallacious reasoning, some of it not too different from the Chewbacca Defense, is quite common. For example, suppose Principal Victoria thinks that, just because she had a bad experience with a person of a particular sex, race, creed, or color, "they must all be like that." Or she believes since a celebrity has endorsed a particular product, then it must necessarily be good for us. Instead of seeking to become an authority in a particular matter, she blindly accepts what some tells us as "The Gospel Truth." Or, she concludes that "there must be no true or false, right or wrong, good or bad beliefs" because "people have so many different beliefs." However, on reflection, we can see why she's not justified in any of these conclusions.

This chapter offers a short logic lesson as an introduction to what philosophers do when they put forward and critique arguments.[1] Logic is the study of the principles of correct reasoning associated with the formation and analysis of arguments. As we've seen already, people don't always abide by these principles. The creators of *South Park*, for the most part, are aware of these logical principles, and

---

[1] For more extensive discussions of logic see Gregory Bassham, William Irwin, Henry Nardone, and James M. Wallace, *Critical Thinking: A Student's Introduction* (New York: McGraw-Hill, 2004); Patrick Hurley, *A Concise Introduction to Logic* (Belmont, CA: Wadsworth Publishing, 2006); Robert Johnson, *Fundamentals of Reasoning: A Logic Book* (Belmont, CA: Wadsworth Publishing, 2002); Anthony Weston, *A Rulebook for Arguments* (Indianapolis: Hackett Publishing, 2000).

purposely violate them to show the absurdities associated with certain beliefs, opinions, ideas, and arguments. In fact, much of *South Park*'s humor concerns logical violations and the absurdities, contradictions, and problems that result. The way people reason correctly, or incorrectly, has real consequences. It affects the policies they adhere to, the laws they make, the beliefs they are willing to die for, and the general way in which they live their lives.

For example, because of Mrs. Broflovski and the town's belief that *The Terrance and Philip Show* promotes immorality, the entire community not only boycotts the show, but also sacrifices members of the community to get the producers of the show to take it off the air. This fictional morality tale parallels parts of reality, and raises questions as to whether TV promotes immorality, as well as what people are willing to do based upon their perceived connection between TV and immorality. Can we draw the general conclusion that a show like *South Park*, even if viewed by children, is bad for *all* children, from evidence that supports the fact that it's bad for *some* children? Further, even if it does promote immorality, is that the kind of thing we are willing to die for? This may seem like a silly question, but the actions of the South Park townspeople get us to think about what kinds of things people are willing to believe or do based upon their faulty reasoning. Consider a somewhat parallel case. Are all Americans immoral? And even if so, should we sacrifice people so as to make our point about them being immoral by flying planes into a skyscraper? Again, how we live our lives, as well as how we affect others' lives, depends upon whether we reason correctly or incorrectly. (You, the reader, may even find what I have said in this paragraph to be logically questionable.) In what follows, we'll consider some basics of logic and, using examples from *South Park* episodes, show some differences between correct and incorrect reasoning.

Dude, Listen to Reason

Logic is the study of the principles of correct reasoning associated with the formation and analysis of arguments. So let's define the word *argument*, and describe its basic components and types. Then, we can talk about correct argument formation and analysis.

An argument consists of two or more claims, one of which is called the *conclusion*. The conclusion is the claim in the argument that is supposed to be supported by, shown to be the case by, demonstrated by, justified by, warranted by, or proved to be the case by the premise or premises. A *premise* is a claim in the argument that is supposed to support, show, demonstrate, justify, warrant, or prove the conclusion. The fundamental purpose of an argument is to persuade or convince someone of the truth of one's concluding claim. In other words, when we put forward an argument, we want others to be persuaded or convinced of the conclusion we arrived at and believe to be true, and we use another claim, or other claims, as supposed support for the truth of that conclusion.

Cochran's fallacious argument can be rephrased, simply, like this: "Because Chewbacca lives on Endor (the premise of the argument), therefore you should acquit my client (the conclusion of the argument)." A complete argument has at least one premise and only one conclusion, but arguments usually have two or more premises. So for example, I was watching a *South Park* re-run last night called "Ike's Wee Wee," and Cartman put forward an argument for why we should be convinced drugs are bad that could be paraphrased like this: "If you do drugs, then you're a hippie; if you're a hippie, then you suck; if you suck, then that's bad (all premises); So, if you do drugs, then that's bad (conclusion)."

Arguments are composed of claims, a concluding claim (the conclusion), and at least one supporting claim (the premise). A *claim* is a statement, proposition, assertion, judgment, declarative sentence, or part of a declarative sentence, resulting from a person's beliefs or opinions, which communicates that something is or is not the case about the self, the world, states of affairs, or reality in general. Claims are either true or false, and again, are the results of beliefs or opinions that people have concerning any part of what they perceive to be reality. We make our beliefs and opinions known through claims. For example, the claims "I am typing this chapter on a laptop" and "Chewbacca is a Wookie" are true, whereas the claims "I was the 40th president of the United States" and "The sun revolves around the earth" are false.

A claim is shown to be true or false as a result of *evidence*, which can take the forms of either direct or indirect testimony of your senses, explanations, the testimony of others, appeal to well-established theories, appeal to appropriate authority, appeal to definitions, and good arguments, among others. So, that I am typing on a laptop is shown to be true by the direct testimony of my own senses, that Chewbacca is a Wookie is true by definition of "Chewbacca," that I was president of the US is false because of the testimony of the senses of others and authorities, and that the sun revolves around the earth is false because of indirect sensory evidence as well as the well-established heliocentric theory. Some claims are difficult, or impossible, to show true or false with evidence. Claims like "God exists," "Abortion is always immoral," and "I have an immortal soul" would fall into this ambiguous category. That is probably why ideas, issues, and arguments surrounding these claims are considered to be "philosophical."

As rational, adult critical thinkers, we have beliefs or opinions that we think are true about reality as we perceive it, and we express those beliefs or opinions in written or spoken claims. But, we can't stop there. We must convince or persuade others as to why we hold these beliefs, and when we do so, we must give a reason or set of reasons (the premises of our argument) for why we hold to a particular belief (the conclusion of our argument). So, for example, in the episode "The Passion of the Jew" Kyle believes strongly that the Jewish community in his hometown should apologize for Jesus' death. If asked why the Jewish community in his hometown, or anyone, should be convinced or persuaded to apologize, Kyle's argument might look like this:

> Premise 1: Since Jews are known to have been partly responsible for the death of Jesus
> Premise 2: And, since an action like this requires that one should apologize
> Premise 3: And, since the Jews in South Park are part of the Jewish community
> _____
> Conclusion: Therefore, the Jews in South Park should apologize for Jesus' death

Let's note a few things about this argument. First, it has been placed into *standard form*. Putting an argument in standard form means placing the premises of the argument first, the conclusion last, and clearly dividing the premise(s) and conclusion with a horizontal line.

This is a handy tool because it helps make the logical form and parts of the argument clear. And, as we'll see later, standard form makes the argument easier to analyze in terms of whether the conclusion follows from the premises as well as whether all the premises are true.

Notice the word *since* at the beginning of the premises and the word *therefore* at the beginning of the conclusion. The word *since* is an example of a premise-indicating word, along with words like *because, for, for the reason that,* and *as,* among others. The word *therefore* is an example of a conclusion-indicating word, along with words like *hence, so, thus, this shows us that, we can conclude that,* and *we can reason/deduce/infer that,* among others. Premise-indicating and conclusion-indicating words are important because they usually let us know that premises and a conclusion are coming in an argument. At times, it can be incredibly difficult to tell if someone is putting forward an argument, so you can look for these indicating words to see if there's an argument in front of you and, further, you can identify what the conclusion and the premise(s) of the argument are. Unfortunately, these indicating words are not always present, and people sometimes place the conclusion anywhere in their argument (sometimes it'll be the first claim, sometimes the second, sometimes the last). In such cases you must supply these words to make the structure and parts of the argument crystal clear.

You're Not Asleep Yet, Are You?

Broadly speaking, there are two different kinds of arguments, *deductive arguments* and *inductive arguments*. In deductive arguments, the speaker intends the conclusion to follow from the premises with absolute certainty such that, if all of the premises are true, then the conclusion must be true without any doubt whatsoever. To say that a conclusion *follows* from a premise means that we are justified in having reasoned appropriately from one claim (the premise) to another claim (the conclusion). Cartman puts forward a deductive argument in "The Tooth Fairy Tats 2000" episode that goes something like this:

> Premise 1: If the boys combine their lost teeth, then they'll get money from the Tooth Fairy

Premise 2: If they get money from the Tooth Fairy, then they can buy a Sega Dreamcast

Conclusion: Hence, if the boys combine their lost teeth, then they can buy a Sega Dreamcast

We can see that, provided that the two premises are true, the conclusion absolutely must be true. We can also see that there is no other conclusion that could correctly be drawn from these premises. In fact, from looking at the premises alone you know the conclusion before even seeing it. The previous argument about Jews apologizing for Jesus' death is also a deductive argument. Just like with the Tooth Fairy argument, if all the premises are true then the conclusion must be true, there is no other conclusion that possibly could be drawn from the premises, and you know exactly what the conclusion is without even seeing it.

In inductive arguments, the speaker intends the conclusion to follow from the premises with a degree of probability or likelihood such that, if all of the premises are true, then the conclusion probably or likely is true, but it is still possible that the conclusion is false. In the "Towelie" episode, the boys notice that when they speak about anything having to do with towels, Towelie shows up, and so they reason like this:

Premise 1: Because in the past, when we mentioned towel-related things, Towelie showed up
Premise 2: And because we will mention something towel-related now

Conclusion: We can conclude that Towelie will show up

We can see that, provided the premises are true, the conclusion is probably or likely true, but not definitely true. It makes sense to conclude that Towelie will show up, given past experience. But the truth of Towelie showing up in the past does not guarantee that, with absolute certainty or without a doubt, Towelie *will* show up. It is still possible that Towelie won't show up, so the conclusion is merely probable or likely. In the episode, Towelie does show up, but he need not necessarily have shown up.

Consider Stan's reasoning at the end of the episode "Scott Tenorman Must Die" after it has been revealed that Cartman orchestrated the death of Scott's parents, the subsequent addition of their bodies to the chili, and Radiohead's witnessing the entire event so as to make fun of Scott for being a woossie.

Premise 1: Since Cartman does horrible things to people for minor offenses (like being cheated out of $16.12)

Premise 2: And since we (the boys) commit, at least, minor offenses against Cartman frequently, and he may retaliate like he did with Scott

Conclusion: Therefore, we had better not piss Cartman off in the future, for fear of retaliation

Again, even if both of the premises are true, it doesn't follow with absolute certainty that the boys had better not piss off Cartman in the future. In fact, as it turns out, the boys piss off Cartman numerous times without receiving the kind of retaliation given poor Scott Tenorman. So, the conclusion is false.

Our goal is not just to form arguments. We need to form *good arguments*, and we need to evaluate the arguments of others. There are good arguments and there are bad arguments in both the deductive and inductive realms. A good argument, in either realm, is one in which the conclusion logically follows from the premises and all of the premises are true. If either one of these conditions is absent, then the argument is bad and should be rejected.

In the deductive realm, that a conclusion follows from premises means that the argument is *valid* (and *invalid* if the conclusion does not follow). When an argument is valid and all the premises are true, the argument is said to be a good, *sound argument*. The conclusion absolutely, positively, without a doubt, is true, and this is a good thing! In the inductive realm, that a conclusion likely will follow from premises means that the argument is *strong* (and *weak* if the conclusion likely does not follow). When an argument is strong and all the premises are true, the argument is said to be a good, *cogent argument*. The conclusion most likely or probably is true, and this is a good thing too!

So, as rational, adult critical thinkers we must always go through this two-step procedure of checking our own arguments and the arguments of others to see if (a) the conclusion follows from the premises (is the argument deductively valid or inductively strong?) and (b) all of the premises are true. If the argument fails to meet either (a) or (b) or both, then we should reject it, thereby rejecting the person's conclusion as either absolutely false or probably false.

For example, Cartman's argument for pooling together the boys' teeth probably is a bad one because Premise 2 seems false, given the information. It is not true that if they get money from the Tooth Fairy then they will be able to buy a Sega Dreamcast, because the Tooth Fairy only gave Cartman $2.00. $2.00 × 4 boys is $8.00 and, provided we are talking about a new one from the store, that is not enough to buy a Sega Dreamcast. So in the case of this particular deductive argument, the conclusion "If the boys combine their teeth, then they can get a Sega Dreamcast" is false.

On the other hand, the Towelie argument was a good one. It was true that the few times they mentioned towel-related things, Towelie showed up. And given this fact, they had a strong case for drawing the conclusion that he would show up again, asking, of course, "Wanna get high?"

If Chewbacca Lives on Endor, You Must Acquit

At times, checking to see if conclusions follow from premises and if premises are true can be very difficult. Some words have multi-level meanings. And some people will try to convince us of the truth of claims in order to deceive us, sell us something, get us to vote for them, become part of their group, or share their ideology. Often, people will try to convince us that a conclusion follows from a premise or premises when, in fact, it does not, kind of like what the cartoon Cochran does with the Chewbacca Defense.

As we have seen in the first section of this chapter, logicians have a special term for these bad arguments in which the conclusion does not follow from a premise. They call it a *fallacy*, and a fallacy occurs when we inappropriately or incorrectly draw a conclusion from reasons that don't support the conclusion. Fallacies are so common that logicians have names for different types of fallacies.

The Chewbacca Defense is an example of a *red herring* fallacy, which gets its name from a police dog exercise in which policemen, while trying to discern the best trail-hunters, use strong-smelling red herring fishes in an attempt to throw dogs off the trail of a scent. In a red herring fallacy, someone uses claims and arguments that have nothing to do with the issue at hand in order to get someone to draw a conclusion that they believe to be true. So, the claims and arguments are the "red herrings" they use to throw you off the "trail" of reasoning that would lead to another, probably more appropriate, conclusion altogether.

In the episode "Weight Gain 4000," Wendy seems to have a legitimate complaint that Cartman cheated to win the essay contest, but people refuse to draw that conclusion given that they are diverted by the idea of Kathy Lee Gifford coming to town. Even after Wendy produces the evidence that Cartman had really handed in a copy of *Walden* as his essay, they simply don't care about drawing the conclusion that Cartman had cheated. In a lot of *South Park* episodes, people are thrown off the track of issues or arguments by other circumstances or events that capture their attention. This is a humorous way for Trey and Matt to make their points about people's faulty and crazy reasoning.

Hasty generalization is a common fallacy often lampooned on *South Park*. In a hasty generalization, a person fallaciously draws a conclusion about characteristics of a whole group based upon premises concerning characteristics of a small sample of the group. Most times, when we think to ourselves "they're all like that" in talking about anything – people, cars, movies, Kenny's extended family – based upon a small sample of the group we're talking about, we commit a hasty generalization. There is usually no way *definitely* to conclude something about the characteristics of an entire group since we have no knowledge of the entire group. The next member of the group we encounter may turn out to have different characteristics from members of the group we know thus far. Any form of prejudice and stereotyping, by definition, constitutes a hasty generalization.

Consider the way Kyle's Jewish cousin, Kyle 2, is stereotyped in the episode "The Entity," or how Mexicans are typecast as lazy, gays are *all* flamboyant like Big Gay Al or Mr. Slave, and African Americans are reverse typecasted as "richers" in "Here Comes the Neighborhood." Even Officer Barbrady commits the fallacy of hasty generalization in the episode "Chickenlover" when, after reading a copy of Ayn Rand's *Atlas Shrugged*, he concludes that all books must be this bad, and reading "totally sucks ass." The creators of *South Park* play on people's hasty generalizations to make their points in episode after episode, probably because not only is prejudice something that *morally* harms people, but it also *logically* "harms" people's thinking as well.

The *slippery slope* is another fallacy often lampooned on *South Park*. This fallacy occurs when one inappropriately concludes that some further chain of events, ideas, or beliefs will follow from some initial event, idea, or belief and, thus, we should reject the initial event, idea, or belief. It is as if there is an unavoidable "slippery" slope that one is on, and there is no way to avoid sliding down it. Mrs. Broflovski's reasoning about the *The Terrance and Philip Show* being taken off the air might go something like this: "If we allow a show like *The Terrance and Philip Show* on the air, then it'll corrupt my kid, then it'll corrupt your kid, then it'll corrupt all of our kids, then shows like this one will crop up all over the TV, then more and more kids will be corrupted, then all of TV will be corrupted, then the corrupt TV producers will corrupt other areas of our life, etc., etc., etc. So, we must take the *The Terrance and Philip Show* off the air; otherwise, it will lead to all of these other corruptions!!!" If I have accurately characterized Mrs. Broflovski's reasoning here, then we can see the slippery slope. It doesn't follow that the corrupt TV producers will corrupt other areas of our life. All of a sudden we're at the bottom of the slope! What the heck just happened!

In the episode "Clubhouses," Mrs. Marsh uses a kind of slippery slope fallacy in combination with a hasty generalization in response to Stan's grabbing a cookie. Here, we can see the obvious humor involved, as she is going through a rough separation time with her husband: "You men are all alike. First you get a cookie and then you criticize the way I dress, and then it's the way I cook! Next you'll be telling me that you need your space, and that I'm sabotaging your creativity! Go ahead Stanley, get your damn cookie!" Her conclusion is obviously that Stan should not grab a cookie because, otherwise, all of these other things will happen. Further, the "you men are all alike" comment is the result of a hasty generalization.

A *false dilemma* is the fallacy of concluding something based upon premises that include only *two* options, when, in fact, there are three or more options. People are inclined to an "all or nothing" approach to matters, and this usually is reflective of a false dilemma in their thinking. In some situation, could it be that we have a little bit of both, so that we get a both-and, rather than an either-or as our conclusion? In the episode "Mr. Hankey, The Christmas Poo" the people of *South Park* have an all-or-nothing kind of thinking when they conclude that the only way not to offend anyone is to rid the Christmas show of any and all Christmas references. This kind of logic has disastrous consequences, as the show is ruined and people wind up fighting over it. Could they have *included* a few other religious traditions, instead of *excluding* all of them?

Now the both-and strategy, which can avoid a false dilemma, might not always have the best consequences. Consider the episode "Chef Goes Nanners" where, in the end, even though a both-and solution is reached and supposed "ethnic diversity" is added to the South Park flag, it is obviously questionable whether such an addition is good, let alone right, for the townsfolk.

An *argument from inappropriate authority* is a fallacy that sounds like what it is, incorrectly drawing a conclusion from premises based upon a non-credible, non-qualified, or illegitimate authority figure. The best way to avoid this fallacy altogether is to become an authority concerning some matter yourself by getting all of the relevant facts, understanding issues, doing research, checking and double-checking your sources, dialoguing with people, having your ideas challenged, defending your position, being open to revise your position, and the like. However, since we can't become authorities on everything, we need to rely upon others.

In the episode "Do the Handicapped Go to Hell?" Fr. Maxi claims that Kyle (who is Jewish) and Timmy (who is limited in his verbal communication) will both go to hell if they don't confess their sins and, apparently, accept Christ as their savior. At first glance, the boys' conclusion that Kyle and Timmy will go to hell if they don't confess and convert seems not to be a case of the fallacy of appeal to inappropriate authority. After all, Fr. Maxi is an authority of the Church. However, if one investigates Church doctrine, one can see that no human being – pope, priest, or layperson – can make pronouncements about who will go to hell or who will not go to hell.

In an *ad hominem* fallacy someone concludes that a person's claims or arguments are false or not worth listening to because of premises that concern an attack on the actions, personality, or ideology of the person putting forward the claim or argument. In other words, instead of focusing on the person's issue, claims, or argument, one attacks the person (*ad hominem* is Latin for *to the man*). This strategy of discrediting a person's argument by discrediting the person is common. But notice, the person and the person's arguments are two distinct things, and they are not logically related to one another.

For example, in the episode "Butt Out" a cartoon Rob Reiner puts forward an argument for why kids in South Park should not smoke, and he goes on a campaign to get a law enacted to ban smoking in the town. However, not only is he portrayed as having a junk food vice, but he wants to use the boys – quite deceptively – to get the law passed. Now, even if Reiner does have a junk food problem and even if he does something immoral in trying to get the boys to help him, what does this have to do with the arguments concerning whether kids should smoke or whether laws against smoking should be passed in South Park? The answer is, absolutely nothing! Yet, we could be led to the conclusion that no law should be set up in South Park against smoking based upon premises that portray Reiner's apparent hypocrisy and deviance. Again, Reiner's hypocrisy and deviance have nothing to do with the arguments for or against smoking.

The Defense Rests

At least part of the appeal of *South Park* has to do with pointing out the flaws in our thinking, and no one is free from blame. We all occasionally forget to check if all of our premises are true, or believe that a conclusion follows from premises when it doesn't. But the biggest logical problem we have has to do with our staunchly held emotional beliefs, the ones that we just can't let go of no matter what evidence and arguments are presented to us. Often times, this logical problem turns into a factual problem, and people suffer as a result. Some people are almost phobic in their fear of letting go of some belief. I am actually afraid to fly, and no amount of evidence or reasoning will get me to feel good about it, period. People can hold to their ideologies in the same crazy way that I hold to the belief that the plane *will* crash when I am 35,000 feet in the air.

In the episode "All About the Mormons," Stan yells at the Mormons for believing in their religion without any proof, and they smile and explain that it's a matter of faith. Without insulting the Mormons, or any religion for that matter, in that moment Stan is hinting at part of what a rational, adult critical thinker should constantly do. As you read the chapters in this book, I ask you to be mindful of claims, arguments, deductive arguments vs. inductive arguments, good vs. bad arguments, and fallacies that are spoken about by the authors. And, hopefully, the authors have avoided fallacies and bad arguments in putting forward their own positions! With this logic lesson in mind, you can be the judge of that.

PART TWO

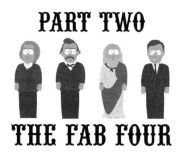

THE FAB FOUR

5

YOU KNOW, I LEARNED SOMETHING TODAY

Stan Marsh and the Ethics of Belief

Henry Jacoby

A wise man, therefore, proportions his belief to the evidence.

David Hume (1711–1776)

If Evidence is Lacking, So What?

People believe all kinds of things for all sorts of reasons; sadly, few pay attention to reasons that involve logic, argument, theory, or evidence. In this regard, the cartoon inhabitants of South Park are no different.

But why should we think critically and rationally? Why does it matter? What harm is there in believing something if it makes you feel good, or provides you with comfort, or gives you hope? If evidence is lacking, so what?

In his classic essay "The Ethics of Belief," the English mathematician and philosopher W.K. Clifford (1845–79) explained the harm when he stated: "Every time we let ourselves believe for unworthy reasons, we weaken our powers of self-control, of doubting, of judicially and fairly weighing evidence." He concluded that it is "wrong always, everywhere, and for anyone, to believe anything upon insufficient evidence."[1]

Amidst the purposely exaggerated craziness and illogic of the citizens of South Park, we are, on occasion, treated to flashes of insight and well thought-out ideas that surprise us. Stan shows off his critical thinking skills as he takes on TV psychics, various cults, and unsupported religious beliefs in a way that would've made Clifford proud. In this chapter, we'll examine how Stan exposes the frauds and the harms they engender, while defending scientific thinking and a healthy skepticism.

Belief and Evidence

We acquire our beliefs in various ways, most notably by observation and authority. The kids believe that Mr. Hankey exists because they see him, but observation is not always trustworthy. Cartman, after all, sees pink Christina Aguilera creatures floating around, but they aren't real. The South Park parents believe the children have ADD because that's the conclusion reached by school psychologists who tested them. Such a belief may be reliable in some circumstances, but not when it comes from the South Park testers, who are fools. Further, we must be careful when relying on authority figures. Scientologists may believe their leaders, who say that there were once frozen alien bodies in the volcanoes of Hawaii. But this is nonsense that should be rejected by any sane person.

We see, then, that rational belief requires evidence. And the more outrageous the belief, the more evidence is required. As Stan told the Mormon family in "All About the Mormons," "If you're going to say things that have been proven wrong, like the first man and woman lived in Missouri and Native Americans came from Jerusalem, then

---

[1] See W.K. Clifford, *The Ethics of Belief and Other Essays*, ed. by Timothy Madigan (Amherst, NY: Prometheus Books, 1999). Epistemology is the area of philosophy concerned with justifying beliefs with evidence. Good introductions to epistemology texts include: Robert Audi, *Epistemology: A Contemporary Introduction* (London: Routledge, 2003); and Jack Crumley, *Introduction to Epistemology* (Columbus, OH: McGraw-Hill, 1998).

you better have something to back it up!" Stan is pointing out here that Mormon beliefs should be rejected unless they can be defended, since they are in addition and contrary to, what are accepted facts. The Mormons here have what philosophers call *the burden of proof*; the obligation is on them to provide the evidence, or proof, for their claims.

In the same episode, two villagers are talking about Joseph Smith. One of them says, "He claims he spoke with God and Jesus." The other one asks, "Well how do you know he didn't?" Is this a fair question? Should claims be accepted if no disproof can be offered?[2] No, the request for disproof is not a request that needs to be answered. The burden of proof always lies with the one who makes the additional claim, not with those who doubt its truth. Otherwise we would be required to entertain *any* belief for which there was no handy disproof. I can't disprove the existence of alien souls inhabiting our bodies, but that doesn't mean I should consider this claim of Scientology to be a meaningful possibility. If our beliefs can't be supported, then they should be rejected or, at least, put aside until further evidence comes about.

Formulating beliefs and making decisions without sufficient evidence leads to trouble. Imagine picking a college, a career, a place to live, a mechanic, a doctor, or anything, for that matter, without reasoning and examining the facts involved. Imagine going through your life just guessing whenever a decision is to be made, or going by how you feel at the moment, or basing decisions on what someone, who may or may not be reliable, has said.

Take as an illustration, the time when Kyle became very ill and, in fact, needed a kidney transplant. But instead, his mother took him to the new "Holistic Healer" in town, Miss Information. At her shop, the townspeople lined up to buy all sorts of useless products from her and her employees who, since they were introduced as Native Americans, must surely know all about healing! Fortunately for Kyle, these "Native Americans" (who turned out to be Cheech and Chong) were honest enough to convince Mrs. Broflovski that Kyle was really sick and should be taken to a real doctor. Stan, who realized from the start that the "healers" were frauds and their methods unscientific,

---

[2] This thinking involves the fallacy of ignorance. For other kinds of fallacious thinking, see Robert Arp's chapter in this volume entitled "The Chewbacca Defense: A *South Park* Logic Lesson."

had been urging this course of action all along. He later tricks Cartman into giving up a kidney, so everything works out well for Kyle in the end. But when we start with beliefs that have been uncritically accepted, the outcome is not usually so fortunate.

Notice too, how closely beliefs are tied to action. In the episode "Trapped in The Closet" Stan tells Tom Cruise that he's not as good an actor as Leonardo Di Caprio, Gene Hackman, or "the guy who played Napoleon Dynamite." This causes poor Tom to become depressed, and he locks himself in the closet. Now, why should a famous actor care what a little boy thinks of his acting skills? Well, he should care if he's a Scientologist and believes, as the current Scientology leaders claim, that the little boy is the reincarnation of Scientology founder L. Ron Hubbard. So the illogical action is caused by a ridiculous belief that is held on the basis, not of any sort of testable evidence (well, they did test Stan's "body thetans" with their "E-Meters" – more unsupported nonsense), but solely on the basis of authority. And the "authority" here is hardly reliable or objective; in fact, later the leading scientologist admits to Stan that it's all made up and he's doing it for the money.

Faith vs. Reason

People often say that their beliefs, especially their religious beliefs, are based on faith. What does this mean? And is this a good idea? First, let's be clear what is meant by *faith* in this context. Sometimes faith refers to a kind of confidence. In the episode "Scott Tenorman Must Die" Cartman was confident that his friends would betray him, and they did. This allowed his plan for revenge on Scott to work perfectly. Cartman, we might say, had faith that his plan would work.

Notice here that this kind of faith is not opposed to reason and evidence. Cartman reasoned that he could accurately predict what his friends would do based on their past actions. This is perfectly reasonable. If, on the other hand, Mr. Garrison had faith that his students would all work hard on their homework assignments, such confidence would be misplaced. He has no good reason to think so. So faith in the sense of being confident may be reasonable or not, depending on one's evidence.

Normally when one talks of religious faith, however, one does not mean confidence based on reason. This kind of faith is in fact *opposed* to reason; quite simply, it is belief without good evidence. After hearing the story of Joseph Smith, a story that Stan points out is unsupported and contrary to known facts, Stan says, "Wait: Mormons actually know this story, and they still believe Joseph Smith was a prophet?" The reply, of course, is "Stan, it's all a matter of faith." So, faith appears to be a kind of fallback position that we take when we can't support our view. Such a move should not be encouraged, for it would render any belief whatsoever acceptable.

Prudential Reasons vs. Evidence

Does a belief have to be supported by evidence to be rational? Can there be other *reasons* that make a belief justified besides evidential ones? Well, philosophers make a distinction between *prudential reasons* and *evidential reasons*. The distinction is easy to illustrate. Suppose that I tell you that John Edward – the self-proclaimed psychic whom Stan puts in his place – really can communicate with the dead. Since you watch *South Park*, you know that John Edward is the "biggest douche in the universe," so you don't believe my claim for a second and demand proof. Suppose I then tell you that if you do believe it, I'll give you lots of money (I show you the briefcase filled with money); but if you don't believe it, I won't (or worse, we can say you'll be killed if you don't believe it!). Now you have a reason to believe that John Edward is not a fraud, and it's a *good reason*. But you still don't have a shred of evidence. Your reason, instead, is a prudential one. It's in your best interest to believe.

Blaise Pascal (1623–62), a French mathematician and philosopher, came up with a well-known attempt to justify religious belief in exactly the same way. His argument has come to be known as Pascal's Wager.[3] Think of belief in God as a bet. If you wager on God (if you

[3]   See Blaise Pascal, *Pascal's Pensées*, trans. by W.F. Trotter (New York: P.F. Collier, 1910). For interesting discussions of the pros and cons of the Wager, see Nicholas Rescher, *Pascal's Wager: A Study of Practical Reasoning in Philosophical Theology* (Notre Dame, IN: University of Notre Dame Press, 1985), and Alan Hájek, "Waging War on Pascal's Wager," *Philosophical Review* 112 (2003), pp. 27–56.

believe) and God exists, you win. God rewards believers with eternal joy and happiness. But if you do not believe and God exists, then you lose. God punishes non-believers with eternal suffering and pain. What if God doesn't exist? Well, in that case the nonbeliever has the truth and the believer doesn't; but whatever positives or negatives result are negligible in comparison to what happens if there is a God. The point is, if you have any chance at all to achieve eternal peace and avoid eternal damnation, you're a fool not to go for it. Prudential reasons reign; it's in your best interest to believe in God.

Notice a few things about Pascal's Wager. First, he's not trying to prove that God exists. If we could prove that there is a God, then the Wager would be pointless (similarly if we could prove that there is no God). Pascal starts by assuming that we don't know either way. Second, Pascal isn't arguing that one should simply have faith. He's instead arguing that religious belief is *reasonable* because it's prudential. Philosophers have offered many criticisms of the Wager, showing that it's not a very good argument for religious belief. Let's look at two of these, as they are nicely illustrated in *South Park*.

You might wonder why God would choose to torture someone for all eternity simply because they don't believe in Him. Isn't God supposed to be perfectly good after all? Why would a good being wish pain and suffering on anyone? In the episode "Cartmanland," Kyle wonders the same thing. Cartman inherits a million dollars and buys an amusement park, while Kyle suffers from hemorrhoid pain. Kyle begins to lose his faith as well as his will to live. If there were a God, he reasons, He wouldn't reward someone like Cartman (who is evil) while allowing me (who is good) to suffer. Kyle says: "Cartman is the biggest asshole in the world. How is it that God gives him a million dollars? Why? How can you do this? There are people starving in Alabama, and you give Cartman a million dollars? If someone like Cartman can get his own theme park, then there is no God. There's no God, dude."

Kyle's parents, in an attempt to restore his faith, tell him that God sometimes causes us to suffer, perhaps to test our faith, and they read him the story of Job. (Incidentally, the idea of God testing us makes little sense; since He is all-knowing, He would already know what we would do, rendering any test pointless.) But the story horrifies Kyle: "That's the most horrible story I've ever heard. Why would God do such horrible things to a good person just to prove a point to Satan?"

Kyle reasons here that if there really were a God, there would be justice in the world. God wouldn't reward someone like Cartman and neither would He allow the good, like Job and Kyle, to suffer.

We can see how all of this applies to Pascal's Wager. Imagine someone who is an extremely good person – loving, honest, helpful, kind – yet she does not believe in God. She thinks one ought to be moral to make the world a better place, let's say, not because God says so or to get some personal reward. Does it really make sense to think that God (who is all good, remember) would allow such a person to be tormented for all eternity?

A second – and much worse problem for Pascal's argument – is that he assumes that we *know* the outcomes of our wager. Pascal says that God rewards believers and punishes nonbelievers. But this is just an assumption. If we had proof of this, we would already know that the religious view of things is true, and thus we wouldn't need a prudential argument. Remember, the point of the Wager is to convince us to believe when we have no evidence of God's existence (or non-existence). Without evidence, there are many possibilities to consider. Perhaps God rewards everyone, or maybe there's no afterlife at all. Maybe God values reason, and punishes those who believe blindly without any evidence. There are endless possibilities.

Even if we could establish that only religious believers get rewarded (and how would we establish that without rendering the Wager pointless?), we still have the problem of *which* religious beliefs to have. In "Do The Handicapped Go To Hell?" we're treated to a bunch of religious folks who, to their horror, find themselves in hell. They are told that they have the *wrong religious beliefs*; only the Mormons go to heaven!

What's The Harm, Dude?

Those who can make you believe absurdities can make you commit atrocities.

Voltaire (1694–1778)

Maybe Pascal's Wager doesn't show us that we *should* believe in God, but still, we might ask, what's the harm? Perhaps we should only have beliefs that are based on reasons, but what's wrong with prudential reasons? In the episode "All About the Mormons" Gary tells Stan: "Maybe us Mormons do believe in crazy stories that make absolutely no sense. And maybe Joseph Smith did make it all up. But I have a great life and a great family, and I have the Book of Mormon to thank for that. The truth is, I don't care if Joseph Smith made it all up." And in "The Biggest Douche in the Universe" John Edward tries to defend himself to Stan when he says: "What I do doesn't hurt anybody. I give people closure and help them cope with life." So, echoing Gary, Stan's Mormon friend, we could similarly say we don't care if Edward is a fraud, as long as what he does makes people feel good. Again, what's the harm?

For one, unsupported beliefs can lead to harmful consequences. In "Timmy 2000" the belief that Timmy has ADD (that he is not just mentally disabled) eventually causes a wild spread of unnecessary prescription drugs and, worse, a belief that the music of Phil Collins is actually good. In "Super Best Friends" some of the followers of magician David Blaine blindly follow him and commit suicide, believing they will go to heaven. And we've already seen how belief in the healing powers of New Age healers almost cost Kyle his life. In each of these cases, the believers feel good about their beliefs; they provide hope or comfort. But they are still extremely dangerous.

A second sort of harm is mental weakness and laziness. As Clifford said, "Every time we let ourselves believe for unworthy reasons, we weaken our powers of self-control, of doubting, of judicially and fairly weighing evidence." His point is that even if one's unsupported belief causes no immediate harm (as in the examples from *South Park*), it still weakens the mind. We become used to accepting ideas uncritically, grow mentally lazy, and this encourages others to do the same. Most of the citizens of South Park rarely use their critical faculties. This makes them easy prey for every cult, fad, or con that comes to town. Think of just about any episode of *South Park*, and you'll find examples of this mental weakness and laziness.

Inquiry, Hard Work, and Progress

To understand a final reason why uncritically accepting unsupported beliefs – however hopeful they might make us feel – is not such a good thing, we turn to Stan at his best. Again, from "The Biggest Douche in the Universe," John Edward challenges Stan: "Everything I tell people is positive and gives them hope; how does that make me a douche?" Stan's reply is brilliant: "Because the big questions in life are tough; why are we here, where are we from, where are we going? But if people believe in asshole douchy liars like you, we're never going to find the real answers to those questions. You aren't just lying, you're slowing down the progress of all mankind, you douche." He follows this up with another terrific speech, this time to the members of Edward's believing audience:

> You see, I learned something today. At first I thought you were all just stupid listening to this douche's advice, but now I understand that you're all here because you're scared. You're scared of death and he offers you some kind of understanding. You all want to believe in it so much, I know you do. You find comfort in the thought that your loved ones are floating around trying to talk to you, but think about it: is that really what you want? To just be floating around after you die having to talk to this asshole? We need to recognize this stuff for what it is: magic tricks. Because whatever is really going on in life and in death is much more amazing than this douche.

We can all learn something today from what Stan has said here. First, he recognizes that it's wrong to dismiss someone with unsupported beliefs as being stupid. We want answers; we need comfort. Sometimes we rely more on emotion than reason to satisfy ourselves, but that doesn't mean we lack intelligence. We poke fun, we often ridicule; but, even in South Park, it's always better when we try for some understanding.

Second, Stan reminds us of Clifford's point that settling for easy answers not only weakens the mind, but also prevents us from finding real answers. In science, philosophy, and any rational pursuit where we require answers to questions, the spirit of inquiry – combined with hard work – is what leads to progress. Settling for magical answers that make us feel good only slows us down.

And speaking of magic, Stan reminds us finally that there's real magic, wonder, and beauty in the universe. As he says, whatever is really going on in life and in death is truly amazing. We don't want to miss it, dude.

6

RESPECT MY AUTHORITA! IS CARTMAN "THE LAW," AND EVEN IF HE IS, WHY SHOULD WE OBEY HIM?

Mark D. White

Get Your Big Wheels Ready

Forget RoboCop, forget T.J. Hooker, forget Officer Barbrady – no one strikes more fear into the hearts of evil-doers than Eric Cartman in the classic "Chickenlover" episode. Dressed in his best Erik Estradas, riding his CHiPped-out Big Wheel with his trusty nightstick at his side, Cartman demands that the fine citizens of South Park "respect my authorita!" He stops Stan's father for speeding (when he wasn't), interrupts an incident of domestic violence at Kenny's house (before joining in), and apprehends the infamous Chickenlover (albeit, after he had already been caught). And yet, Cartman is an inspiration to us all, embodying the qualities we hope for in police officers whom we trust with our day-to-day safety.

Settle down, Kyle, I'm only kidding – of course, Cartman doesn't strike us as the most imposing law-enforcement figure (though his figure is rather imposing in itself). But I'm sure we've all seen real police officers that inspire less respect than they should. (Insert your favorite donut joke or Barney Fife reference here.) But we still have respect for what they represent – law and order. (CH-CHUNG!) No, I didn't forget what show I'm writing about. This chapter is about what obligates us as citizens to obey the law, no matter what form it may take, even a corpulent little potty-mouth with delusions of grandeur.

66

In their brilliance, Matt Stone and Trey Parker (with episode co-writer David Goodman) raised several important philosophical issues when they made Eric Cartman a representative of "the law" in South Park. Why should we listen to him? Why should we respect his "authorita"? Why should we respect *any* police officer, or more generally, why should we respect the law at all? What is "the law," and who decides what it is? And what is the relationship between law and morality, if there even is one? These are all questions debated in the philosophy of law, otherwise known as legal philosophy or *jurisprudence*. Philosophers since ancient times have disagreed on these issues, and we will meet a few of them along the way. (Be nice, Cartman.) So get your Big Wheels ready, because we're going for a ride. (And watch out for Kenny – no one dies in my chapter.)

Commands, Threats, and Authorita

Let's start with a biggie – what is "the law" anyway? I'm not asking what is the law regarding murder, parallel parking, or having conjugal relations with chickens. When I say "the law" I mean something much more general, such as when we say we have respect for the law, or that we live under the rule of law. In other words, what makes the particular laws listed above part of "the law?" Or, what makes Eric Cartman "the law?" And why isn't simply anyone "the law," such as Chef or Mr. Hankey?

A man named John Austin is going to help us answer these questions.[1] A nineteenth-century legal scholar, Austin described a theory of law that came to be known as the *command theory of law*, because he saw law as consisting of commands backed by threats. The government tells us not to make love to chickens, so if we decide to make love to a chicken anyway, we are punished (hopefully by being someone else's "chicken" in the big house!). Each command backed by

---

[1] Austin's most important work is *The Providence of Jurisprudence Determined* (1832), and excerpts can be found in most legal philosophy collections, such as Joel Feinberg and Jules Coleman's *Philosophy of Law*, seventh edition (Belmont, CA: Wadsworth Publishing, 2003) or Timothy Shiell's *Legal Philosophy: Selected Readings* (Belmont, CA: Wadsworth Publishing, 1993).

threat of a sanction is a law, and the entire body of such commands is "the law" – there is no sense of law as a system in Austin's writings.

There's more to say about Austin, but let's use what we've got so far. Does this description of law fit Cartman? When he orders Stan's father out of his car, and threatens to whack him in the shins with his nightstick if he doesn't obey, Cartman has issued a command backed by a sanction. So according to what we know so far about Austin, Cartman is the law.

But this can't be right, can it? Just because he orders people around and threatens to beat them? Anyone can do that, even Stan's dad at Little League games, but that doesn't make him "the law." Not surprisingly, this part of Austin's theory has been criticized as applying just as well to a gunman robbing a bank as to a police officer ordering him to stop, because it implies that anyone threatening physical violence to get what one wants is "the law." What's missing here is some sense of authority or *pedigree*, which would explain why we have more respect for an unarmed police officer than an armed mugger, or for Officer Barbrady compared to Eric Cartman.

Of course, Austin recognized that the law does not consist of just anybody's commands, even if backed by effective threats, but must be issued by someone in authority. Austin called this person the *sovereign*. The word itself doesn't answer much – can Cartman just declare himself the sovereign (if someone tells him what it means)? If he can't, someone would have to make him the sovereign, and who could do that but – the sovereign? But who made that person the sovereign?

"Mpm-pr-rpm-mrm-mp!" That's right, Kenny – there has to be more to this sovereign concept than just calling yourself the sovereign, or getting someone else to say it (and then who made that person sovereign, and so on). Austin had two conditions for recognizing the true sovereign: that person (or group) must be habitually obeyed by most of the citizens "subject" to him, and that person must not regularly obey anyone else. Any person (or group) that meets these requirements would be sovereign over people, and that person or group's commands would be law.

In terms of Austin's theory of law, this does take care of the gunman problem, since the bank robber is not habitually obeyed by most people – at most, just by the bank clerk he's robbing at any particular time! So the mugger is certainly not a sovereign. Then what about Eric Cartman, or any police officer for that matter? They are not writing the laws, merely enforcing them, so perhaps that is the wrong question to ask. But then, who is the sovereign in the United States, or the United Kingdom, or any modern democracy?

That's how Austin gets into trouble again. His idea of the sovereign was better suited for the days of kings and queens, when these privileged individuals reigned over their subjects, imposing their commands but obeying no one else's. But this idea doesn't translate very well to modern democracies. Who is the sovereign, for instance, in the United States – the President? Congress? the Supreme Court? (Use the British parliament and prime minister if you like, guv'na.) OK, maybe the separation of powers confuses the issue, so let's just say "the federal government." But the members of the federal government are – in theory, anyway – subject to their own laws, and Austin's sovereign is subject to no one, not even himself. And who elects these folks – we, the people. So are we the sovereign? It's enough to make your head spin like Moses at Jewbilee!

Getting to the "Hart" of the Matter

So Austin's idea of the sovereign doesn't hold water anymore, but the more general concept of pedigree is still important. The law has to come from some place of authority, and legal scholars still debate the ultimate source of it. One of Austin's fiercest critics, and the father of modern legal philosophy, a man named H.L.A. Hart, said that the law is best understood as a system of rules.[2] He split these rules into two types: primary and secondary rules. Primary rules tell us what to do or what not to do. When Cartman pulls over Stan's dad for driving 40 mph in a 40 mph zone, he is stating and enforcing a primary rule (however nonsensically).

Primary rules are laws as we usually think of them, but they don't answer the authority question – that's what secondary rules are for. Secondary rules are "rules about rules," and the most important secondary rule is the rule of recognition, which tells us which primary rules are valid or not. This is Hart's version of pedigree, and he argued that it is better suited to explaining various features of the law

---

[2] Hart's classic work is *The Concept of Law* (Oxford: Oxford University Press, 1961).

than Austin's idea of the sovereign. For instance, in the United States, the Constitution is the rule of recognition – it lays out the three branches of the federal government, as well as defining the laws they can and can't pass. (Does this work perfectly? Of course not, but to be fair, Hart never claimed it did.) Even in the days of kings and queens, there were certain rules of succession – in England, for example, to this day the crown traditionally passes to the oldest son first, then younger sons, then daughters and, if necessary, to various other relations. This hasn't always worked perfectly either, as shown by the Wars of the Roses and other conflicts for the crown throughout English history. But as with the Constitution, it served as a guide to recognizing which laws were or weren't to be obeyed.

How does this relate to our boy Cartman? What is the rule of recognition that would recognize his commands as valid in South Park? Well, Officer Barbrady deputized him, so if we recognize his authority to deputize Cartman, then we may have to respect Cartman. But where does Barbrady's authority come from? He cited Article 39 section 2 of the South Park police code when he deputized the boys, but that just shifts the focus of the problem. What gives that document the authority to establish a police force?

Starts to sound like the chicken(lover) and the egg, doesn't it? There is a bit of that to Hart's concept of rules of recognition, and that is little improvement over Austin's idea of the sovereign. In the US, the Constitution is only as valid as the people believe it to be, and if the American people lose faith in it, it will begin to lose its power as the foundation of the American government and legal system. As I mentioned before, even the rules of succession in the British monarchy, which were (fairly) straightforward, lost their power when not applied consistently. (Next time the Booktastic Bus rolls around, read up on Lady Jane Grey, who was Queen of England for about as long as Kenny lasts in any given *South Park* episode, with a very tenuous claim to the throne.)

Why Obey the Law at All, Dude?

OK, let's say we accept that Cartman does represent the law in South Park. But that doesn't answer this question: why should we obey the law at all? In other words, what obligation do we have to obey the law? Are we morally obligated to obey the law? Or do laws reflect morality, so if we behave morally, we're automatically obeying the law, which makes the law irrelevant? And what if laws demand immoral acts – what obligation do we have then?

Let's go way back to Plato, who often wrote philosophy in the form of dialogues involving another ancient philosopher (and Plato's teacher), Socrates. In the dialogue named *Crito*, Socrates is in jail, waiting to be executed for questioning the Greek gods (talk about authority issues!).[3] His friend Crito visits to try to convince Socrates to break free. After a lot of back and forth – very big with ancient philosophers, who must have had a lot of time on their hands – Socrates replies that when a citizen decides to live in a certain area, with its own government and laws, he agrees to live by those laws. After all, if he does not like them, he can leave. (If he can't, that's another story.) Think of it this way: you benefit from other people obeying the law, and you owe these people the benefit of obeying the law yourself. If you exempted yourself from the laws that everyone else is bound to, then you are receiving the benefits of the law unfairly, and that is wrong.

Many philosophers have made similar arguments, which all come down to reciprocity – citizens owe either the government or their fellow citizens (or both) for benefits they receive from the law. But these arguments make a critical assumption – that all laws are good laws, ones that benefit the people subject to them. Everyone benefits from laws against murder – even potential murderers, who are protected from being killed by other murderers! (There's the reciprocity point again – murderers would violate a law that they benefit from themselves.) We all benefit from traffic laws, because they allow us to drive without hitting each other (too much), whether we're driving a hybrid Pious or Mr. Garrison's "IT."

But what about laws that don't provide any benefit to all? Consider laws that have prevented people of a particular gender, race, or ethnic group from voting, or working in particular jobs, or riding in certain seats on the bus. Did Rosa Parks benefit from the law that would have forced her to the back of the bus? Of course not – but we all benefited from her refusal to obey that law. This discussion leads to an argument made by thinkers such as Saint Thomas Aquinas and

---

[3] Excerpts from this dialogue can also be found in most legal philosophy books (including the two cited above).

Dr. Martin Luther King, that even if there is a reason to obey the law in general, bad laws in particular deserve no respect, and as in Ms. Parks' case, some deserve disobedience.

Aquinas put it very succinctly: bad laws are no laws at all.[4] In other words, we are under no obligation to obey a bad law. To Aquinas, the true law is God's law, and man's laws are just approximations – or abominations, if man gets them wrong. Since we are always bound to God's law, we are also bound to ignore man-made law if it conflicts with the word of God.

Aquinas' view of law is called "natural law," and was originally strongly tied to religion, but modern thought on natural law is more secular. Immanuel Kant (1724–1804), the famous eighteenth-century philosopher, had a theory of law derived from his theory of ethics, which were in many ways hostile to religion, including his cherished Pietist upbringing. Martin Luther King, though a deeply religious man who drew on Aquinas' writings, also talked about unjust laws purely in political terms, as laws imposed on a minority that the majority itself does not follow. Finally, Ronald Dworkin, one of the most highly regarded legal philosophers of our time, casts his variant of natural law thinking in terms of moral principles essential to the legal system itself, not as part of any particular religious tradition. What all of these writers have in common is that they believe there is more to the law than just merely what particular lawmakers pass at any particular time.[5]

Let's Ask Another Guy with Three Initials – They're Smart . . .

OK, so we shouldn't obey bad laws, but let's rule those laws out. (After all, Cartman's not writing any laws, a fact for which all in

---

[4] Aquinas' most important legal writings are contained in his famous *Summa Theologica*, questions 90–97. See, for example, *Thomas Aquinas: Treatise on Law*, trans. by Stanley Parry (New York: Henry Regnery, 1964).

[5] For Kant, see *Kant: The Metaphysics of Morals*, ed. by Mary Gregor (Cambridge: Cambridge University Press, 1996); for King, see his famous "Letter from Birmingham Jail," included in most legal philosophy collections and published as *Letter from Birmingham Jail* (New York: Harper Collins, 1994); and for Dworkin, see *Taking Rights Seriously* (Cambridge, MA: Harvard University Press, 1978).

South Park should be thankful!) Even if we just count the good laws, the laws that truly help protect our selves and our property, still we can ask: what obligation do we have to follow these laws? The arguments based on reciprocity that we saw before seem to make sense, but a modern philosopher named M.B.E. Smith argues that they really don't hold water.[6] (I wish I had three first initials – how about M.A.D. White?)

First, Smith says that if we didn't ask for a benefit, we don't owe anything for it. If we did, then we would be forced to pay for things we don't want all the time. Someone could mow my lawn or wash my car and expect me to pay for it, even though I didn't ask to have these things done. While we certainly benefit from laws, we never actually asked for them, and therefore we don't owe anything back. Second, there are other ways to reciprocate for benefits – you shouldn't necessarily have to pledge total subservience and obedience, which is what a strict obligation to obey the law would imply. (But I bet Cartman's mom would love that idea!)

Smith says that the reciprocity argument works better if phrased in terms of fairness, as philosophers H.L.A. Hart and John Rawls did.[7] Everybody else obeys the law, so you should too – to break the law yourself would be unfair. But this still connects back to receiving benefit and not returning it, which assumes that each person actually does benefit from everybody else obeying the law, and likewise suffers some harm if someone breaks the law. But is someone harmed every time a law is broken? If Ms. Choksondik runs a stop sign at 4 a.m. with no one around, has she hurt anybody? Has she taken advantage of everybody else's obedience and hurt them in exchange? It is hard to see how, and Smith concludes that the understanding of reciprocity as fairness works better in small groups, not societies as a whole, in which one person's behavior often affects few if any other people.

Smith takes on Plato as well. (The three initials help – think of what Plato could have done with some initials!) Plato's argument was

---

[6] M.B.E. Smith's article is titled "Is There a Prima Facie Obligation to Obey the Law?" and originally appeared in the *Yale Law Journal* 82 (1973).

[7] On this topic, see Hart's article "Are There Any Natural Rights?" *Philosophical Review* 64 (1955), pp. 175–91, and Rawls' article "Legal Obligation and the Duty of Fair Play" in his *Collected Papers*, ed. by Samuel Freeman (Cambridge, MA: Harvard University Press, 1999), pp. 117–29.

based on something that philosophers call implicit consent to a *social contract*, a hypothetical agreement between a government and its citizens that everyone would have consented to if they had been given the chance. Remember that his point was that if you decide to live in a certain area, you (implicitly) agree to abide by its laws. The problem with this is simple – one can say "I didn't agree to nothin'," followed by something more colorful (if we're talking about one of our boys in *South Park*). If the social contract is hypothetical, and no one actually agreed to it anyway, what force does it have in defending an obligation to obey the law? This is not to say that social contract theory is not useful as a thought experiment, but Smith (and others) argue that it does not carry enough weight to ground this idea.

So what does Smith conclude? He denies any obligation to obey the law, even good laws. Why? Because if a law is a good law, then it presumably prohibits us from doing something truly wrong or bad, and we have a moral obligation not to do these things anyway. The fact that they are also against the law does not make that obligation any stronger, so there is no independent obligation to obey the law. Take murder, for instance – the law against unjustified killing prohibits an act that is clearly wrong, whether it is against the law or not. Does the fact that it is against the law make the act of killing any worse? I would think it's about as bad as it can get, and being illegal doesn't make it any worse. Since breaking the law doesn't add much "bad" to the act of killing, how could we be obligated not to break it? Smith argues that we're not – the only true obligation is the one not to kill, and the law simply attaches a penalty if we do kill someone. (The same logic applies to chicken-loving, harboring Romanian quintuplets, or what have you.)

The Big Question: Law and Morality

There is one problem with the argument above – that there is a moral obligation to do the things the law commands, so the law has no independent force to oblige us – and it's a big one. It assumes a connection between the law and morality that scholars in the natural law tradition like Aquinas accept, but many legal philosophers don't, going back to John Austin and Jeremy Bentham. These scholars are called *legal positivists*, and they believe that law should be understood as the laws passed by those in authority, with no necessary moral foundation.

H.L.A. Hart, a leading positivist, admitted that morality and the law often deal with similar things, like murder, theft, or doing the nasty with chickens, but there is no *necessary* link between the two. If laws are simply identified by a rule of recognition, then there is nothing to say these laws also have to coincide with morality. And if law has no moral foundation, there is no moral reason to do what the law commands, so the only reason to obey the law is, well, because it's the law. So there must be an obligation to obey the law, and we're back to Hart's argument based on fairness that we discussed above.

These are not easy questions – the interesting ones never are! Law and morality are both ways to control people's behavior and ensure a civil society, but their interaction is very complex, and much of the work being done today in legal philosophy deals with this issue. Most legal philosophers today would be considered legal positivists, though there are still prominent natural law theorists to put up a good fight. (Let's hope they don't meet at their kids' Little League games, though.)

As fans of the series are aware, *South Park* is a very philosophical show – issues of ethics, religion, and race, just to name a few, are raised in almost every episode, hidden (or not) among clever satire, talking poo, and fart jokes. The show also highlights topics of legal philosophy, such as the legitimacy of Eric Cartman as a representative of the law in South Park, and the nature of law in general. What seems like a simple question – what is law? – turns out to be one of the most perplexing questions in philosophy.

But just because it's a very philosophical question doesn't mean it's not important for real world people like us (or even cartoon folks like those who live in South Park). As Matt and Trey have shown time and time again, we live in a world filled with evil dictators, corrupt and inept democracies, and everything in between. Most good satire pokes fun at our political leaders, elected or not, but that leads us again to the question: with leaders like these, what makes their laws legitimate? In a sense, the legitimacy of laws is ultimately traced to the legitimacy of government (as we saw when we talked about the rule of recognition and the US Constitution). It is easy to question the legitimacy of a dictatorship, but we can also question democracies.

What obligation does a person have to a government that she didn't elect?

Recall the scene from *Monty Python and the Holy Grail* where an English peasant says, "well I didn't vote for you!" upon meeting Arthur, self-proclaimed King of the Britons. Confused as she may have been about her political environment (covered in shit as she was), her question highlights feelings we all may have, and that legal philosophers still struggle with.[8] And whatever answer they come up with, we can count on Matt and Trey to make some hilarious, insightful commentary on it, even if the words come out of the mouth of an unlikely philosopher like Eric Cartman.

---

[8] For more on the link between obligation to obey the law and the legitimacy of the state, see William Edmundson's article "State of the Art: The Duty to Obey the Law," *Legal Theory* 10 (2004), pp. 215–59, as well as his collection of articles on the topic, *The Duty to Obey the Law: Selected Philosophical Readings* (Lanham, MD: Rowman & Littlefield, 1999).

7

OH MY GOD! THEY KILLED KENNY ... AGAIN

Kenny and Existentialism

Karin Fry

Kenny's Existential Crisis

Any fan of *South Park* knows that, until season 6, Kenny gets killed in almost every episode. While the Christmas episode from the first season shows a cheering and relieved Kenny who avoids destruction (presumably because it is *Christmas*), generally speaking, Kenny's death is inevitable. We know it's coming – it's just a matter of how, and in what new and inventive way, he will meet his demise. Ozzy Osbourne bites his head off, Saddam Hussein shoots him, he internally combusts, he is frozen in carbonite, decapitated, stabbed, electrocuted, micro-waved, drowned . . . the list goes on and on. Since Kenny was killed off for a year in the sixth season, he does not die nearly as often, but we still assume that when grave danger is near, he'll be the victim. Of course, the premise is absurd since Kenny is miraculously revived in each episode, and no explanation is given for his resurrection. Still, the joke never gets old, and we eagerly await his death along with Stan and Kyle's retort: "Oh God. They killed Kenny. You bastards!" Stan and Kyle immediately get over the injustice of Kenny's death, of course, and move on as if nothing happened, and Cartman rarely notices at all. But, for a brief second, we laugh at the absurdity of Kenny's dire situation.

Believe it or not, there are parallels between Kenny's weekly mortal struggle and the philosophical school of *existentialism*. Existentialism is a philosophical movement that arose in the nineteenth and twentieth centuries in Europe. Although there are a wide variety of existentialists, and a great deal of debate concerning the definition of existentialism and which thinkers "count" as existentialists, there are some common themes among them. Jean-Paul Sartre (1905–1980), a famous French existentialist, wrote an essay in the 1940s that sought to define this movement, suggesting the one thing that existentialists have in common is their view of humanity.[1] While many philosophies claim that humans have a purpose in life that has been decided in advance by God or nature, Sartre rejects this view. That is not to say that all existentialists are atheists, but whether or not a person believes in God does not change the fact that the meaning of human life and the state of the world is decidedly a human affair. For existentialists, there can be no comfort in seeking some divine plan, or using fate or destiny as an excuse for why an event occurred.

Sartre defines an existentialist as anyone who thinks that existence precedes essence for humans. This means that humans are born first and then, through their decisions and actions, construct their essential character traits – like whether they are a good or bad people, kind or cruel, or humorous or boring (Sartre, p. 28). It is not predetermined by God or genetics that Cartman be the kind of person he is, and he could choose to be like Stan and Kyle instead. Since a person's character traits are not predetermined, Sartre thinks that we are solely responsible for who we are. The question of "who" is extremely important to the existentialists, since all people must face up to the task of deciding for themselves what is important to them, and what kind of people they are going to be.

So who is Kenny? Since Kenny mumbles every bit of dialogue he is given, this is a tough question. One thing we do know is that Kenny is poor and his family is on welfare. Kenny's dad is an alcoholic who's unemployed. His mom wears an "I'm with stupid" tee shirt, and they are so poor that they eat frozen waffles for dinner – as Cartman notes "without side dishes." They also literally live on the wrong side of the tracks in South Park, which Cartman calls the ghetto, and there are rats in his house. According to existentialists, these facts about

---

[1] See Jean-Paul Sartre, "Existentialism and Humanism," in *Jean-Paul Sartre: Basic Writings*, ed. by Stephen Priest (London: Routledge, 2001), pp. 25–46. Subsequent citations as (Sartre, p. "x") in the text.

Kenny's situation do not imply anything about the character of Kenny himself. It is not divinely ordained that Kenny be born into a poor family, and there is nothing about the fact that Kenny is born into meager circumstances that will predetermine what kind of person he will be or what kind of future is open to him.

The second thing we know about Kenny is that he has an unusual relation with mortality. There is usually no explanation given for why Kenny dies, or why he can come back to life. A partial explanation occurs in the episode "Cartman Joins NAMBLA." After Kenny is run over by an ambulance taking his pregnant mother to the hospital, Mrs. McCormick has another son who they name Kenny in honor of his dead brother. The episode ends with the McCormicks noting that this has happened 52 times before, suggesting that each Kenny is a new one. The audience is not meant to take this joke too seriously though, especially since no reason is given for the accelerated growth pattern of the new Kennys. Generally speaking, the humor lies in the fact that there is no explanation for why Kenny must die, or why he can come back in the next episode. Since Kenny cannot speak, his character is less developed than the other boys, and his primary function is to die for the sake of a laugh and come back as if nothing happened.

Kenny seems to be unusually fated to his perilous condition. By contrast, for Sartre, there is no fate or destiny and, though we do not choose to be mortal and would prefer to keep on living, almost all factors in our lives are the result of our free choice, so no one would be condemned to such a predetermined fate. In the episode "Cripple Fight," it is suggested that perhaps Kenny is doomed beyond measure. When Timmy is trying to get rid of Jimmy – the other "handicapable" child in South Park – he gives him an orange parka like Kenny's. Immediately, Jimmy is bombarded with a safe falling from the buildings above, a near-car accident, a bird swooping down to capture him, gunshots, a fire, a stampeding herd of cows, and even the space shuttle nearly crashing into him. Jimmy lives, but clearly in the world of South Park, Kenny does have a particular fate, and seems to be under a curse that he has not chosen. Kenny's fate of repetitive death is something that he must face alone, and seems to be part of his essence.

Kenny may not choose the fact that he dies (or that he dies over and over again) but, from an existentialist perspective, Kenny does have responsibility for how he reacts to his mortal situation. The way that Kenny reacts to what the world throws at him helps to define who he is as a person. On many occasions, Kenny seems to know that he is doomed and makes prudent decisions to avoid danger, like when he chooses to take Home Economics, rather than shop, as the visions of circular saws, drills, and other dangerous equipment swirl in his head. Occasionally, he shivers and cowers when danger is near. Other times, he seems blissfully ignorant of his impending doom, like when Charles Manson escapes from prison and takes the boys to the mall, and Kenny happily walks off with him alone. Ironically, Kenny does not die at Manson's hands. Rather, the police shoot him when Manson is trying to surrender. Unfortunately, the orange of his parka also matches the orange of a penitentiary uniform. At times, Kenny responds to his death by heroically sacrificing himself for the group, like in the film *South Park: Bigger, Longer & Uncut* when Kenny chooses to go back to hell, so that things can get back to normal between the Americans and Canadians and the war can stop. Sometimes, at least, Kenny actively chooses his response to the situation and positively contributes to the definition of his character.

Authentically choosing one's character is important to the existentialists. Removing the possibility of a predetermined life plan means there are no excuses for who a person chooses to be. Since this is the only chance we have to live our lives, it's very important to make choices that matter to us, rather than following along with the crowd or succumbing to social pressures. Kenny has choices to make, and those choices define his character.

The Purposeful Death

Unlike Sartre's view, one of Kenny's deaths actually has a predetermined purpose. In the episode "Best Friends Forever" Kenny is run over by a bus, but this time, it's part of God's plan. Kenny is the only human to reach level 60 in the video game "Heaven vs. Hell" which, unbeknownst to Kenny, is merely a test for using identical talents to direct the real battle that is about to take place between the armies of heaven and hell. Kenny's death is not entirely predetermined since, if

God knew Kenny would do the best on the video game, there would be no need to distribute the game worldwide as a test. However, as the winner of the game, Kenny's death is sanctioned by God. Kenny is needed to battle the armies of Satan.

There is a plan and a reason for Kenny's death, at last! But of course, we as humans miss it entirely. Making clear references to the removal of Terry Schiavo's feeding tube in Florida in 2005, Kenny is unfortunately kept alive in a persistent vegetative state, making his direction of the armies of heaven impossible. His soul becomes stuck in his body in the hospital room, and Cartman takes the case to the Supreme Court so that he can inherit the legally dead Kenny's video game. Eventually the humans do the right thing – they killed Kenny. Kenny is able to defeat the armies of Satan and save heaven.

So, given the fact that there is a divine plan and purpose for Kenny's death does this mean that, in this case, his death is no longer in line with the existentialist perspective? No. Even if there is a divinely inspired plan, the citizens of South Park cannot know it. As Jean-Paul Sartre says, the actual existence of God would change nothing from an existentialist perspective since, even if there is a plan or purpose, we cannot know it; therefore, we are still left with the need to choose for ourselves (Sartre, p. 46). Prior to being run over by the bus, Kenny knows nothing about the "divine" plan. Kenny's mom nags Kenny for playing the video game stating that, if he died tomorrow, he would wish he did more with his life than play video games for two weeks straight. She's wrong, but Kenny doesn't know it. So it is left to Kenny to make the decisions for his life without the consolation in knowledge of a divine plan.

Who are "The Bastards"?

Existentialist philosophy stresses the need for humans to take their mortality seriously. Sometimes Kenny's death is not the result of anyone who is easily identifiable as responsible. When Kenny is struck by lightning, Stan and Kyle scream "Oh my God. They killed Kenny. You Bastards!" Kenny's girlfriend from the third season, Kelly, is the first to ask Stan and Kyle, who are "they?" Stan and Kyle of course have no real response and just assert, "you know . . . they."

Stan and Kyle scream out of anger and frustration with the condition of mortality itself, and the wretchedness of the human condition. Existentialists believe that we do not choose our mortality. Rather, we are abandoned in the universe, and mortality limits our freedom. When Kyle and Stan scream curses, they briefly touch on the injustice of our mortality. For humans, there are no clear answers concerning why we are here, or why we have to die.

The universe does indeed seem cruel for Kenny. He dies so many times and in so many different ways. But on top of that, no one seems to care that Kenny dies. The characters care when their other friends die. When Kyle is sick and dying of kidney failure Stan says, "if a friend died, I don't know what I'd do." Kenny is visibly annoyed by this comment and is later hit by a piano, with no remorse shown by his friends. The one person who seems to care at all (aside from Kenny's parents) is Kenny's girlfriend, Kelly. Unlike the rest of Kenny's so-called friends, she actually gives him CPR and saves him when he gets struck by lightning. Typically, Stan and Kyle curse those responsible and move on as if nothing happened. They never try to help him or call an ambulance.

The only episode where Kenny's death has a lasting impact on the boys is in "Kenny Dies," when he dies of a terminal disease and is in fact killed off for about a year. By the fifth season, Stone and Parker acknowledge that they are sick of making Kenny die, and they decide to kill him off.[2] The entire joke of the episode is that, this time, the boys actually care that Kenny is diagnosed with a terminal illness. Stan can't bear to see Kenny in his hospital bed and misses the chance to say goodbye to him. The prior deaths are forgotten, and cheesy piano music chimes in to add emotional weight to the boys' sadness. Overwhelmed with grief, Cartman actually cries and is moved to hug Kyle. Cartman then goes to Washington to get the politicians to repeal the ban on stem cell research so that he can save his friend. Speaking through tears, Cartman says, "I love Kenny McCormick, and I want you to love him too." Of course, later we discover that for Cartman, at least, it was all an act. He wanted to get the stem cell research ban repealed and attempt to make his own Shaky's Pizza restaurant with stem cells.

---

[2] DVD mini-commentary from *South Park: The Complete Fifth Season*.

The Absurd

Kenny is subjected to the cruel fates, which kill him over and over again, and none of his friends seem to care. He certainly points out the ambivalence of the universe, and moves one to question whether life is worth anything at all, if it can be yanked away at any moment for no apparent reason. The question of whether life has meaning and is worth living was especially important to Albert Camus (1913–1960), who called the question of suicide the "fundamental question of philosophy." Originally from Algeria during the French occupation, Camus grew up in poverty, like Kenny. He became a playwright, author, and journalist, moving to Paris in 1940 and witnessing the German occupation of France. Camus was an active part of the French resistance, and later attained fame with his existentialist novels, including *The Stranger* and *The Plague*.[3]

In 1942 Camus wrote *The Myth of Sisyphus*, which discusses the Greek myth of Sisyphus, who is condemned by the gods for stealing their secrets. As punishment, Sisyphus is forced to roll a heavy rock to the top of a steep hill, only to have it roll back to the bottom. Sisyphus must continue this seemingly pointless task for eternity because the gods knew that there is "no more dreadful punishment than futile and hopeless labor."[4] Camus describes Sisyphus as the absurd hero who is being punished with an existence that accomplishes nothing.

For Camus, the myth is a metaphor for the absurdity of life. Just as the workman must face each day with the same repetitive task, Sisyphus must push the rock again. This is bearable for the average person because she hasn't thought about it, but Sisyphus is starkly conscious of the absurdity of his task, making his pointless existence even harder to face. Camus describes the feeling of facing the absurdity of the average life in the following way: "Rising, street car, four hours in the office or the factory, meal, streetcar, four hours of work,

---

[3] Camus rejected the labeling of his work as existentialist, and preferred the term "absurdist." However, usually Camus' work is classified as existentialist. See Albert Camus, *Lyrical and Critical Essays* (New York: Alfred A. Knopf, 1968), p. 345.

[4] Albert Camus, *The Myth of Sisyphus*, trans. by Justin O'Brian (New York: Vintage Books, 1955), p. 119. Subsequent citations as (Camus, p. "x") in the text.

meal, sleep, and Monday Tuesday Wednesday Thursday Friday and Saturday according to the same rhythm – this path is easily followed most of the time. But one day the 'why' arises and everything begins in that weariness tinged with amazement" (Camus, pp. 12–13). Life for the average person is humdrum, involving a repetitious schedule of work, food, and sleep. This is bearable so long as one does not think about it, but once one is conscious of the situation, there is great frustration and despair. For Camus, we are all like Sisyphus pushing the rock up to the top of the hill each day, only for it to roll to the bottom again, and knowing that we will have to do it again the next day.

The moment of consciousness is important for Camus, since it marks a gap between the way the world is, and the way we want it to be. Humans want an explanation of the purpose or meaning of life, and they want to know that their actions matter in the grand scheme of things. When bad things happen, humans need an explanation and they want to know there is a purpose to all events. Camus calls the feeling that arises when humans notice that the world cannot be fully explained in a rational manner as the feeling of the *absurd*. Following the thought of Friedrich Nietzsche (1844–1900), Camus thought that God was dead, since belief in religious answers was waning in Europe.[5] The loss of belief left humans alienated in the world, without a conclusive direction or plan to interpret events. The absurd occurs with the clash between the human desire for rational explanation and the inability to obtain it (Camus, pp. 29–30). Camus describes the absurd as a struggle that "implies a total absence of hope, a continual rejection, and a conscious dissatisfaction" (Camus, p. 31). Once Sisyphus knows his sentence, his daily existence becomes absurd, since his labor seems pointless. The typical reaction to the realization of the absurd is to either seek a positive solution, to escape the dilemma through religion or some other type of hopeful philosophy, or to become nihilistic and suicidal. Camus rejects both approaches, since both deny the facts of the matter for consolation in a solution, rather than acknowledging the fact that life is absurd. For Camus, one must face the absurd and accept it.

[5] See selections from Nietzsche's *The Gay Science* and *Thus Spoke Zarathustra*, in *The Portable Nietzsche*, trans. by Walter Kaufmann (New York: Viking Books, 1959).

Kenny's life and death can also be viewed as absurd. We want to know why he is killed over and over again, though we never get a full explanation. Kenny's labor is to die and, for the most part, people laugh or fail to notice. This is a doubly existential punishment because not only is it absurd and meaningless like Sisyphus' task, but it also directly concerns Kenny's mortality, the most popular existential theme. The indifferent attitude towards Kenny's death is the attitude of the absurd, since it reflects the indifference of the universe to human mortality. So like Sisyphus, who pushes the boulder every day, Kenny must also address his fate without consolation in answers. The same thing happens in almost every episode and Kenny must face it. He is killed only to be resurrected, and killed again. Like Sisyphus, he must push the same boulder every day, without a comforting story about why his life is meaningful. Even though we may not repetitively die like Kenny, we are all like Kenny to the extent that we must face the absurdity of life.

Kenny, The Absurd Hero

For Camus, Sisyphus is an absurd hero, not because he is sentenced to a repetitive daily grind and is aware of this fact, but because of how he chooses to respond to his punishment. Sisyphus is conscious of his absurd condition, but still chooses to face it and accept it. The moment that most interests Camus is when Sisyphus walks back down the hill towards his rock. When Sisyphus walks down the hill, Camus thinks he is "superior to his fate. He is stronger than his rock" (Camus, p. 121). The absurd hero acknowledges that life has no inherent meaning, but nonetheless continues to live. Camus describes this as a position of revolt because the absurd is acknowledged, but it does not give way to resignation (Camus, pp. 53–4). The absurd hero lives a life without appeal, with no consolations or certain answers. Sisyphus says "yes" to his fate, and does not reject it, despair, or think he can get out of it. What is most important is that Sisyphus is free of illusion, and he takes no consolation in comforting fairy tales concerning the meaning of life.[6] Sisyphus' struggle is truly his

---

[6] Brian Masters, *Camus: A Study* (London: Heinemann, 1974), p. 47.

own and it is up to him to decide its value, since there will never be answers concerning life's purpose.

Interestingly enough, when the absurdity of life is acknowledged, Camus believes that a person achieves lucidity and clarity. The absurdity of life is clear to Sisyphus in his pushing the rock and, yet, he accepts the struggle. It is the continual struggle that is important, and Camus thinks that the struggle back towards the heights is "enough to fill a man's heart" (Camus, p. 123). For Camus, Sisyphus has a silent joy because he says *yes* to his absurd task, just as Kenny seems to embrace his comic function.

Kenny dies each episode to make us laugh at ourselves, at mortality, and at hackneyed plot devices that sacrifice the least developed character for the sake of dramatic tension. Though Kenny seems completely aware of his situation and often intentionally sacrifices himself or nervously awaits his demise he, like Sisyphus, continues to say "yes" to his task and makes meaning for himself, despite the absurdity of life. Camus concludes that "one must imagine Sisyphus happy," since he has accepted the absurd (Camus, p. 123). If Kenny has come to terms with his repetitive death, then Camus would say that Kenny is happy too.

8

THE PHILOSOPHICAL PASSION OF THE JEW

Kyle the Philosopher

William J. Devlin

More Than Just the Token Jewish Character

Like the other boys, Kyle appears two-dimensional. But there's more to him. He's more than just the token Jewish character. He's a passionate child whose chaotic mishaps with the other boys lead him to become more reflective, as he thinks deeply about the significance of their actions, both in terms of their moral consequences and in terms of what they imply about life and the world. In short, Kyle is the philosopher of South Park. He is a lover of wisdom, pursuing truth above all else (at least sometimes). For instance, in the episode "Cartmanland" Kyle questions how it could be that God, who apparently has a say in making the world a good place, allows Cartman to inherit one million dollars and buy his own amusement park. In "Tooth Fairy Tats 2000" Kyle becomes distraught when the boys discover that the Tooth Fairy doesn't really exist and begins to speculate about what other things adults have lied to him about. In "Toilet Paper" only Kyle really considers the moral problems of seeking revenge on Mrs. Driebel, after TPing her house. Because of Kyle's moral outlook the other boys sometimes keep their mischief from him. Just recall the episode "Two Days Before the Day After Tomorrow," where Stan and Cartman crash a speedboat into a beaver dam, causing the neighboring town to flood.

The Socratic Method and Ike's Wee Wee

In the episode "The Super Best Friends," when the boys watch David Blaine perform magic tricks in South Park, Kyle becomes intrigued by his performance and wants to learn more. At the workshop, he comes to realize that he isn't happy and that he hasn't fully reached his potential in life yet. As he tells his mother, "I had no idea how unhappy I was until today." We may be inclined to dismiss Kyle's revelation as the predictable outcome of a young impressionable mind being brainwashed by the sinister and maniacal Blaine. But Kyle's discoveries are not unique to this one occasion. Whether presenting his case to his parents for money to buy a Chinpokomon, or suggesting to his synagogue that the Jews need to make atonement for the crucifixion of Jesus, Kyle struggles to find the right thing to do in each situation. Indeed, Kyle seeks to find and understand the *good life*, the life constituted by doing the right thing – the life that gives meaning to the person living it.

The search for the good life sets Kyle on the path of philosophical questioning. His awareness that he is unhappy echoes Socrates (470–399 BCE) who, in Plato's (427–347 BCE) *Apology*, tells us that a person may falsely believe that he or she is happy.[1] Like Socrates, Kyle doesn't simply want to believe he is happy; rather, he wants to *know* that he *really* is happy, and not fooling himself. For Socrates, "The unexamined life is not worth living." The good life entails that you examine your life – know thyself – as well as the assumed values in your own tradition. Such values need to be re-examined to determine whether or not they are true and absolutely real. If they are not true, they should be discarded. But if they are true, then they should be properly defined and understood so that they serve as ideals to live by. This lifestyle of questioning, challenging, and defining the truths of the world is known as the *dialectic*, and serves as the foundation for the Socratic approach in philosophy of living a life in pursuit of knowledge.

The *Socratic method* involved questioning those who claimed to know and engaging people in philosophical dialogue in an attempt

[1] See Plato, *Plato's Five Dialogues: Euthyphro, Apology, Crito, Meno, Phaedo*, trans. by G.M.A. Grube (Indianapolis: Hackett Publishing, 2002).

to define the fundamental nature or essence of some idea or thing. Whether it was a question of virtue, piety, goodness, friendship, or soul, Socrates sought a proper definition of the idea or thing. If a universal definition could be found, then one could apply the definition to one's own particular life. For example, if I know what *virtue* or *piety* or *goodness* mean, in essence, then I will know how to act virtuously, or I can actually be pious, or I could begin to live the good life.

Kyle, like Socrates, cannot find happiness by following narrow tradition. Christians may have Santa during the Christmas holiday, but Kyle has Mr. Hankey, a more universal figure who serves as the picture of benevolence and joy to *all* people. Mr. Hankey satisfies the Socratic approach insofar as he is universal rather than particular. With the help of his Christmas Poo, Kyle is able to transcend the standard view of Christmas from the Christian tradition, and come to an understanding of the compassionate values that apply to all people, from all different traditions.

Kyle further demonstrates this Socratic lifestyle, continuing to pursue knowledge. For instance, when Kyle discovers that his younger brother, Ike, is being forced by the family to undergo circumcision, he becomes protective of Ike and is determined to prevent Ike from undergoing such "barbarism." But when he discovers that Ike is adopted, Kyle initially falls back on the unreflective response that since Ike is not related by blood, he has no responsibility to care for him. Thus Kyle confronts the question, what is family? His initial implicit answer is "those for whom we care that are related by blood." If Ike is family, then Kyle believes that the right thing to do would be to help him and save him from the circumcision. But with this initial definition of family in mind, Kyle no longer sees helping Ike as the right thing to do.

Fortunately, like Socrates, Kyle engages in dialectic, but this time he questions himself. As a result, Kyle determines that his initial definition of family is unsuccessful. He "learns something today," namely, that family is not limited by bloodline, but instead is open to others we love and care about. This new broader definition of family includes not simply his blood relatives, but also Ike, Stan, Kenny, and even Cartman. With firm knowledge and a definition of family in hand, Kyle determines the right way to act: he becomes reinvigorated with the belief that he *must* protect Ike from the upcoming circumcision, and so does what he can to prevent it. Of course, Kyle isn't perfect. If he had only used the Socratic method to discover the true definition of circumcision he wouldn't have had this trouble in the first place. After all, his parents weren't going to have Ike's wee-wee cut off.

Is God Dead? Cartman's Money and Kyle's Hemorrhoid

In the episode "Cartmanland" Kyle's account of the good life is challenged. As a Jew, Kyle believes that all good ultimately comes from God's will and grace. If God exists, then God ultimately sets the world right. But when Kyle learns that Cartman has inherited one million dollars, he finds it an "impossible" event. To make matters worse, Kyle gets a hemorrhoid and suffers greatly. Frustrated with God, Kyle complains "all my life I was raised to believe in Jehovah! To believe that we should all behave a certain way and good things will come to us. I make mistakes, but every week I try to better myself. I'm always saying, 'You know, I learned something today' and what does this so-called God give me in return? A hemorrhoid. He doesn't make sense!" Unable to come to rational terms with this situation, Kyle calls both the pursuit of the good life and the existence of God into question: "I finally figured it out. You see, if someone like Cartman can get a million dollars and his own theme park, then there is no God. There's no God, dude."

Friedrich Nietzsche (1844–1900) reached the same conclusion as Kyle did – there is no God.[2] It's not that God once lived and now has died. Rather, God never existed. God was created through the

---

[2] See selections from Nietzsche's *The Gay Science* and *Thus Spoke Zarathustra*, in *The Portable Nietzsche*, trans. by Walter Kaufmann (New York: Viking Books, 1959). Technically, the "death of God" was not so much a pronouncement of atheism as it was a description and prediction of the state of genuine belief in the God of Christianity. God, like a "party" with just three frat boys and some cheap beer, is dead. As an atheist, though, Nietzsche thought it was good that God is dead. No need to try to liven up this particular party.

imagination of people who felt they needed such a mighty and powerful being to guarantee a meaningful life. If God does not exist, then there is no good life, and life is without meaning. This is a very serious matter for Nietzsche, for by getting rid of God in our lives, our original view of a meaningful life is lost. Why should I bother striving to do what is right? Why shouldn't I just be a selfish jerk like Cartman? Nietzsche calls this result *nihilism*, or the view that there is no meaning or value to our lives and to the world. Since Kyle comes to agree with Nietzsche that God doesn't exist, he lapses into nihilism. With no meaning to life, his health deteriorates due to the hemorrhoid, and it looks as though Kyle is going to die. As the doctor explains: "I don't understand it. He's not fighting the infected hemorrhoid at all. It's like he, like he's lost all hope; he's just given up on life . . . Little fella's just lost his will to live."

Now, Nietzsche's advice to Kyle would be to see his struggle with the hemorrhoid as a metaphor for life. Human beings are constantly changing, constantly in a state of becoming. But our becoming doesn't have a pre-set direction; rather, we give ourselves a direction. We give ourselves meaning in life. Thus, human beings are creators and inventors of meaning. Whether we create Jehovah and the Jewish lifestyle, or a life like Mephisto's – geared towards cloning animals so that they have four asses – it is the individual who creates the meaningful life and the direction towards it. The Nietzschean ideal is the *overman*, the person who dynamically and continuously creates and betters himself. Just as Kyle fights the hemorrhoid, so too, the overman continuously struggles and strives to overcome and create himself in new ways.

But, alas, Kyle fails to become the *overman*. Rather than focus on his own struggle and self-creation, he is distracted and weakened by his envy and resentment of Cartman. While he acknowledges the meaninglessness of it all, Kyle retreats to the previous Socratic lifestyle of making sense of the world through universal definitions. Only when he learns that Cartman has lost his inheritance does Kyle effectively fight the hemorrhoid and recover. Now that Cartman is once again alone and miserable, Kyle sees the world can be set right. The good life is possible once again. Kyle *can* live a meaningful life, one in which good people are rewarded and selfish people are unhappy, and this means for Kyle that God does exist. As he tells God: "You *are* up there!"

Do You Think Dan Rather is Real?

While Socrates takes it for granted that there are things like virtue, piety, and goodness "out there" in reality, other philosophers hold that before we can begin to discover what sorts of things exist in the world, we need to first determine what human beings can really know. What do we *really* know in life? What things are we certain about? What do we know *really* exists in the world? How do we know it? How do we justify our beliefs? These questions are central to the branch of philosophy known as *epistemology*.

Many of Kyle's beliefs are justified through his parents and teachers. But in the episode "The Tooth Fairy Tats 2000," when the boys discover that there's no Tooth Fairy, Kyle is in shock: "That can't be. *My* parents wouldn't lie to me." He confronts his father, who admits that the Tooth Fairy isn't real. Kyle worries that his source of justification is now unreliable, since his parents may lie to him about anything. And if he cannot trust his source, then he cannot say with certainty that he knows anything. Everything could be "all made up" so that "nothing's real."

Kyle slips further and further into *skepticism*, the view that what is typically taken to be knowledge may, in fact, not be justified. First, he begins to doubt the reality of other people he previously accepted as being real: "What about Dan Rather? Do you think he's real?" Next, he begins to wonder whether or not he himself is real: "Oh my God, what if *I'm* not real? I mean, what if I'm just part of my *parents'* reality? What if this is all just somebody's dream?" For all Kyle knows, he could be living a life of illusion like Neo in *The Matrix*.

Without a way to justify his beliefs, Kyle is unable to find any certainty about the world, including himself. The world around him could very well be a dream, and he too may only be part of a dream. While he previously thought he was real, he does not know even if he, himself, exists. Feeling lost, Kyle might turn to philosophy. He might read a number of books concerning what we can know about reality, the most important of which is *Meditations on First Philosophy* by René Descartes (1596–1650).[3] Like Kyle, Descartes

---

[3] See René Descartes, *Discourse on Method and Meditations on First Philosophy*, trans. by Donald Cress (Indianapolis: Hackett Publishing, 1999).

becomes dissatisfied with what he has learned from his upbringing. Having studied philosophy as a student, Descartes wonders whether or not the tradition from Socrates until his own time was correct concerning what they said about the world. In order to find certainty about the things he has come to believe to be true – that is, in order to find absolute, clear, indubitable knowledge – Descartes tries to doubt the truth of everything that he possibly can, no matter how far fetched his doubts may seem. Thus, Descartes becomes a skeptic in order to come up with absolute and certain knowledge. Descartes calls this process of meticulously and methodically doubting everything one can in order to obtain certainty, *systematic doubt.*

Like Kyle, Descartes comes to the skeptical view that this whole world and all of our experiences may be part of a dream. Or, for all he knows, there could be an Evil Deceiver who has God-like powers and has manipulated him into thinking that the world he experiences is real and that he is real. Like Kyle, then, Descartes holds that this world may very well be a dream and he may not exist. Further, both find this utter skepticism to be overwhelming. Descartes, for instance, feels as if he is drowning in a whirlpool of doubt and disbelief. He feels as though he can no longer function in the world given that he is left without any apparent certainty. The case is no better for Kyle: "I can't deal with it, Stan. I mean, all the stuff I've been reading; I really don't think I exist! Sometimes I think I can see time slowing down and my own existence fading."

Descartes, however, ultimately saves himself from drowning in his doubt by coming to realize that there is one thing he cannot doubt: his own existence as a thinking thing. Even if there is an Evil Deceiver or *Matrix* that makes me believe in a world that is not real, I still cannot doubt that I exist as a thinking thing. In order to doubt that I exist, I must be thinking, since doubting requires thinking. But since I am thinking, I must exist, since thinking entails existence. And so, we get Descartes' famous line: "I think, therefore I am." Descartes' own existence as one who thinks is certain and indubitable knowledge. Kyle comes to the same conclusion as Descartes: "You know, I learned something today. You see, the basis of all reasoning is the mind's awareness of itself. What we think, the external objects we perceive are all like actors that come on and off stage. But our consciousness, the stage itself, is always present to us." Now that he is justified in believing he is a conscious, thinking thing, Kyle is set to resume his pursuit of the good life.

What Have We Learned Today?

Like Socrates, Kyle pursues the good life by trying to come to know the virtues that help him determine the right thing to do. And while he doesn't completely embody the idea that life is open to creation (including God), Kyle's open-minded investigation into the world allows him to challenge the existence of God and see what the loss of God would entail. Further, Kyle's inquisitive nature makes him reflect upon what he really knows to be true, which he comes to discover after a meticulous examination of everything that he can doubt. Kyle *is* the philosopher of South Park.

PART THREE

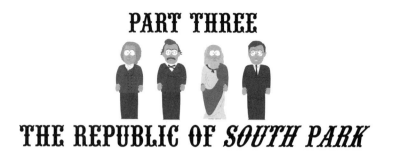

THE REPUBLIC OF *SOUTH PARK*

9

THE INVISIBLE GNOMES AND THE INVISIBLE HAND

South Park and Libertarian Philosophy

Paul A. Cantor

High Philosophy and Low Comedy

The critics of *South Park* – and they are legion – bitterly complain about its relentless obscenity and potty humor. And they have a legitimate point. But if one wanted to mount a high-minded defense of the show's low-minded vulgarity, one might go all the way back to Plato (427–347 BCE) to find a link between philosophy and obscenity. Toward the end of his dialogue *Symposium*, a young Athenian nobleman named Alcibiades offers a striking image of the power of Socrates. He compares the philosopher's speeches to a statue of the satyr Silenus, which is ugly on the outside but which, when opened up, reveals a beautiful interior: "If you choose to listen to Socrates' discourses you would feel them at first to be quite ridiculous; on the outside they are clothed with such absurd words and phrases. His talk is of pack-asses, smiths, cobblers, and tanners, so that anyone inexpert and thoughtless might laugh his speeches to scorn. But when these are opened, you will discover that they are the only speeches which have any sense in them."[1]

---

[1] Plato, *Symposium*, trans. by W.R.M. Lamb, in *Plato: Lysis, Symposium, Gorgias* (Cambridge, MA: Harvard University Press, 1925), p. 239.

These words characterize equally well the contrast between the vulgar surface and the philosophical depth of the dialogue in which they are spoken. The *Symposium* contains some of the most soaring and profound philosophical speculations ever written. And yet in the middle of the dialogue the comic poet Aristophanes comes down with a bad case of hiccoughs that prevents him from speaking in turn. By the end of the dialogue, all the characters except Socrates have consumed so much wine that they pass out in a collective drunken stupor. In a dialogue about the spiritual and physical dimensions of love, Plato suggests that, however philosophical we may wax in our speeches, we remain creatures of the body and can never entirely escape its crude bodily functions. In the way that the *Symposium* moves back and forth between the ridiculous and the sublime, Plato seems to be making a statement about philosophy – that it has something in common with low comedy. Both philosophy and obscene humor fly in the face of conventional opinion.

I'm not sure what Plato would have made of *South Park*, but his Silenus image fits the show quite well. *South Park* is at one and the same time the most vulgar and the most philosophical show ever to appear on television. Its vulgarity is of course the first thing one notices about it, given its obsession with farting, shitting, vomiting, and every other excretory possibility. As Plato's dialogue suggests, it's all too easy to become fixated on the vulgar and obscene surface of *South Park*, rejecting out of hand a show that chose to make a Christmas icon out of a talking turd named Mr. Hankey. But if one is patient with *South Park*, and gives the show the benefit of the doubt, it turns out to be genuinely thought provoking, taking up one serious issue after another, from environmentalism and animal rights to assisted suicide and sexual harassment. And, as we shall see, the show approaches all these issues from a distinct philosophical position, what is known as libertarianism, the philosophy of freedom. I know of no television program that has so consistently pursued a philosophical agenda, week after week, season after season. If anything, the show can become too didactic, with episodes often culminating in a character delivering a speech that offers a surprisingly balanced and nuanced account of the issue at hand.

Plato's *Symposium* is useful for showing that vulgarity and philosophical thought are not necessarily antithetical. Before dismissing *South Park*, we should recall that some of the greatest comic writers

– Aristophanes, Chaucer, Rabelais, Shakespeare, Ben Jonson, Voltaire, Jonathan Swift – plumbed the depths of obscenity even as they rose to the heights of philosophical thought. The same intellectual courage that emboldened them to defy conventional proprieties empowered them to reject conventional ideas and break through the intellectual frontiers of their day. Without claiming that *South Park* deserves to rank with such distinguished predecessors, I will say that the show descends from a long tradition of comedy that ever since ancient Athens has combined obscenity with philosophy. There are almost as many fart jokes in Aristophanes' play *The Clouds* as there are in a typical episode of *The Terrance and Philip Show* in *South Park*. In fact, in the earliest dramatic representation of Socrates that has come down to us, he is making fart jokes as he tries to explain to a dumb Athenian named Strepsiades that thunder is a purely natural phenomenon and not the work of the great god Zeus: "First think of the tiny fart that your intestines make. Then consider the heavens: their infinite farting is thunder. For thunder and farting are, in principle, one and the same."[2] Cartman couldn't have said it better.

Speaking the Unspeakable

Those who condemn *South Park* for being offensive need to be reminded that comedy is by its very nature offensive. It derives its energy from its transgressive power, its ability to break taboos, to speak the unspeakable. Comedians are always pushing the envelope, probing to see how much they can get away with in violating the speech codes of their day. Comedy is a social safety valve. We laugh precisely because the comedian momentarily liberates us from the restrictions that conventional society imposes on us. We applaud the comedian because he says right out in front of an audience what, supposedly, nobody is allowed to say in public. Paradoxically, then, the more permissive American society has become, the harder it has become to write comedy. As censorship laws have been relaxed, and people have been allowed to say and show almost anything in movies

---

[2] Aristophanes, *The Clouds*, trans. by William Arrowsmith (New York: New American Library, 1962), p. 45.

and television – above all to deal with formerly taboo sexual material – comedy writers like Parker and Stone must have begun to wonder if there was any way left to offend an audience.

The genius of Parker and Stone was to see that in our day a new frontier of comic transgression has opened up because of the phenomenon known as political correctness. Our age may have tried to dispense with the conventional pieties of earlier generations, but it has developed new pieties of its own. They may not look like the traditional pieties, but they are enforced in the same old way, with social pressures and sometimes even legal sanctions punishing people who dare to violate the new taboos. Many of our colleges and universities today have speech codes, which seek to define what can and cannot be said on campus, and in particular to prohibit anything that might be interpreted as demeaning someone because of his or her race, religion, gender, handicap, and a whole series of other protected categories. Sex may no longer be taboo in our society, but sexism now is. *Seinfeld* was probably the first television comedy that systematically violated the new taboos of political correctness. The show repeatedly made fun of contemporary sensitivities about such issues as sexual orientation, ethnic identity, feminism, and handicapped people. *Seinfeld* proved that being politically incorrect can be hilariously funny in today's moral and intellectual climate, and *South Park* was quick to follow its lead.

The show has mercilessly satirized all forms of political correctness – anti-hate crime legislation, tolerance indoctrination in the schools, Hollywood do-gooding of all kinds, including environmentalism and anti-smoking campaigns, the Americans with Disabilities Act and the Special Olympics – the list goes on and on. It's hard to single out the most politically incorrect moment in the history of *South Park*, but I'll nominate the spectacular "cripple fight" in the fifth season episode of that name – and indeed just look at the politically incorrect name to describe what happens when two "differently abled," or rather "handi-capable" boys named Timmy and Jimmy square off for a violent – and interminable – battle in the streets of South Park. The show obviously relishes the sheer shock value of moments such as this. But more is going on here than transgressing the boundaries of good taste just for transgression's sake. This is where the philosophy of libertarianism enters the picture in *South Park*. The show criticizes political correctness in the name of freedom.

A Plague on Both Your Houses

That is why *South Park* is in fact an equal opportunity satirist; it often makes fun of the old pieties as well as the new, savaging both the right and the left insofar as they both seek to restrict freedom. "Cripple Fight" is an excellent example of the balance and even-handedness of *South Park*, and the way it can offend both ends of the political spectrum. The episode deals in typical *South Park* fashion with a contemporary controversy, one that has even made it into the courts: whether homosexuals should be allowed to lead Boy Scout troops. The episode makes fun of the old-fashioned types in the town who insist on denying a troop leadership to Big Gay Al (a recurrent character whose name says it all). It turns out that the ostensibly straight man the Boy Scouts choose to replace Big Gay Al is a real pedophile who starts abusing the boys immediately by photographing them naked. As it frequently does, *South Park*, even as it stereotypes homosexuals, displays sympathy for them and their right to live their lives as they see fit. But just as the episode seems to be simply taking the side of those who condemn the Boy Scouts for homophobia, it swerves in an unexpected direction. Big Gay Al himself defends the right of the Boy Scouts to exclude homosexuals on the principle of freedom of association. An organization should be able to set up its own rules and the law should not be able to impose society's notions of political correctness on a private group. This episode represents *South Park* at its best – looking at a complicated issue from both sides and coming up with a judicious resolution of the issue. And the principle on which the issue is resolved is freedom. As the episode shows, Big Gay Al should be free to be homosexual, but the Boy Scouts should also be free as an organization to make their own rules and exclude him from a leadership post if they want to.

Nothing could be more calculated to make *South Park* offensive to the politically correct than this libertarianism, for if applied consistently it would dismantle the whole apparatus of speech control and thought manipulation that do-gooders have tried to construct to protect their favored minorities. Libertarianism is a philosophy of radical freedom, and particularly celebrates the free market as a form of social organization. As a philosophy, it descends from the thinking of the Scottish Enlightenment in the eighteenth century, social philosophers such as Adam Smith (1723–1790), who argued for free trade and the reduction of government intervention in the economy. Libertarianism is especially grounded in the work of the Austrian School of economics, and above all the writings of Ludwig von Mises (1881–1973) and Friedrich Hayek (1899–1992), who offer the most uncompromising defense of unfettered economic activity as the key to prosperity and progress.[3] The word *libertarianism* was popularized by Murray Rothbard (1926–1995), a student of Mises, who developed the most radical critique of state interference in economic and social life – a philosophy of freedom that borders on anarchism.[4]

With its support for unconditional freedom in all areas of life, libertarianism defies categorization in terms of the standard one-dimensional political spectrum of right and left. In opposition to the collectivist and anti-capitalist vision of the left, libertarians reject all forms of economic planning and want people to be left alone to pursue their self-interest as they see fit. But in contrast to conservatives, libertarians also oppose social legislation, and generally favor the legalization of drugs and the abolition of all censorship and anti-pornography laws. Parker and Stone have publicly identified themselves as libertarians, which might explain why their show ends up offending both liberals and conservatives. As Parker has said: "We avoid extremes but we hate liberals more than conservatives, and we hate them."[5] This does seem to be an accurate assessment of the leanings of the show – even though it is no friend of the right, *South Park* is more likely to go after leftwing causes.

---

[3] Mises' most famous book is *Human Action: A Treatise on Economics* (New Haven, CT: Yale University Press, 1949) and Hayek's is *The Road to Serfdom* (Chicago: University of Chicago Press, 1944).

[4] Rothbard articulates his libertarian philosophy most fully in *The Ethics of Liberty* (New York: New York University Press, 2002) and *For a New Liberty: The Libertarian Manifesto* (New York: Macmillan, 1978). Perhaps the clearest introduction to the economic principles underlying libertarianism is Henry Hazlitt's *Economics in One Lesson* (San Francisco: Laissez Faire Books, 1996), originally published in 1946.

[5] As quoted in Brian C. Anderson, *South Park Conservatives: The Revolt Against Liberal Media Bias* (Washington, DC: Regnery, 2005), p. 178.

Defending the Undefendable

Thus the libertarianism of Parker and Stone places them at odds with the intellectual establishment of contemporary America. In the academic world, much of the media, and a large part of the entertainment business, especially the Hollywood elite, anti-capitalist views generally prevail.[6] Studies have shown that businessmen are usually portrayed in an unfavorable light in movies and television.[7] *South Park* takes particular delight in skewering the Hollywood stars who exploit their celebrity to conduct liberal or leftwing campaigns against the workings of the free market (Barbra Streisand, Rob Reiner, Sally Struthers, and George Clooney are among the celebrities the show has pilloried). Nothing is more distinctive about *South Park* than its willingness to celebrate the free market, and even to come to the defense of what is evidently the most hated institution in Hollywood, the corporation. For example, in the episode "Die Hippie Die," Cartman fights the countercultural forces that invade South Park and mindlessly blame all the troubles of America on "the corporations."

Of all *South Park* episodes, "Gnomes" offers the most fully developed defense of capitalism, and I will attempt a comprehensive interpretation of it in order to demonstrate how genuinely intelligent and

---

[6] For an analysis of why such groups turn against capitalism, see Ludwig von Mises, *The Anti-Capitalistic Mentality* (Princeton, NJ: D. Van Nostrand, 1956) and especially pp. 30–3 for the turn against capitalism in Hollywood.

[7] A perfect example of Hollywood's negative portrayal of businessmen is the cruel banker Mr. Potter in the classic *It's a Wonderful Life* (dir. Frank Capra, 1946). For a comprehensive survey of the portrayal of businessmen in American popular culture, see the chapter "The culture industry's representation of business" in Don Lavoie and Emily Chamlee-Wright, *Culture and Enterprise: The Development, Representation and Morality of Business* (London: Routledge, 2000), pp. 80–103. Here are some representative figures from media studies: "Of all the antagonists studied in over 30 years of programming, businessmen were twice as likely to play the role of antagonist than any other identifiable occupation. Business characters are nearly three times as likely to be criminals, relative to other occupations on television. They represent 12 percent of all characters in identifiable occupations, but account for 32 percent of crimes. Forty-four percent of all vice crimes such as prostitution and drug trafficking committed on television, and 40 percent of TV murders, are perpetrated by business people" (p. 84).

thoughtful the show can be. Like the episode "Something Wall-Mart This Way Comes," "Gnomes" deals with a common charge against the free market – that it allows large corporations to drive small businesses into the ground, much to the detriment of consumers. In "Gnomes" a national coffee chain called Harbucks – an obvious reference to Starbucks – comes to South Park and tries to buy out the local Tweek Bros. coffee shop. Mr. Tweek casts himself as the hero of the story, a small business David battling a corporate Goliath. The episode satirizes the cheap anti-capitalist rhetoric in which such conflicts are usually formulated in contemporary America, with the small business shown to be purely good and the giant corporation shown to be purely evil. "Gnomes" systematically deconstructs this simplistic opposition.

In the conventional picture, the small businessman is presented as somehow being a public servant, unconcerned with profits, simply a friend to his customers, whereas the corporation is presented as greedy and uncaring, doing nothing for the consumer. "Gnomes" shows instead that Mr. Tweek is just as self-interested as any corporation, and he is in fact cannier in promoting himself than Harbucks is. The Harbucks representative, John Postem, is blunt and gruff, an utterly charmless man who thinks he can just state the bare economic truth and get away with it: "Hey, this is a capitalist country, pal – get used to it." The great irony of the episode is that the supposedly sophisticated corporation completely mishandles public relations, naively believing that the superiority of its product will be enough to ensure its triumph in the marketplace.

The common charge against large corporations is that, with their financial resources, they are able to exploit the power of advertising to put their small rivals out of business. But in "Gnomes," Harbucks is no match for the advertising savvy of Mr. Tweek. He cleverly turns his disadvantage into an advantage, coming up with the perfect slogan in his circumstances: "Tweek offers a simpler coffee for a simpler America." He thereby exploits his underdog position as a small businessman, at the same time preying upon his customers' nostalgia for an older and presumably simpler America. The episode constantly dwells on the fact that Mr. Tweek is just as slick at advertising as any corporation. He keeps launching into commercials for his coffee, accompanied by soft guitar mood music and purple advertising prose; his coffee is "special like an Arizona sunrise or a juniper wet with dew." His son may be appalled by "the metaphors" (actually they're similes), but Mr. Tweek knows just what will appeal to his nature-loving, yuppie customers.

"Gnomes" thus undermines any notion that Mr. Tweek is morally superior to the corporation he's fighting, and in fact the episode suggests that he may be a good deal worse. Going over the top as it always does, *South Park* reveals that the coffee shop owner has for years been overcaffeinating his son Tweek (one of the regulars in the show) and is in fact responsible for the boy's hypernervousness. Moreover, when faced with the threat from Harbucks, Mr. Tweek seeks sympathy by declaring: "I may have to shut down and sell my son Tweek into slavery." It sounds as if his greed exceeds Harbucks'. But the worst thing about Mr. Tweek is that he's not content with using his slick advertising to compete with Harbucks in a free market. Instead, he goes after Harbucks politically, trying to enlist the government on his side to prevent the national chain from coming to South Park. "Gnomes" thus portrays the campaign against large corporations as just one more sorry episode in the long history of businessmen seeking economic protectionism – the kind of business/government alliance Adam Smith wrote against in *The Wealth of Nations*. Far from the standard Marxist portrayal of monopoly power as the inevitable result of free competition, *South Park* shows that it results only when one business gets the government to intervene on its behalf and restrict free entry into the marketplace.

The Town of South Park vs. Harbucks

Mr. Tweek gets his chance when he finds out that his son and the other boys have been assigned to write a report on a current event. Offering to write the paper for the children, he inveigles them into a topic very much in his self-interest: "how large corporations take over little family-owned businesses," or, more pointedly, "how the corporate machine is ruining America." Kyle can barely get out the polysyllabic words when he delivers the ghostwritten report in class: "As the voluminous corporate automaton bulldozes its way . . ." This language obviously parodies the exaggerated and overinflated anti-capitalist rhetoric of the contemporary left. But the report is a big hit with local officials and soon, much to Mr. Tweek's delight, the mayor is sponsoring Proposition 10, an ordinance that will ban Harbucks from South Park.

In the debate over Prop 10, "Gnomes" portrays the way the media are biased against capitalism and the way the public is manipulated into anti-business attitudes. The boys are enlisted to argue for Prop 10 and the man from Harbucks to argue against it. The presentation is slanted from the beginning, when the moderator announces: "On my left, five innocent, starry-eyed boys from Middle America" and "On my right, a big, fat, smelly corporate guy from New York." Postem tries to make a rational argument, grounded in principle: "This country is founded on free enterprise." But the boys triumph in the debate with a somewhat less cogent argument, as Cartman sagely proclaims: "This guy sucks ass." The television commercial in favor of Prop 10 is no less fraudulent than the debate. Again, "Gnomes" points out that anti-corporate advertising can be just as slick as corporate. In particular, the episode shows that the left is willing to go to any length in its anti-corporate crusade, exploiting children to tug at the heartstrings of its target audience. In a wonderful parody of a liberal political commercial, the boys are paraded out in a patriotic scene featuring the American flag, while the "Battle Hymn of the Republic" plays softly in the background. Meanwhile, the announcer solemnly intones: "Prop 10 is about children. Vote yes on Prop 10 or else you hate children." The ad is "paid for by Citizens for a Fair and Equal Way to Get Harbucks Out of Town Forever." *South Park* loves to expose the illogic of liberal and left-wing crusaders, and the anti-Harbucks campaign is filled with one non-sequitur after another. Pushing the last of the liberal buttons, one woman challenges the Harbucks representative: "How many Native Americans did you slaughter to make that coffee?"

Prop 10 seems to be headed for an easy victory at the polls until the boys encounter some friendly gnomes, who explain corporations to them. At the last minute, in one of the most didactic of the *South Park* concluding message scenes, the boys announce to the puzzled townspeople that they have reversed their position on Prop 10. In the spirit of libertarianism, Kyle proclaims something rarely heard on television outside of a John Stossel report: "Big corporations are good. Because without big corporations we wouldn't have things like cars and computers and canned soup." And Stan comes to the defense of the dreaded Harbucks: "Even Harbucks started off as a small, little business. But because it made such great coffee, and because they ran their business so well, they managed to grow until they became the corporate powerhouse it is today. And that is why we should all let Harbucks stay."

At this point the townspeople do something remarkable – they stop listening to all the political rhetoric and actually taste the rival coffees for themselves. And they discover that Mrs. Tweek (who has been disgusted by her husband's devious tactics) is telling the truth when she says: "Harbucks Coffee got to where it is by being the best." Indeed, as one of the townspeople observes: "It doesn't have that bland, raw sewage taste that Tweek's coffee has." "Gnomes" ends by suggesting that it is only fair that businesses battle it out, not in the political arena, but in the marketplace, and let the best product win. Postem offers Mr. Tweek the job of running the local franchise and everybody is happy. Politics is a zero-sum, winner-take-all game, in which one business triumphs only by using government power to eliminate a rival, but in the voluntary exchanges a free market makes possible, all parties benefit from a transaction. Harbucks makes its profit, and Mr. Tweek can continue earning a living without selling his son into slavery, but above all the people of South Park get to enjoy a better brand of coffee.[8] Contrary to the anti-corporate propaganda normally coming out of Hollywood, *South Park* argues that, in the absence of government intervention, corporations get where they are by serving the public, not by exploiting it. As Ludwig von Mises makes the point:

---

[8] Not being a coffee drinker myself, I cannot comment on the question of whether Starbucks is actually better than any particular local brew. I am simply presenting the situation as it is laid out in "Gnomes," but I realize that the issue of Starbucks coffee is controversial. In fact, no episode of *South Park* I have taught has raised as much raw passion, indignation, and hostility among students as "Gnomes" has. I'm not sure why, but I think it has something to do with the defensiveness of elitists confronted with their own elitism. What many intellectuals hold against capitalism is precisely the fact that it has made available to the masses luxuries formerly reserved to an elite, including their double lattes. I have heard every tired argument against capitalism raised with regard to Starbucks, including the old canard that the company lowers prices to drive out the local competition with the aim of then raising prices once it has a monopoly. Since the barriers to entry in the coffee business are very low, of course Starbucks has never reached that monopoly position and never will.

The profit system makes those men prosper who have succeeded in filling the wants of the people in the best possible and cheapest way. Wealth can be acquired only by serving the consumers. The capitalists lose their funds as soon as they fail to invest them in those lines in which they satisfy best the demands of the public. In a daily repeated plebiscite in which every penny gives a right to vote the consumers determine who should own and run the plants, shops and farms.[9]

The Great Gnome Mystery Solved

But what about the gnomes, who, after all, give the episode its title? Where do they fit in? I never could understand how the subplot in "Gnomes" related to the main plot until I was lecturing on the episode at a summer institute and my colleague Michael Valdez Moses made a breakthrough that allowed us to put together the episode as a whole. In the subplot, Tweek complains to anybody who will listen that every night at 3:30 a.m. gnomes sneak into his bedroom and steal his underpants. But nobody else can see this remarkable phenomenon happening, not even when the other boys stay up late with Tweek to observe it, not even when the emboldened gnomes start robbing underpants in broad daylight in the mayor's office. We know two things about these strange beings: they are gnomes and they are normally invisible. Both facts point in the direction of capitalism. As in the phrase "gnomes of Zurich," which refers to bankers, gnomes are often associated with the world of finance. In the first opera of Wagner's Ring Cycle, *Das Rheingold*, the gnome Alberich serves as a symbol of the capitalist exploiter – and he forges the Tarnhelm, a cap of invisibility.[10] The idea of invisibility calls to mind Adam Smith's famous notion of the "invisible hand" that guides the free market.[11]

---

[9]   Mises, *Anti-Capitalistic Mentality*, p. 2.
[10]   George Bernard Shaw offers this interpretation of Alberich; see his *The Perfect Wagnerite* (1898) in George Bernard Shaw, *Major Critical Essays* (London: Penguin, 1986), pp. 198, 205.
[11]   For the way H.G. Wells uses invisibility as a symbol of capitalism, see my essay "*The Invisible Man* and the Invisible Hand: H.G. Wells's Critique of Capitalism," *American Scholar* 68 (1999), pp. 89–102.

In short, the underpants gnomes are an image of capitalism and the way it is normally – and mistakenly – pictured by its opponents. The gnomes represent the ordinary business activity that is always going on in plain sight of everyone, but which they fail to notice and fail to understand. The people of South Park are unaware that the ceaseless activity of large corporations like Harbucks is necessary to provide them with all the goods they enjoy in their daily lives. They take it for granted that the shelves of their supermarkets will always be amply stocked with a wide variety of goods and never appreciate all the capitalist entrepreneurs who make that abundance possible.

What is worse, the ordinary citizens misinterpret capitalist activity as theft. They focus only on what businessmen take from them – their money – and forget about what they get in return, all the goods and services. Above all, people have no understanding of the basic facts of economics and have no idea of why businessmen deserve the profits they earn. Business is a complete mystery to them – it seems to be a matter of gnomes sneaking around in the shadows and mischievously heaping up piles of goods for no apparent purpose. Friedrich Hayek noted this long-standing tendency to misinterpret normal business activities as sinister:

> Such distrust and fear have . . . led ordinary people . . . to regard trade
> . . . as suspicious, inferior, dishonest, and contemptible . . . Activities
> that appear to add to available wealth, "out of nothing," without
> physical creation and by merely rearranging what already exists, stink
> of sorcery . . . That a mere change of hands should lead to a gain in
> value to all participants, that it need not mean gain to one at the
> expense of the others (or what has come to be called exploitation),
> was and is nonetheless intuitively difficult to grasp . . . Many people
> continue to find the mental feats associated with trade easy to discount
> even when they do not attribute them to sorcery, or see them as
> depending on trick or fraud or cunning deceit.[12]

Even the gnomes do not understand what they are doing. Perhaps *South Park* is suggesting that the real problem is that businessmen themselves lack the economic knowledge they would need to explain their activity to the public and justify their profits. When the boys ask

[12] F.A. Hayek, *The Fatal Conceit: The Errors of Socialism* (Chicago: University of Chicago Press, 1988), pp. 90, 91, 93.

the gnomes to tell them about corporations, all they can offer is this enigmatic diagram of the stages of their business:

Phase 1	*Phase 2*	*Phase 3*
Collect Underpants	?	Profit

This chart basically encapsulates the economic illiteracy of the American public. They can see no connection between the activities businessmen undertake and the profits they make. What businessmen actually contribute to the economy is a big question mark to them. The fact that businessmen are rewarded for taking risks, correctly anticipating consumer demands, and efficiently financing, organizing, and managing production is lost on most people. They would rather complain about the obscene profits of corporations and condemn their power in the marketplace.

The "invisible hand" passage of Smith's *Wealth of Nations* reads like a gloss on the "Gnomes" episode of *South Park*:

> As every individual, therefore, endeavours as much as he can both to employ his capital in the support of domestick industry, and so to direct that industry that its produce may be of the greatest value; every individual necessarily labours to render the annual revenue of the society as great as he can. He genuinely, indeed, neither intends to promote the publick interest, nor knows how much he is promoting it. By preferring the support of domestick to that of foreign industry, he intends only his own security, and by directing that industry in such a manner as its produce may be of the greatest value, he intends only his own gain, and he is in this, as in many other cases, led by an invisible hand to promote an end which was no part of his intention. Nor is it always the worse for the society that it was no part of it. By pursuing his own interest he frequently promotes that of the society more effectively than when he really intends to promote it. I have never known much good done by those who affected to trade for the publick good.[13]

The "Gnomes" episode of *South Park* exemplifies this idea of the "invisible hand." The economy does not need to be guided by the very visible and heavy hand of government regulation for the public

---

[13] Adam Smith, *An Enquiry into the Nature and Causes of the Wealth of Nations* (Indianapolis: Liberty Classics, 1981), Vol. I, p. 456.

interest to be served. Without any central planning, the free market produces a prosperous economic order. The free interaction of producers and consumers and the constant interplay of supply and demand work so that people generally have access to the goods they want. Like Adam Smith, Parker and Stone are deeply suspicious of people who speak about the public good and condemn the private pursuit of profit. As we see in the case of Mr. Tweek, such people are usually hypocrites, pursuing their self-interest under the cover of championing the public interest. And the much-maligned gnomes of the world, the corporations, while openly pursuing their own profit, end up serving the public interest by providing the goods and services people really want. In this rational justification of the free market, *South Park* embodies the spirit of libertarian philosophy and challenges the anti-capitalist mentality of much of Hollywood. Gnomes of the world unite! You have nothing to lose but your bad image.

10

SOUTH PARK AND THE OPEN SOCIETY

Defending Democracy Through Satire

David Valleau Curtis and Gerald J. Erion

Unfettered Intellectual Inquiry or Potty Humor?

At first glance, *South Park* seems to offer little more than crude animation and tasteless jokes expressed with a juvenile and offensive vulgarity. However, as media theorist Douglas Rushkoff argues in his book *Media Virus!*, a sophisticated social criticism sometimes lurks beneath the surface of seemingly inane cartoons, comics, video games, and the like.[1] Such is the case with *South Park*; indeed, we can draw an oblique social criticism from the show that illustrates some of the fundamental principles of democratic political philosophy introduced by such great thinkers as Karl Popper and Thomas Jefferson.

For instance, consider *South Park*'s treatment of overzealous political activists. Though the show's core duo of Kyle and Stan play

---

[1] Douglas Rushkoff, *Media Virus! Hidden Agendas in Popular Culture* (New York: Ballantine Books, 1994); see especially chapter 4, "Kids' TV," pp. 100–25 and chapter 6, "Alternative Media," pp. 179–209.

relatively centered roles, many of the remaining cast members are caricatured extremists who serve as objects of the show's funniest and most clever jokes. Cartman, for example, often plays a buffoonish exaggeration of a right-wing conservative. On the other hand, Hollywood celebrities like Rob Reiner appear as liberal fanatics whose views have little connection to the mainstream. And religious extremists of all types receive particularly harsh ridicule; indeed, anyone familiar with *South Park* knows this is one of the main reasons the show is so regularly targeted for censorship, boycott, or cancellation.

Perhaps extremists receive such unflattering portrayals on *South Park* because of the threat that they can sometimes pose to the very free expression that makes the show possible. Consider this pronouncement from *South Park* co-creator Trey Parker, made during an extended interview with his partner Matt Stone on the PBS program *The Charlie Rose Show*: "What we say with the show is not anything new, but I think it is something that is great to put out there. It is that the people screaming on this side and the people screaming on that side are the same people, and it's OK to be someone in the middle, laughing at both of them."[2] So, it could be noteworthy that *South Park*'s scripts do not silence extremists; instead, extremists are allowed to express their views (or in some cases, allowed to express caricatured versions of their views), which are then held up for examination and subsequent ridicule. While extremists are tolerated, then, they are not permitted to suppress the sort of free expression that is vital to the show itself.

In this chapter, we'll examine characters and situations from *South Park* to explore such possibilities. Along the way, we'll consider some of the important democratic concepts and arguments presented by thinkers like Popper and Jefferson. Of particular interest will be the role of free expression and unfettered intellectual inquiry – even when such expression and inquiry are offensive – in a democratic society. In the end, we'll see that Popper and others have understood this sort of freedom to be absolutely *essential* to a healthy democracy.

---

[2] *The Charlie Rose Show*, September 26, 2005; abbreviated hereafter as *CRS*.

Karl Popper, the Open Society, and Its Enemies

Though his name might be unfamiliar to most, Karl Popper (1902–1994) was one of the most important and influential philosophers of the twentieth century. An Austrian by birth, Popper made major contributions to philosophical thinking about knowledge and science. However, it is his celebrated critique of totalitarian governments that most concerns us here, since we can see important elements of this critique in numerous *South Park* episodes.

Popper's critique of totalitarianism is based upon his distinction between a *closed society* and an *open society*. To Popper, a closed society is one in which social customs are especially rigid and resistant to criticism. The most significant characteristic of a closed society is "the lack of distinction between the customary or conventional regularities of social life and the regularities found in 'nature'; and this goes often together with the belief that both are enforced by a supernatural will."[3] Consequently, the rules and customs of closed societies are relatively clear and uncontested. "The right way is always determined by taboos, by magical tribal institutions which can never become objects of critical consideration" (*OS*, p. 168). It's no surprise, then, that ways of life in closed societies rarely change. When changes do occur, they are more like "religious conversions" or "the introduction of new magical taboos" than careful, rational attempts to improve the lives of the society's members (*OS*, p. 168).

On the other hand, Popper's *open society* is one where customs are open to the "rational reflection" of its members (*OS*, p. 169). In an open society, this reflection and its associated public discussion can be significant and consequential, and ultimately can produce changes in the society's taboos, rules, and codified laws. In fact, this power extends even to whole governments, as Popper maintains that the key mark of a democracy is its ability to facilitate wholesale governmental changes without violence.[4]

---

[3] Karl Popper, *The Open Society and Its Enemies* (London: G. Routledge and Sons, 1945), p. 168; abbreviated hereafter as *OS*.

[4] "Prediction and Prophecy in the Social Sciences," in Popper's *Conjectures and Refutations* (New York: Basic Books, 1962), pp. 344–5. See also Popper's "Public Opinion and Liberal Principles" contained in the same volume, pp. 346–54.

Popper's critique of closed totalitarian societies is, in large part, a practical one. To Popper, the most successful societies will be those that are able to apply the uninhibited criticism at the heart of the scientific method to whatever new social problems they may face. As Bryan Magee writes, "because problem-solving calls for the bold propounding of trial solutions which are then subjected to criticism and error elimination, [Popper] wants forms of society which permit of the untrammeled assertion of differing proposals, followed by criticism, followed by the genuine possibility of change in the light of criticism."[5] So, open societies are preferable because they permit – or even better, *promote* – a free and critical exchange of ideas. This ultimately leaves them more flexible than closed societies, and thus more capable of dealing in creative ways with all of the problems that inevitably confront them.

Of course, not every society is an open society, nor is every open society as open as it should be. Given his experiences in Europe just before World War II, Popper was particularly interested in the question of why democracies are sometimes attracted to the closed totalitarianism of, for instance, Nazism or Fascism. As a result, he devotes considerable attention to this issue in both *The Open Society and Its Enemies* and his later book, *The Poverty of Historicism*. The bulk of Popper's work here investigates the political philosophies of Plato (427–347 BCE) and Karl Marx (1818–1883), but what's most important is that Popper generally seems to understand those on both the extreme right wing and the extreme left wing of the political spectrum as "enemies of the open society." Representatives of both extremes have difficulty tolerating the free and open public discussion that is so essential to an open society. Moreover, both are impatient with the imperfections inherent in the democratic process, and both are too quick to reject the possibility that their views might be mistaken.

South Park and the "Enemies"

Despite the over-the-top presentation of most *South Park* episodes, it seems likely that co-creators Parker and Stone would share Popper's

---

[5] Bryan Magee, *Karl Popper* (New York: Viking, 1973), pp. 70–1.

distrust of political extremism. Time and time again, they develop characters and situations aimed at ridiculing various "enemies" of the open society. For Parker and Stone, as much as for Popper, democracy is endangered by totalitarian threats from both the political right and the political left. Recall Parker's claim during the *Charlie Rose* interview that "the people screaming on this side and the people screaming on that side are the same people, and it's OK to be someone in the middle, laughing at both of them." While the strategy of Parker and Stone is not so much to argue with extremists as to mock them, there is no question that they consistently single out fanatics of all sorts for especially vicious treatment.

Consider Cartman. He is typically portrayed as a ridiculous, albeit unusually young, right-wing fanatic. Anti-democratic and authoritarian, Cartman is a selfish bully who finds heartless humor in the misfortunes of others. He makes fun of Kenny for being poor, and for having an alcoholic father. He teases Kyle for being Jewish; indeed, his anti-Semitism is so strong that he sees nothing wrong with dressing up as Adolf Hitler for Halloween. Cartman also has a curious hostility for those he sees as "hippies," and he abuses his pets Mister Kitty and Fluffy the Pig. In fantasizing about a career in law enforcement, Cartman yearns, not to help people or serve his community, but to have others, as he drawls, "respect my authorita." (To our horror and amusement, Cartman actually manages to get himself deputized in the episode "Chickenlover.") For these and countless other sins and character defects, Cartman rarely makes it through an episode without being mocked or otherwise punished (and with penalties up to and including crucifixion).

Parker and Stone satirize the political left as well, especially when left-wing politics lead to the sort of hypocrisy inconsistent with a proper open society. For example, in the episode "Ike's Wee Wee," Mr. Mackey attempts to convince Kyle, Stan, and the rest of Mr. Garrison's class that smoking, alcohol, and drugs are bad. Alas, his presentation does not reveal a sophisticated understanding of substance abuse or addiction. Instead, in a rather paternalistic and condescending lecture, Mr. Mackey simply tells the children: "Smoking's bad; you shouldn't smoke. And, uh, alcohol is bad; you shouldn't drink alcohol. And, uh, as for drugs, well, drugs are bad; you shouldn't do drugs." Eager to enhance the drug awareness of South Park's children, Mr. Mackey then passes around a sample of marijuana for their examination. The sample disappears (at the hands of Mr. Garrison, it turns out), and Mr. Mackey is promptly fired by Principal Victoria. With no money, no job, and ultimately nowhere to live, Mr. Mackey becomes a drug addict himself. (His recovery at the Betty Ford Clinic is, ironically, facilitated by a counselor who has him repeat the slogan, "Drugs are bad.")

The left-wing liberalism of many Hollywood celebrities also receives brutal treatment on *South Park*. Indeed, Parker and Stone seem to reserve some of their most merciless attacks for outspoken stars like Tom Cruise and Rob Reiner. For his part, Reiner appears willing to lie, cheat, and sacrifice Cartman's life in order to further his heavy-handed anti-tobacco agenda in the episode "Butt Out." And just after the disputed November 2000 Presidential election, Rosie O'Donnell visits South Park to resolve an unsettled kindergarten election involving her nephew in the episode "Trapper Keeper." After O'Donnell suggests some questionable vote recount strategies, Mr. Garrison erupts: "People like you preach tolerance and open-mindedness all the time, but when it comes to Middle America, you think we're all evil and stupid country yokels who need your political enlightenment! Well, just because you're on TV doesn't mean you know crap about the government!" Thus, *South Park* exhibits a clear pattern of criticism for extremist "enemies of the open society," whether right-wing fascist types or sanctimonious liberal celebrities.

Not Tolerating a Tolerance for Intolerance

Our discussion of Popper's contributions to democratic political philosophy must include one last component, which Popper dubs the *paradox of tolerance*. According to Popper, the sort of tolerance required to keep a democracy healthy requires, ironically, an *intolerance* for intolerance. In other words, those who refuse to let others ask questions and speak their minds ought to be prevented from doing so; otherwise, the open discussion that is so essential to a healthy democracy will become impossible to maintain. As he puts it: "If we extend unlimited tolerance even to those who are intolerant, if we are not prepared to defend a tolerant society against the onslaught of the intolerant, then the tolerant will be destroyed, and tolerance with them" (*OS*, p. 546).

A special concern for criticizing and countering intolerance might explain *South Park*'s surprisingly nasty treatment of groups like the Church of Scientology. Popularized by the endorsement of such celebrities (and *South Park* foils) as Tom Cruise and John Travolta, the Church of Scientology also suffers from the widely held perception that it seeks to silence former members and others who criticize its beliefs and practices. In fact, Isaac Hayes, the Scientologist who had long provided a voice for the beloved character Chef, left the show in 2006 because of its treatment of Scientology in episodes like "Trapped in the Closet." (One can only imagine his horror had he stuck around for "The Return of Chef," an episode produced just after his departure in which Chef joins a cult-like group called "The Super Adventure Club." Moreover, his lines in "The Return of Chef" were voiced by splicing together bits of his singing and dialogue from earlier episodes in a particularly awkward but clever way.)

Indeed, *South Park*'s willingness to criticize intolerance earned the show a Peabody Award in April of 2006. According to Peabody Awards Program director Horace Newcomb: "We see [*South Park*] as a bold show that deals with issues of censorship and social and cultural topics. My line on *South Park* is that it properly offends everybody by design and by doing so it reminds us all that it's probably a good idea to be tolerant."[6]

Thomas Jefferson and the Foundations of Modern Democracy

Before we conclude, let's connect Popper's ideas to those of his predecessors, especially since Popper self-consciously viewed himself in the tradition of earlier philosophers. For instance, students of American history may notice similarities between Popper's views on free and open expression and those of the great political leader and scholar, Thomas Jefferson (1743–1826). Jefferson was the primary

---

[6] Interview with Josh Grossberg, " 'South Park,' 'Galactica' Peabody'd," *E! Online*, April 5, 2006.

author of the American Declaration of Independence (1776) and was among the foremost intellectuals of the revolutionary era. Under the influence of some of the same thinkers who later inspired Popper – especially Francis Bacon (1561–1626) and John Locke (1632–1704) – Jefferson pursued a wide range of philosophical interests throughout his lifetime. He was by all accounts deeply committed to freedom of thought and expression, a commitment manifested most notably in his steadfast defense of religious freedom and tolerance.

While it might be easy for us to take religious freedom for granted these days, Jefferson lived shortly after the very long and very bloody conflict that engulfed Europe following the Protestant Reformation. He knew very well, then, the high social and political costs of religious discrimination, coercion, and war. Jefferson's preeminent contribution to the defense of religious liberty was his Virginia Bill for Establishing Religious Freedom, a document first drafted in 1777 and passed into law in 1786. So proud of the Bill was Jefferson that it was one of the three items that he listed in his self-penned "Epitaph" of 1826.[7]

Rereading the Bill today, it's easy to discern a Popper-like conviction that free and unfettered inquiry is the only satisfactory method for gaining knowledge, whether regarding important matters of science, politics, religion, or anything else. "Truth," Jefferson writes, "is great and will prevail if left to herself; she is the proper and sufficient antagonist to error, and has nothing to fear from the conflict unless by human interposition disarmed of her natural weapons, free argument and debate." Moreover, Jefferson continues, "errors cease to be dangerous when it is freely permitted to contradict them." There is even something of a divine justification for free inquiry here, as when Jefferson proclaims in his preamble that "God hath created the mind free." Jefferson concludes the Bill with the bold universal declaration that "the rights hereby asserted are of the natural rights of mankind."[8] Thus, Boyd writes in his editor's footnotes to the Bill:

---

[7] The other two items were his writing of the Declaration of Independence and his founding of the University of Virginia; it is interesting to note the omission from this list of his two terms as President of the United States. See the "Epitaph" in Jefferson's *Writings*, ed. by Merrill D. Peterson (New York: Literary Classics of the US, 1984), pp. 706–7.

[8] All quotations from *Writings*, pp. 346–8.

"The Preamble to [Jefferson's] Bill provided philosophical justification, as of natural right, not merely to the ideas of religious toleration and separation of state and church but also for the right of the individual to complete intellectual liberty – 'the opinions of men are not the object of civil government, nor under its jurisdiction.' "[9]

Someone in the Middle

Given our earlier discussion of *South Park*'s treatment of the Church of Scientology, and given the show's infamous and insensitive ridicule of Christianity, Judaism, Islam, Mormonism, and other faiths, these are points worth remembering. According to Jefferson, who lived in the aftermath of tremendous religious violence, "free argument and debate" are the proper means for settling contentious issues. And according to Popper, "rational reflection" supplemented by open public discussion is the most effective way to solve complex social problems. As for *South Park*'s creators, consider Stone's comments during his interview with Parker on *The Charlie Rose Show*: "Where we live is, like, the liberalest liberal part of the world. There's a groupthink, and you only get to some new truth by argument and by dissent, and so we just play devil's advocate all of the time." We can therefore understand *South Park* within a wider intellectual context that champions free – and sometimes offensive – investigation and expression, just as the Peabody judges have done. Instead of limiting discussion about difficult issues when it becomes uncomfortable, Popper, Jefferson, Parker, Stone, and others are willing to tolerate such expression for its greater benefits.

To summarize, then, *South Park* offers us much more than vulgar language, crude potty humor, and shock for shock's sake. We learn something by paying close attention to the show's tacit criticism of overzealous left-wing and right-wing political extremists: "It's OK to be someone in the middle, laughing at both of them."

---

[9] From Julian P. Boyd (ed.), *The Papers of Thomas Jefferson* (Princeton, NJ: Princeton University Press, 1950), vol. 2, p. 547.

11

"VOTE OR DIE, BITCH" – THE MYTH THAT EVERY VOTE COUNTS AND THE PITFALLS OF A TWO-PARTY SYSTEM

John Scott Gray

Douches and Turds, Y'all

In the 2004 episode "Douche or Turd" *South Park* parodied the American election process. After the initial selection of nominees for a new school mascot, the boys are forced to select between a Giant Douche and a Turd Sandwich in a run-off. Stan doesn't care about the issue and decides not to vote, until Puff Daddy enlightens him with his "Vote or Die" campaign. Stan reconsiders the value of the election process, in the end casting a vote for the Turd Sandwich, who loses in a landslide. How important was Stan's vote, given that the election was a landslide? Would the vote have been more valuable had the final margin of victory been closer? And how important is a vote that is limited to what are widely seen as only two viable, yet unsavory options?

Questions like these are addressed in *political philosophy*, the branch of philosophy concerned with evaluating political institutions and the ways in which those institutions are constructed. In light of *South Park*'s parody of the election process, this chapter will briefly consider these questions by analyzing the enfranchisement of the vote in the United States over the last two hundred years and discussing the voting irregularities of the 2000 and 2004 Presidential elections.

This chapter also will consider the problem of choice within a two-party system, given the *South Park* PETA member's comment that every election is "always between a giant douche and a turd sandwich."

Yeah, Boy . . . Getting, Keeping, and Using the Right to Vote

Most Americans take the right to vote for granted, but the founding fathers viewed voting as a privilege of the white, male landowners who made up the aristocracy. Initially, in national elections voters directly elected only members of the House of Representatives, with the Presidency decided by the Electoral College and the Senate appointed by the various state legislatures. Over time, however, ten amendments to the Constitution dealt either directly or indirectly with elections. Of these changes, among the most important are the 15th amendment of 1870 giving freed male slaves the right (at least in principle) to vote, the 17th amendment of 1913 providing for direct election of Senators, the 19th amendment of 1920 giving women the right to vote, and the 26th amendment of 1971 making the minimum voting age eighteen.[1]

Given the suffering and hardships so many people had to endure to win the right to vote, one might think that nearly every eligible American would cast a ballot. But just like Stan in the "Douche or Turd" episode, many Americans choose not to vote. Nearly 40 percent of eligible voters chose *not* to vote in the general election of 2004, and over one million actual voters chose not to cast a ballot for the Presidential race. While the general trend in voter turnout has been downward since the 1960s (turnout at 63.1 percent in 1960), the numbers for the Bush-Kerry election are surprising given the controversy that surrounded the 2000 election. Data from Dr. Michael McDonald's "United States Elections Project" shows that tens of millions of possible voters chose not to make the trip to their local ballot box, perhaps echoing Stan's desire not to vote because of his lack of

---

[1] The text of the Constitution can be found in most US government textbooks, such as Steffen Schmidt, Mack Shelley, and Barbara Bardes, *American Government and Politics Today* (Belmont, CA: Wadsworth, 2001).

interest in the two nominees, or maybe feeling that a single vote did not matter in the larger scheme of things.[2] Regardless, Stan's resistance mirrors general trends in our political arena. Is this trend merely a symbol of a growing sense of apathy or is something more going on?

Gettin' Schooled at College, Dawg

In 2000 post-election polls many people expressed the view that the voters didn't have much say in the process of nominating Presidential candidates or in the final selection of the Chief Executive. One might be tempted to write this sentiment off as due to the controversies surrounding the counting of ballots in Florida and the controversial court proceedings that ultimately upheld the initial results, giving the state's electoral votes – and the Presidency – to George W. Bush, but political commentators also point to other reasons for this disillusionment. Notably, elections are often decided by millions of votes (at least in terms of the popular vote), and the Electoral College separates some potential voters from the process of selecting a President.[3]

Because most Presidential elections boil down to roughly ten prime battleground states (such as Ohio, Florida, and Pennsylvania in the 2004 election), potential voters in other states may not be as motivated to take action, both in terms of volunteering to campaign

---

[2] Michael P. McDonald, "Up, Up and Away! Voter Participation in the 2004 Presidential Election," *The Forum: A Journal of Applied Research in Contemporary Politics* 2 (2004). Complete data from the project can be found at the following web address: www.elections.gmu.edu/voter_turnout.htm.

[3] Discussion of these assertions can be found in Thomas E. Patterson, *The Vanishing Voter* (New York: Alfred A. Knopf, 2002), hereafter cited as (Patterson, p. "x") in the text. For further discussions of recent voter behavior, see Alan Abramowitz, *Voice of the People: Elections and Voting in the United States* (New York: McGraw Hill, 2004); André Blais, *To Vote or Not to Vote? The Merits and Limits of Rational Choice Theory* (Pittsburgh: University of Pittsburgh Press, 2000), hereafter cited as (Blais, p. "x"); Geoffrey Brennan and Loren Lomasky, *Democracy and Decision: The Pure Theory of Electoral Preference* (New York: Cambridge University Press, 1993), hereafter cited as (BL, p. "x") in the text; Donald Green, *Get Out the Vote!* (Washington, DC: Brookings Institution Press, 2004); Steven E. Schier, *You Call This an Election? America's Peculiar Democracy* (Washington, DC: Georgetown University Press, 2003), hereafter cited as (Schier, p. "x") in the text.

before the election or voting on election day itself. In essence, the Electoral College turns more than half of the country into mere spectators.[4] Stan feels that his vote didn't matter, when his candidate loses by a margin of 1,410 votes to only 36. His father disagrees, and his mother goes so far as to say that you can't judge the merits of a vote by whether or not a given candidate wins. Still, Stan's feeling of helplessness isn't unreasonable. Very few races are close enough for a single vote to actually change the outcome.

Unfortunately, the Electoral College is only one of America's *disincentives* to vote. Another disincentive is the early network projections on election night, declaring who has won the election before many polls have closed. Early poll closing times are another factor, with 26 states requiring people to vote before 7:30 p.m. The complicated registration process, handled independently by the states, also confuses the matter for many. The frequency and number of elections in the United States, including primaries, general elections, run-offs, mid-terms, odd-year locals, and special elections, is sometimes said to lead to "voter fatigue." Furthermore, the fact that elections are held on a Tuesday, instead of on a holiday or weekend (unlike many other democracies), further compounds the problem of people not voting (Patterson, ch. 5 and Blais, ch. 1).

Yo . . . Your Candidate is In the House

Stan is plagued by people telling him to vote only because they believe he will vote for their choice for mascot. Kyle tells Kenny: "We have got to make Stan understand the importance of voting, because he'll definitely vote for our guy." At one point, after Puff Daddy's first intervention, Stan temporarily decides to cast a vote, a move cheered on by Kyle until he realizes that Stan is actually voting for Cartman's candidate. Kyle criticizes Stan's decision, with Stan replying, "I thought I was supposed to make my own decision." Kyle responds, "Well yeah, but not if your decision is for Turd Sandwich! What the

---

[4] For an explanation and discussion of the United States Electoral College, see Robert Bennett, *Taming the Electoral College* (Stanford: Stanford University Press, 2006).

hell is wrong with you?" Cartman also campaigns hard, as he and Butters use candy to try and sway undecided voters, including Clyde. Cartman even offers to help Stan cast his vote, promising a steak dinner after the process is completed. Stan remains resistant to this kind of ploy, however, and refuses to be manipulated into making a choice.

Not even kindergarteners are safe from pressure and tricks. In the episode "Trapper Keeper" the class is called upon to elect a new class president, but the election comes to a stalemate when Flora is unable to choose between Filmore and Kyle's little brother, Ike. The vote is tied at six each, and Mr. Garrison tells Flora that she has the last winning vote. He can't read her handwritten ballot, so he directly asks her who she picked. She says that she doesn't know, but Mr. Garrison forces the issue, telling her that she has to pick one, Filmore or Ike. As Flora tries to decide, the other kids argue, trying to get her to cast her deciding vote for their pick. The situation escalates when Rosie O'Donnell, Filmore's aunt, comes on the scene to help make sure "that the kids that voted for my nephew don't get cheated," calling for recount after recount. Mr. Garrison stands up to Rosie, saying that "half the kids in the class didn't vote for your nephew, so what about them? You don't give a crap about them because they're not on your side!" In the end, Filmore drops out because he doesn't want to play the stupid game anymore, letting Ike become class president. Ike promptly declares that he pooped his pants, and the class begins to finger-paint.

The C to the H to the O to the I to the C to the E

The philosopher John Locke (1632–1704) argued that political authority comes from the consent of the people.[5] Clearly, the vote is one of the primary avenues by which that consent is granted. When Stan refuses to vote for one of the two new school mascots, one could very easily argue that, in essence, he is rejecting the "authorita" of

---

[5] John Locke, *Two Treatises of Government* (New York: Cambridge University Press, 1988), p. 407.

both of the candidates to represent him. Although Stan might be alone in his protest of the process in South Park, he is joined by nearly half of all eligible Americans in every Presidential election – and by nearly two-thirds during midterm elections.

Although in the US many people feel perfectly at ease not voting, Stan feels immense pressure from his family and friends. Kyle reminds him of Puff Daddy's Vote or Die campaign and P Diddy himself brings home the "die" option by whipping out a gun from his back pocket, cocking it, and pointing it squarely at Stan. The threats of violence from Puff Daddy and banishment from South Park mirror the social pressures that motivate some people to vote out of duty (Blais, p. 8).

You Wanna Third Party, G?

Stan initially resists voting because of his feelings about the two candidates, but in the end he admits "I learned that I'd better get used to having to pick between a douche and a turd sandwich because it's usually the choice I'll have." Perhaps if Stan didn't feel that his choices were limited to those two options, or Flora to her two choices, they might feel more inclined to vote. Similarly, while US voters can cast a ballot for third parties (including the Green, Libertarian, Constitution, and Natural Law parties), those options are usually not seen as legitimate. The games of Presidential politics are slanted toward the major parties, with the closed nature of the debates and the winner-take-all elections (48 of the 50 states award all of the electoral college votes in that state to the candidate who wins a simple majority of the votes).

Stan's choice between the douche and the turd is captured in a song played as he finally votes: "Let's get out the vote! Let's make our voices heard! We've been given the right to choose between a douche and a turd. It's democracy in action! Put your freedom to the test. A big fat turd or a stupid douche. Which do you like best?" This distasteful dualism is even more troublesome for voters who see themselves as voting within a framework of self-expression or self-definition. According to Brennan and Lomasky, "If individuals do genuinely vote merely as an act of self-expression . . . Surely individuals need a larger repertoire of political positions than two in order to define themselves and/or express their political affections" (BL, pp. 119–20). Our two-party system doesn't make enough room for third parties. If, however, we attempted to incorporate some of the advantages of a proportional representation system, instead of our winner-take-all districts, we might find third parties getting more attention. A proportional representation system is one in which the percentage of votes received by a party matches the percentage of seats they obtain in the legislature. Even if proportional representation were only applied to the Electoral College system, such that the percentage of the vote in that state would translate into the number of electoral votes received for that candidate, we might find more people getting involved in the election process.

Stability in the Political Ghetto, My Homey

Having noted its flaws, we still have to marvel at the stability of our system. During the uncertain days that followed Election Day, 2000, there was very little serious political unrest and no real violence. Our political system continued to work and, ultimately, most Americans accepted the winner as legitimate, even if they did not agree with his selection. This respect for the system of government might simply be due to America's reverence for its national institutions (Schier, pp. 19–20). This respect might also be due to a faith that we are, rightly or wrongly, better off in our system than we would be in any other.

Americans who choose not to vote on Election Day may simply be too distracted by the day-to-day events of busy lives, they may choose not to vote as a form of protest against a system, or against candidates, that they object to, or they may not cast ballots because they do not believe that their vote matters. The question that we need to consider in light of Stan's dilemma calls for us to reflect on ways to improve our democratic system, given the absence of so many voters. More work must be done in political philosophy to investigate the reasons for the absence of so many voters from our political community and to alleviate the problems. Just as Stan is left thinking of his reasons to vote, Americans as a whole also must find ways to make our political decisions.

PART FOUR

ETHICS: DUDE . . . GAY MUSLIMS DON'T EAT VEAL

12

THEY SATIRIZED MY PROPHET...
THOSE BASTARDS! *SOUTH PARK*
AND BLASPHEMY

David R. Koepsell

This Is My Faith, And You Shouldn't Make Fun Of It!

South Park is a show born in blasphemy. Its very first, un-aired episode (from 1995) was entitled "Jesus vs. Santa: The Spirit of Christmas" and involves a fight scene in which Jesus employs judo and hurls profanities at Jolly Ole St. Nick. Since this auspicious start, *South Park*'s creators have spared no major religion from their taunts and mockery. Targets of the *South Park* kids' mockery have included Judaism, Mormonism, Buddhism, Hinduism, Catholicism, and Islam. Yet, in this day of cartoon riots and terror bombings fueled by religious rage and sectarian hatred, how can we justify what some consider fuel for the flames? Is there a role for mockery in public discourse of even the most cherished beliefs of billions of believers, or does *South Park* go too far? Answering these questions involves discussing whether there are topics that are off limits for public dialogue, satire, or other forms of discourse, as well as whether and to what degree there is an individual duty to self-censor certain forms of speech concerning "offensive" topics.

No one has ever accused *South Park* of being the pinnacle of good taste. In fact, the filth and offense that Cartman, Stan, Kyle, and Kenny (however muffled) spew are an inherent part of its spectacle, if not its charm. In the past decade, affronts to religious belief have abounded, but a number of particularly offensive ones now command our attention, thanks to some other events also involving cartoons. In 2006, riots erupted across Europe and much of the Muslim world due to a Danish newspaper's publishing a series of rather lame cartoons depicting the Prophet Mohammed. Such depictions are forbidden according to some interpretations of Islamic law. Also in 2006, Isaac Hayes left the show as the voice of Chef due to "religious intolerance" toward his own religion, Scientology.

In the midst of the culturally charged 2006 climate, Comedy Central censored an episode that depicted, in a brilliant bit of double satire, the Prophet Mohammed delivering a helmet to Peter in a mock episode of *Family Guy*. The sudden censorship was an odd move, given *South Park*'s long history of religious mockery, none of which had garnered nearly as much attention prior to 2006's cartoon wars.

Has the public climate changed so radically that, all of a sudden, religious mockery is off-limits, or did *South Park* cross some line? The former seems most likely, and we are experiencing a cyclical up-tick in tension among religious groups as well as a renewed sensitivity. Historically, religion has been fair game for mockery, satire, and ridicule. In fact, *South Park* has done a brilliant – and offensive – job of mocking, satirizing, and ridiculing religion with little-to-no controversy for ten years. Let's look at the history and breadth of their blasphemy.

In the episode "Jewbilee," Kenny poses as a Jew to join Kyle at "Jew Scouts" where the young Jewish "squirts" make macaroni pictures and soap sculptures for a delighted Moses. In the same episode, Kyle admonishes Kenny: "It's not stupid, Kenny! This is my faith, and you shouldn't make fun of it!" Nonetheless, the entire episode proceeds to do just that.

In "Are You There God? It's Me, Jesus!" Jesus is initially treated like the millennial version of Punxsutawney Phil as a predictor of the apocalypse. When Jesus realizes that people are waiting for a sign from him, he goes to his "dad" saying that, if he could help Jesus with a sign, it would help with his "one big shot at a comeback." God refuses and Jesus arranges a concert with Rod Stewart . . . in Las Vegas, of course. God himself fails to appear readily at the big Las Vegas-Jesus-Rod Stewart event, and the audience becomes angry enough to try to crucify Jesus *again*. In a touching finale, God *does* appear, only to explain to the boys that they will never have menstrual cycles.

Parker and Stone spare no major faith and, in "The Super Best Friends," they skewer several at once. When Jesus attempts, and fails, to break the cult-like spell cast by magician David Blaine, he turns to the Super Best Friends, a sort of ecumenical Justice League which includes Lao Tse, Mohammed, Krishna, Joseph Smith, and "Sea Man." Among the jolly blasphemy bandied about in this episode, Mohammed is given the power to shoot fire from his hands, Joseph Smith has magical ice-breath, and Lao Tse can "link mentally with fish." Finally, despite their super powers, the Super Best Friends are advised by Moses on the best way to defeat a Blaine-animated Lincoln monument. It involves Lao Tse using his "powers of Taoism" to animate a giant stone John Wilkes Booth. Interestingly, Mohammed's depiction in this episode was not censored by Comedy Central, and as far as we know, no riots ensued.

While sexual abuse scandals peaked in the daily news, "Red Hot Catholic Love" aired in August, 2002. Besides portraying pederasty as an expected and normal portion of the priesthood, the episode reveals that a 20-foot giant Queen Spider runs the Vatican and interprets Catholic law. Offenses against Judaism and Christianity abound in "A Ladder to Heaven," "Christian Hard Rock," and "The Passion of the Jew." There's more Jesus/Santa hilarity in "Red Sleigh Down," and Catholics got slapped again – this time through a mocking reference to a miraculous icon of Mary that bleeds from its ass – in "Bloody Mary."

Finally, Joseph Smith makes another appearance in the episode "All About Mormons," where Stan and his family learn about Mormonism after Stan befriends a young Mormon kid named Gary. The story of Mormonism is not-so-subtly critiqued by a chorus that sings, "dumb, dumb, dumb, dumb" with each episode in the tale. When Stan finally decides the story is unbelievable, Gary, his new little Mormon friend, tells him to believe whatever he wants, but not to denounce him because he has a nice family and they were only ever trying to be nice, not to convert Stan and his family. Then, in a rare moment of Mormon obscenity, Gary tells them to "suck my balls."

And so, as we see, *South Park* has been littered, not with just offense and mere critique, but also with what, in earlier times, would have been considered punishable blasphemy. Thank the Super Best Friends for free speech!

Suck My Balls – Is Nothing Sacred?

No, frankly, not on *South Park*. But in the first half of the twentieth century, long before the show bravely shattered all pretense of taste, blasphemy could get you thrown in jail, even in the United States with its groundbreaking First Amendment.

The First Amendment protects speech, but not absolutely. Despite its plain guarantee of "freedom of speech," courts, legislatures, and custom have long prohibited certain forms of speech. Notably, and of no comfort to Parker and Stone, obscenity is not protected, and local communities set the standards for obscenity. Besides obscenity, blasphemy itself was punished for some time. In the United States, a contract for leasing rooms as a forum for lectures concerning the potential truth of Christ's teachings was held to be illegal as late as 1867. In 1870, a Pennsylvania court held that the "Infidel Society of Philadelphia" was not entitled to receive a bequest because it was illegal, despite the legal incorporation of the society, and the technically correct manner of the bequest's language and execution.[1] Prosecutions for blasphemy were for some time supplanted by prosecutions for "obscenity." Notably, Charles C. Moore of Lexington, Kentucky edited the freethought journal *Blue Grass Blade* and was prosecuted under the state's obscenity laws, subsequently serving jail time in 1899. The crime was publishing speculation as to the divine nature of Jesus. In 1891 Moses Harman, the editor of an anarchist publication named *Lucifer the Light Bearer* published in Topeka, Kansas, also served jail time for publishing obscene materials speculating about established religious dogmas.[2] As Cartman would say, that dude was just asking for trouble.

In 1940 the Supreme Court finally extended the protections of the First Amendment to religious criticism and religious argument. For more than a hundred years, blasphemers had been routinely prosecuted

---

[1] *Zeisweiss vs. James*, 63, Pa. 465.
[2] See Fred Whitehead and Verle Muhrer, *Free Thought on the American Frontier* (Amherst, NY: Prometheus Press, 1992).

under antiquated anti-blasphemy laws throughout the United States. In *Cantwell vs. Connecticut*, the Supreme Court essentially nullified state and local blasphemy ordinances that had been in effect, enforced, and responsible for people being jailed for public challenges to the dominant religion – Christianity. The court's ruling echoes the reasoning of the philosopher John Stuart Mill (1806–1873). In his treatise *On Liberty*, Mill makes a compelling case for free and open dialogue on every topic, including those held most sacred by church and state. He argues that only free and open discussion can shake out the truth of any matter, lest it become mere dogma. But then Mill made himself liable to prosecution for his lectures, calling into question the divine authority of the Bible in 1851.[3]

Despite the 1940 ruling in *Cantwell*, two years later, the same court refused to extend their reasoning to "profanity," whatever the fuck that is. In *Chaplinsky vs. New Hampshire*, Justice Frank Murphy ruled that profanity enjoyed no First Amendment protection in a case in which a Jehovah's Witness – clearly tired of knocking on doors – proclaimed publicly that all religion was a "racket" and, then, while being arrested called the cop a "God damned racketeer" and a "damned fascist." The court reasoned that these exclamations were not a part of the "exposition of ideas," and the social interest in order and morality clearly outweighed any potential benefit from those words. As Leonard Levy points out, the *Chaplinsky* decision "violates the establishment clause of [the First] amendment by favoring religious beliefs over nonreligious beliefs."[4] This is because "profanity," unlike mere "obscenity," invokes the name of God.

Now, in these enlightened times, neither profanity nor blasphemy is routinely punished, and freedom of speech is extended to the likes of *South Park*, as long as no nipples make an appearance. But, despite the legal protection now seemingly afforded the rampant profanity and blasphemy of *South Park*, we should ask whether there's any virtue in self-censorship, tolerance, kindness, and humility, before considering Comedy Central's outright and unprecedented censorship of the show.

[3] John Stuart Mill, *On Liberty* (New York: Penguin, 1975). See *The Infidel Tradition: From Paine to Bradlaugh*, ed. by Macmillan Publishers (New York: Macmillan, 1976), p. 206.

[4] Leonard Levy, *Blasphemy: Verbal Offense Against the Sacred, from Moses to Salman Rushdie* (Chapel Hill: University of North Carolina Press, 1993).

Can't We all Just Get Along?

Nah, not really. That is, unless we all agree not to take affronts to our cherished beliefs personally and, oh, not to kill each other over them, too. Now, under their convention on human rights, a renewed effort has appeared in the European Community – where there is no First Amendment – to revive old notions of human rights so as to punish those who denigrate any religion. Similarly, there was a failed effort in response to the Danish cartoon controversy and other disputes to expand Britain's blasphemy statute to protect religions other than their official, state religion. These attempts have followed a line of reasoning that holds certain beliefs beyond mockery, beyond criticism, and beyond question. Is there a human right to have one's beliefs so valued by others?

While the Human Rights Commission in Europe believes so, it is difficult to make an honest philosophical argument for that point of view. Nonetheless, in 1983, the Commission held as much, basing its decision obliquely on the European Convention on Human Rights, Article 10. The case involved a fellow named Lemon who published a poem entitled "The Love That Dares to Speak Its Name," which was held blasphemous by the crown, and censored. Lemon took his case to the European Human Rights Commission, alleging that the censorship violated his rights of free expression under the EU charter, Article 10. The commission found that, in fact, the British blasphemy law was too vague for Lemon to conclude his poem was proscribed by it, and that the law may have been too restrictive for a "democratic society." However, the commission found that the law did protect the rights of others and was necessary in a democratic society. The commission held that there was a civil right "not to be offended in [one's] religious feelings by publications." The commission thus found that the law itself did not violate Lemon's human rights, although its use in his case was unwarranted.[5]

Yet, under the US Constitution, blasphemy could not be legitimately prosecuted, at least for now. Instead, speech may be restricted

---

[5] *Lemon vs. UK*, Decision of the Commission, May 7, 1982. 5 E.H.R.R 123, para. 11. Also see Sheldon Leader, "Blasphemy and Human Rights," *Modern Law Review* 46 (1983), pp. 338–45.

for other, valid, secular purposes. This is so because elevating *any particular* faith's belief-set above others and beyond criticism, or even ridicule, would violate the establishment clause of the First Amendment, while elevating *every* faith's belief-set to that level would elevate religion over other sorts of belief and severely curtail speech. Specifically, one could garner absolute protection from criticism simply by declaring one's set of beliefs "religious," seeking tax-exempt status, and suing those who dare question you . . . just like Scientologists. Ooops! Did I say that? Let's *pretend* I did, and look closely at Comedy Central's reactions to the Islam/*The Family Guy* and "Tom Cruise Trapped in the Closet" episodes, both of which aired within six months of each other in 2005–2006, and both of which were censored by the network.

2005–2006: Comedy Central Caves

South Park laid a double-whammy on Comedy Central, Scientology, *Family Guy*, and Tom Cruise in two episodes that aired within six months of each other. The episode "Tom Cruise Trapped in the Closet" finds Stan attracted to Scientology to heal his alleged depression. Stan learns the Scientology dogma while being made into a sort of messiah for their religion. In a none-too-subtle and largely unrelated aside, Tom Cruise gets trapped in a closet, and refuses to come out . . . of the closet. After this episode aired Isaac Hayes, who played Chef, quit the show, citing the show's "intolerance" of religious beliefs (like this was a new thing). In the episode, Stan learns the actual dogma of Scientology in brief. The "president" of Scientology tells Stan a short version of the story of Xenu, based directly on the actual Scientology OT III document. This is accompanied by an onscreen caption reading, "THIS IS WHAT SCIENTOLOGISTS ACTUALLY BELIEVE."

Recall that the same device was used in the "All About Mormons" episode, elucidating the actual beliefs of the Church of Jesus Christ of Latter Day Saints. But recall also that it was interspersed with the "dumb, dumb, dumb, dumb" chant. The harshest critique of Scientology comes from Stan's honest desire to transform the church from a profit-making venture into a force of good in people's lives.

By a long shot, this show was more kind to Scientology than was "All About Mormons" to Mormonism. Yet, Comedy Central did not re-air the episode after its November 16, 2006 debut, and had suggested it would not until it was announced on July 12, 2006, that it would indeed rerun it.[6]

In "Cartoon Wars (II)," which aired in April, 2006, levels of parody intertwine. Combining the revelation that *Family Guy* is really created by manatees with the appearance of a Bart Simpson-like character who shares Cartman's loathing for *Family Guy*, this episode skewers Comedy Central itself by comparing it to a fictional Fox network that is allegedly censoring the appearance of the Prophet Mohammed in a fictional episode of *Family Guy*. The episode was itself actually censored, and a clip featuring the Prophet (as seen in "Super Best Friends") delivering a "salmon helmet" to Peter was replaced by a black screen with text: "Mohammed hands Peter a football helmet." Then another caption follows, with the distinctly sour tone "Comedy Central refuses to show an image of Mohammed on their network." It cuts back to the citizens of South Park saying how it wasn't bad at all, not offensive or degrading. The show then cuts to a shot of terrorist leader Al Zawahari, vowing revenge. The revenge is an al Qaeda cartoon featuring various Americans, President G.W. Bush, and Jesus all pooping on one another. Of course, the fact that Comedy Central chose not to censor that scene, much more objectively objectionable than Mohammed delivering a football helmet to Peter from *Family Guy*, has never been explained. Moreover, Parker and Stone have depicted Mohammed on *South Park* for years, as he makes an appearance, along with numerous other characters, in the rapid-fire musical montage opening.

Is *South Park* Responsible for the Decline of Western Civilization?

Frankly, every generation has its *South Park*. It was *The Simpsons* more than a decade ago; before that, the explicit lyrics of 2 Live Crew

---

[6] Gina Serpe, "Airwaves Again Safe for *South Park* Scientology Spoof," *E! Online News*, July 12, 2006.

and, before that, punk music. And before that, it was rock 'n' roll, drugs, hoop skirts, two-piece bathing suits, chewing gum, sarsaparilla – you get the picture. There's always a scapegoat. Civilization isn't declining. The very fact that there were no cartoon riots in the US – nor have there been *South Park* riots – indicates that freedom of speech is working. Tolerance does not require silence, nor does it require an absence of criticism, mockery, or even ridicule.

In fact, many of the blasphemous episodes of *South Park* make that point. In "The Passion of the Jew," Stan lectures Mel Gibson, who insists that being a good Christian requires enjoying Gibson's *The Passion*. "No, dude, if you wanna be Christian, that's cool, but, you should follow what Jesus taught instead of how he got killed. Focusing on how he got killed is what people did in the Dark Ages and it ends up with really bad results." In "Red Hot Catholic Love" Randy, having once again learned a lesson from his son, reclaims his faith, observing: "He's [Priest Maxi] right, Sharon. We don't have to believe every word of the Bible. They're just stories to help us to live by. We shouldn't toss away the lessons of the Bible just because some assholes in Italy screwed it up." Finally, in "All About Mormons," Gary, the little Mormon kid, teaches the lesson that Parker and Stone frequently teach in their messed-up way:

> Look, maybe us Mormons do believe in crazy stories that make abso-lutely no sense, and maybe Joseph Smith did make it all up, but I have a great life, and a great family, and I have the Book of Mormon to thank for that. The truth is, I don't care if Joseph Smith made it up, because what the church teaches now is loving your family, being nice, and helping people. And even though people in *this* town might think that's stupid, I still choose to believe in it. All I ever did was try to be your friend, Stan, but you're so high and mighty you couldn't look past my religion and just be my friend back. You've got a lot of grow-ing up to do buddy.

South Park's ultimately pragmatic view of religion is just this. They mock not the belief, but the believer, and credit believers where their lives reflect good, ethical practice. They also point out hypocrisy wher-ever possible. Because the show treats nothing as sacred, this lesson comes across as genuine rather than as preaching. By mocking every-thing, the lessons that actually come through have a deeper meaning. So what good did Comedy Central do by censoring a depiction of

Mohammed giving someone a helmet? What positive impact is there from refusing to re-air an episode that explains the actual tenets of Scientology? In fact, *South Park*'s continual quest for reason, and its mockery of irrationality, is legitimate cultural criticism. The mockery of religion is subordinate to mockery of society, a society that over-reacts to perceived affronts. There's plenty to be offended by in *South Park*, and it's all treated on an equal basis. Nothing is sacred, and that's what comedy is about. To quote Gary, from the end of the soliloquy above, if you don't like it, Comedy Central, "suck my balls!"

13

YOU CAN'T GET MARRIED, YOU'RE FAGGOTS

Mrs. Garrison and the Gay Marriage Debate

Jacob M. Held

Fags are Gettin' Married Over My Dead Body

Gay marriage is an issue that very few people have little or no opinion about. To make matters worse, almost everybody's position, whether for or against, is based on a really bad argument. Most recently, the issue of gay marriage reared its head when Congress introduced and voted on an amendment to the Constitution that would have defined marriage as a union between a man and a woman.[1] As with most controversial topics, *South Park* also had its say. And *South Park* seems a fitting place for the debate, especially with characters like Mr./Mrs. Garrison, Mr. Slave, and Big Gay Al.

This chapter is going to center around one particular episode of *South Park*, "Follow That Egg!" In this episode, Mrs. Garrison attempts to rekindle her relationship with Mr. Slave, but the reunion doesn't go as planned. Mr. Slave is going to marry Big Gay Al as soon as the Colorado governor signs the Bill authorizing same-sex marriages. Mrs. Garrison vows to put an end to the Bill, claiming, "Fags are getting' married over my dead body." She then begins her crusade

---

[1]   Senate Joint Resolution 1, S.J. Res. 1, the "Marriage Protection Amendment." The motion for cloture was rejected with 49 voting Yea, 48 voting Nay, and 3 abstentions.

against gay marriage arguing from tradition, the holy sacrament of marriage, and that we must think of the children.

There are many arguments for and against gay marriage. In what follows, I will look at the most familiar arguments on both sides and demonstrate how they usually miss the point, are entirely irrelevant, or are just bad arguments. In so doing, I hope to map out the landscape of the gay marriage debate and show how barren it is. I conclude with a case for gay marriage rooted in America's political liberal tradition of negative liberty.

My God, Nature, and the Dictionary Say "No!" The Worst Arguments Against Gay Marriage

The basic religious argument is simply that, according to one's religion, homosexuality is a sin or marriage is a holy sacrament between a man and a woman, or both. Many religiously minded people take this issue seriously, and they have the right to their religious beliefs. But we are not a theocracy and our rights are not and should not be determined by religious traditions. We live under a constitution, not Leviticus. We obey a rule of law, not your pastor or priest. Whoever your god is, whatever book you think communicates this god's laws, and however you interpret them is irrelevant to a debate about the distribution of rights and privileges. We are a secular nation. So the religious argument may be convincing to you personally, but that is as far as it can go, unless Jesus Christ actually gets a public access call-in show, in which case we could actually get his take on the matter and he could enter the political discourse! Mrs. Garrison does argue that marriage is a holy sacrament, but even she doesn't push the point. She knows that marriage as debated in the same-sex marriage debate is a secular issue of rights and privileges, not a theological matter.

The argument from definition is another argument against gay marriage and simply says that marriage is defined as a union between a man and a woman; so gay marriage can't be marriage. This is trivially true. If we define marriage in this way then same-sex unions, whatever else they might be, can't be marriage. But the last time I checked, we didn't refer constitutional issues or matters of rights to Webster. We need more than a dictionary to understand the issues at hand here. To be charitable, let's presume that what someone offering the definition argument means is that marriage is essentially a union between a man and a woman. But what could this mean? If it's just about gender then as Mrs. Garrison pointed out to Mr. Slave, since he is now legally a woman, if Mr. Slave is going to marry anyone he has to marry Mrs. Garrison. But surely this isn't consistent with what opponents of gay marriage intend. When they speak of marriage there must be something else, because how can a Mrs. Garrison and Mr. Slave marriage be acceptable for those who wish to maintain the sanctity of marriage?

What this argument usually boils down to is not just opposite sexes, but procreation; the essence of marriage is the connection of opposites for procreation.[2] A marriage is essentially between a man and woman because they are the ones who can have children. But this presumes a moral order inherent in simple biological or natural fact. If this moral order reduces to a theological position, then it is unacceptable for the reasons above. If it's not theological, it still would have the consequence of denying marriage to post-menopausal women, sterile couples, or even those couples who willfully choose not to have children. They all violate the sanctity of marriage by denying its procreative purpose. To avoid this problem, some say it is about the fact that a man and woman could have children, that is, if everything worked properly they could procreate, whereas gays can't possibly have children. It is inherent in gay relationships that they are not procreative. But this fails to address childless couples who choose to be childless and remarriages of post-menopausal woman. In fact, this whole argument seems to simply reduce to the fact that the possession of complementary sexual organs is the only necessary condition for marriage. This seems incredibly arbitrary when talking about the distribution of rights and privileges. Apparently, just because my wife and I "fit together" we are granted certain rights others are not, that

---

[2] See Sam Schulman, "Gay Marriage – and Marriage," in *Contemporary Moral Problems*, ed. by James E. White (Belmont, CA: Wadsworth Publishing, 2006), pp. 285–93.

is, we enjoy the position of a privileged class because of our genders, not because of our capacity to have children, love for each other, or any other factor that might seem relevant for marriage. If I have characterized this argument correctly, then not only is the argument dogmatic (marriage is between a man and woman because only a man and woman can get married for no other reason than that one is a man and the other a woman), but it betrays a simple bigotry: "Gays can't get married because they're gay." End of story, no further explanation needed. I just believe it, or feel strongly about it.

But rights are too important to be left to the irrational moral sentiments or visceral reactions of others, and the law is not about enforcing the morality of the majority.[3] We need reasons why we grant rights to some and not to others. Reasons are what hold our society together and afford all of us an equal voice.

So maybe there is something more to the position against gay marriage, in fact there would have to be. So what about the more traditional argument that marriage has always been between a man and a woman? Aside from being questionable,[4] let's presume it's true. So what! Slavery was a tradition with a long lineage, so was the oppression of women. Tradition does not prove that something is acceptable, merely that others have accepted it. But the traditionalists must know this, because they always insert in this argument that traditional marriage has endured because it works so well and it is a fundamental institution of society. George Bush (a.k.a., Turd Sandwich) has remarked: "Ages of experience have taught humanity that the commitment of a husband and wife to love and to serve one another promotes the welfare of children and the stability of society."[5] Let's go with that, because the simple fact that something has been done for a long time means very little.

---

[3] See Ronald Dworkin, *Taking Rights Seriously* (Cambridge, MA: Harvard University Press, 1978), ch. 10, "Liberty and Moralism." Hereafter cited as (Dworkin, p. "x") in the text.

[4] Some have argued that historical data show that the equivalent to gay marriage has existed in the past. For a good summary of this position, see *Same-Sex Marriage: Pro and Con: A Reader*, ed. by Andrew Sullivan (New York: Vintage Books, 2004), ch. 1, "For the First Time Ever? Same-Sex Marriage in History."

[5] George W. Bush, "The President Speaks: President George W. Bush, February 24, 2004," in *Same-Sex Marriage: Pro and Con: A Reader*, p. 343.

You Think Kids Can Be Raised by Queers? The Argument from Harm and the Slippery Slope

Maybe the problem with gay marriage is that it will harm society. This is a legitimate concern, and one that needs to be addressed. Marriage has played a very important role in society and it is a valuable institution. It should be protected and probably promoted. So in what way will gay marriage destroy it or prevent heterosexual marriage from continuing to function? Will it destroy the institution of marriage itself? Whether or not Mr. Slave and Big Gay Al get married has no impact whatsoever on my actual marriage. Yet, opponents of gay marriage argue that it will devalue marriage. Aside from the questionable implication – it will undermine marriage because gays will make a mockery of it; supposedly because they are gay – this doesn't seem plausible. Gays want marriage rights because they value the institution and want in on it. Heterosexuals will still be able to marry (and divorce) as they always have. Maybe it's about the children?

Mrs. Garrison is quick to point out to the governor that if gays are allowed to marry, then they will want adoption rights. Think of the children! Bill O'Reilly has made the same case, arguing that nature made it a man and woman because they are best suited to raise children.[6] The only problem with this claim is that all existing information fails to show that kids raised in families with gay parents are harmed by this fact and are in any way disadvantaged, harmed, or otherwise maladjusted.[7] Some of the concerns themselves seem

---

[6] Aside from the questionable premise that nature intends anything (he must mean a god), it presumes that what qualifies one to be a parent is the proper genitals, not any set of parenting skills. He made this comment on "The O'Reilly Factor," air date June 5, 2006, and no doubt countless other times.

[7] When faced with this many opponents to gay marriage, like O'Reilly, fall back on the claim that they just don't believe gays can raise kids as well as straights. Apparently facts and logic are irrelevant for the forming of their opinions; all they need are good old-fashioned gut reactions. Stephen Colbert would be proud. For this type of view, see James Q. Wilson, "Against Homosexual Marriage," and Hadley Arkes, "The Role of Nature," in *Same-Sex Marriage: Pro and Con: A Reader*; Stephen Knight, "How Domestic Partnerships and Gay Marriage Threaten the Family," in *Same-Sex Marriage: The Moral and Legal Debate*, ed. by Robert M. Baird and Stuart E. Rosenbaum (Amherst, NY: Prometheus Books, 1996).

ludicrous. People argue that these children will have a distorted sense of sexual identity.[8] But no study has shown this to be the case and, even if it did, this argument presumes that current understandings of sexual identity are normatively superior to alternative conceptions and this claim is itself contentious. People also argue that these children will suffer from social isolation or ridicule. But is this a good argument? The fact that Mrs. Garrison is willing to rip on Stan and Kyle's "freak egg" because it has two daddies is her problem, not the egg's or gay parents' problem. Consider her reasoning: the egg can't be raised by gay parents because if it is, she, and people like her, will pick on it and cause it to be maladjusted, thus proving that gay parents can't raise healthy children. The problem isn't with the gay parents. Instead of telling a group of people that they can't have family rights and must remain social outcasts because too many of us are bigoted, perhaps we should fight against bigotry. Let's argue for moral progress rather than acquiescence to bigotry and hatred. Regardless, if marriage is about fitness as parents, then where is the test for straight parents that would guarantee they are qualified to have children? Did Butters' parents have to demonstrate their fitness as parents before they could conceive, have, and mess him up? There just aren't any demonstrable harmful effects that arise from gay marriage either with regard to the institution itself or children. But maybe it is what will necessarily follow from gay marriage that needs to be feared and prevented.

The slippery slope argument is by far the most popular and the one most people think to be decisive against gay marriage. The basic structure of this argument is: if you claim that you can't deny gays the right to marry because gender is not a good reason to limit marriage rights, then you have to admit that all limitations on marriage are unacceptable. So if you allow gays to marry, then you will have to allow polygamy, polyandry, and even incestuous marriage. Who knows, somebody might even want to marry their cat! Many believe this argument to be sound because they do not see a legitimate way to distinguish between gay marriage and these other more "questionable" types of relationships. For them, allowing one means you must allow them all. There are many ways to respond to this argument.

---

[8] See Charlotte Patterson, "Children of Lesbian and Gay Parents: Summary of Research Findings," in *Same-Sex Marriage: Pro and Con: A Reader*, pp. 240–5.

First, gay marriage is different from these other types of marriage in an important way: there is no foreseeable harm in allowing gay marriage, whereas polygamy and incestuous marriage arguably harm the interests of society, but more on this later. The easiest way to respond is to simply point out that speculation about the possibility of negative outcomes is not a good reason to deny a set of rights to one group. One could have argued against the Supreme Court's ruling in *Loving vs. Virginia* in which the court ruled anti-interracial marriage legislation unconstitutional on the same basis, that is, if you allow the races to mix next thing you know gays will want to marry and then polygamists and so forth.[9] But none would have taken this seriously. Gay marriage should stand or fall on its own merits, not as a result of the hyped and unjustified fears of its detractors, even if they are such stand up citizens as Mrs. Garrison.

At the heart of the opponents' arguments is a genuine concern, and one that needs to be taken seriously; namely, the good of society. If one boils down the above arguments, you can see two basic approaches. The first is simply to claim that gay marriage just is wrong, that you oppose it for personal reasons and, so, it shouldn't be allowed. But revulsion, personal disgust, or visceral reactions are not moral positions – they are mere reactions, and they do not make for admissible arguments for public policy (Dworkin, ch. 10). My rights are not contingent on your opinion of me or of my lifestyle. Unfortunately, just as with Mrs. Garrison, most people simply oppose gay marriage because they are morally opposed to homosexuality in general, and they construct arguments after the fact to try and rationalize, or justify, their foregone conclusions. Mrs. Garrison's arguments are simply a way for her to allow her own jealousy into a public policy debate through the backdoor (tasteless pun intended). The second and only legitimate argument voiced above is the claim that gay marriage will have a demonstrable negative impact on society whether it is through the undermining of traditional marriage and family values, harming children, or leading to truly harmful consequences like polygamy and incestuous marriage.

America's liberal heritage is rooted in the notion of negative liberty best expressed in J.S. Mill's (1806–1873) Harm Principle: "The only purpose for which power can be rightfully exercised over any

---

[9] *Loving vs. Virginia*, 388 US 1967.

member of a civilized community, against his will, is to prevent harm to others."[10] Mill claims that before the government can restrict a behavior it has to demonstrate that that behavior causes a demonstrable harm to others. This notion of liberty, the claim that liberty is freedom from encroachment and I have the right to self-determination so long as it harms no one, is a founding principle of American democracy. With respect to natural rights, Thomas Paine (1737–1809) claimed we had "all those rights of acting as an individual for his own comfort and happiness, which are not injurious to the natural rights of others." And civil rights are those secured through a social contract that guarantees our natural rights.[11] The majority's moral condemnation is no good reason to limit one's rights. In fact, this is the basic reasoning the Supreme Court used to demonstrate the unconstitutionality of anti-sodomy laws.[12] It is the same reasoning that can be used to demonstrate that there is no compelling reason to deny marriage rights to gays.

They're Going to Allow Queers and Homos to Get Married, Huh? The Arguments for Gay Marriage

There are two common arguments for gay marriage, the argument from equal rights and the argument that gay marriage would benefit society. The equal rights argument can be summarized as the simple claim that what gays are demanding are the same rights that straights have, and that sexual orientation is not an adequate reason to deny one class of individuals this particular set of rights. Denying gays the right to marry is, it is argued, discrimination equivalent to that historically suffered by other minority groups like women and African Americans.

---

[10]   John Stuart Mill, *On Liberty and The Subjection of Women* (Hertfordshire: Wordsworth Editions, 1996), p. 13.
[11]   Thomas Paine, *Rights of Man* in *Collected Writings* (New York: Literary Classics of the United States, 1995), p. 464.
[12]   See Justice Kennedy's majority opinion in *Lawrence vs. Texas*.

This argument seems to be based on a fundamental misunderstanding. Gays do not want equal rights; they want the creation of an entirely new category of rights. The historical civil rights movements have been based on the idea that all people should have the same rights. So if men can vote, then women ought to be afforded the right also. But gay marriage is different. As it stands, nobody has the right to marry a person of the same sex. Straights do not possess that right any more than gays. And the right that straights have, to marry one partner of the opposite sex, is also shared by gays.[13] Mr. Slave could marry Mrs. Garrison. What proponents of gay marriage want is a new right, namely, the right to marry a member of the same sex, which would carry with it equivalent rights and privileges to marriage and, ideally, both would be subsumed under the same laws through a legal redefining of marriage. Whatever else this might be, it is not an equal rights issue and to claim that it is betrays a fundamental misunderstanding of the issue at stake, the redefinition of marriage rights. This might be a civil rights issue, but it is not about equal rights.

The other often-made case for gay marriage is that gay marriage will have the same stabilizing and beneficial effect on society that traditional marriage has had, so if it is a good enough reason to maintain traditional marriage, then it is an equally good reason to promote gay marriage.[14] This argument claims that gay marriage will help stabilize the gay community, promote family values in a community that could benefit from them, provide loving and nurturing homes and families to children who might otherwise not have them, and, in general, benefit society. Mr. Slave and society could only benefit by allowing Big Gay Al to marry, and perhaps temper some of Mr. Slave's otherwise less than desirable proclivities (poor Lemmiwinks!). There has been little research on this matter and, to tie this into the final and perhaps best argument for gay marriage, all that needs to be said is this: at worst gay marriage doesn't hurt society and at best it helps.

---

[13] See Richard McDonough, "Is Same-Sex Marriage an Equal-Rights Issue?" *Public Affairs Quarterly* 19 (2005), pp. 51–63.

[14] See Jonathan Rauch, "Who Needs Marriage?" in *Contemporary Moral Problems*, ed. by James E. White (Belmont, CA: Wadsworth Publishing, 2006), pp. 294–302. Hereafter, cited as (Rauch, p. "x") in the text.

Teacher, Our Egg is Fine – Gays Can Get Married

The best case for gay marriage is that there is no compelling, legitimate case against it. Gays don't have to make the case for themselves; rather, others have to make a case against them. Mrs. Garrison can't rely on tradition, holiness, or the children to condemn gay marriage. She must acknowledge that she only wants the ban because she doesn't want to see Mr. Slave married to anybody that isn't her. But without good reason, her personal feelings do not count as a good foundation for her argument.

Let's recognize that marriage is not something that is freely handed out. We have certain restrictions on it. You can only marry one person of a certain age and of the opposite sex, and not a close relative. But marriage is also fairly permissive. Rapists and child molesters can get married, so can transgendered individuals and even gays, so long as they meet the requirements above.[15] These restrictions and allowances are all justified based on the principle of harm. One can't deny the right to marry felons because there is no compelling reason to exclude them from this arrangement. But, so it has been argued, we must restrict marriage because it is too important to allow it to degenerate, and we can't allow harmful practices, so we don't allow polygamy, incestuous marriage, or underage marriages. But each of these cases is made based on the fact that there is a demonstrable and relevant harm caused by allowing them. To allow underage marriages is to allow the exploitation of children who require protection. To allow incestuous marriages undermines the family structure since it makes relatives accessible sexual targets and thus creates insecurity and instability in the family unit, and the family is too important to be destroyed. The case against polygamy is similar; namely, it is harmful to women and has negative repercussions on society. But the case of gay marriage is different.

Many of our rights are *negative* rights, or rights to non-interference. The only justifiable way government can interfere in our right to

---

[15] See M.D.A. Freeman, "Not Such a Queer Idea: Is There a Case for Same Sex Marriages?" *Journal of Applied Philosophy* 16 (1999), pp. 1–17.

self-determination is to prevent harm. So if there is no immanent harm, there is no reason for government to interfere. Applied to gay marriage this would allow us to say that since gay marriage is not a demonstrable threat to society in the way that other alternative forms of marriage might be, then there is no justifiable reason to ban it or outlaw the practice – as might be the case if a gay marriage amendment to the Constitution were ever passed. But this is a far cry from the claim that gays ought to be allowed to marry. Rights are tricky things. Showing that there is no reason to deny a right doesn't demonstrate a compelling reason to create it. It might just be a matter of being hands-off and letting people do what they want to do in their private lives. But gays want the right to marry, so they must make an effective case for the creation of equivalent marriage rights for themselves.

Once it has been shown that there is no reason to deny the right to gay marriage, it can be shown why the right should be granted, and the reason has to do with the importance of family. Marriage is about the family and although the family has traditionally been one man and one woman raising naturally born children, this doesn't mean this is how it has to be. In the episode "Follow That Egg!" Stan and Kyle functioned much better as parents than did Stan and Bebe. Cartman broke his egg. So clearly, being straight isn't enough to be a good parent, just like being gay isn't sufficient to prove one is unqualified to be a parent. Families are functional units that form the cohesive base of society and provide for child rearing and stability. But there is nothing in this definition demanding that this be accomplished by one man and one woman, for their naturally born children. Adoptions can work. Single parent families can work, and would more often with governmental support. So too, gay families have worked in the past. Although a cliché, it is true that there are many ways to be a family.[16] If the family's role is to serve a function, namely, to raise children and to be a stabilizing force on society, and if there is no reason to suspect that gays can't also serve this function and may even help to strengthen it, then they should be allowed to join in for the benefit of all of us. In fact, Defense of Marriage Acts never actually promote the welfare of the family, they simply deny

---

[16] See Larry A. Hickman, "Making the Family Functional: The Case for Same-Sex Marriage," *Same-Sex Marriage: The Moral and Legal Debate*, pp. 192–202.

gays the right to marry. But there are much greater threats to marriage. As John Kerry (a.k.a., Giant Douche) noted with respect to the 1996 DOMA act, "If this were truly a defense of marriage act, it would expand the learning experience for would-be husbands and wives. It would provide for counseling for troubled marriages . . . treatment on demand for those with alcohol and substance abuse [problems] . . . it would expand the Violence Against Women Act."[17] He goes on and on. Defending marriage is important, but gays are not the threat. In fact, it would probably be better for a child of a gay parent if that parent were accepted by society, had his commitment to his partner publicly recognized and secured through a system of rights and privileges, instead of living in a society in which he is taught to be ashamed of his gay dad.

With all of this said, let me make it clear that I don't think all opponents of gay marriage are bigoted. They probably would not endorse Mrs. Garrison's solution of a "fag drag." Some have genuine and legitimate concerns about gay marriage and an institution they believe, correctly, to be at the heart of society – the family. But if all your arguments fail and you are left with merely your visceral reaction, your moral indignation or distaste and nothing else, then although you are allowed your opinion you can't reasonably demand that your moral preference be the guiding principle of public policy, especially at the expense of others. Likewise, proponents of gay marriage must make their case and understand that there are legitimate concerns surrounding the institution of marriage. It is not something to be taken lightly.

Being Butt Buddies Isn't the Same as Being Married

In "Follow That Egg!" the governor of Colorado comes up with an ingenious solution to the problem of gay marriage. Gays will be given the same rights as married couples, but it will be called something different. Gays will get the rights they want and opponents won't have

---

[17] John F. Kerry, "Senate Debate on the Defense of Marriage Act: September 10, 1996," *Same-Sex Marriage: Pro and Con: A Reader*, p. 232.

the word *marriage* "tainted" by the inclusion of gays. Gay married couples will instead be called "Butt buddies." (And, since nobody cares about dykes, we don't have to worry about them.) Mr. Slave lisps, "We want to be treated equally." (Yes, he is so gay he can lisp a sentence without a single "s" in it.) The governor claims they are; they will have all the same rights but they will be "Butt buddies," not married. And everybody's happy, right?

No. This isn't being treated equally in the relevant sense. Gay marriage is about rights, but it is more about family and acceptance. Gays want marriage rights because they want to be included in society. Jonathan Rauch notes: "One of the main benefits of publicly recognized marriages is that it binds couples together not only in their own eyes, but also in the eyes of society at large" (Rauch, p. 301). It is about social recognition. But to use a different word to denote gay marriage sets it off as different and inferior. It doesn't treat gays as equals but, rather, reaffirms their second-class citizenship. Some people who oppose gay marriage are for civil unions – or "butt buddies" – because, although they recognize the rights issue, they don't want to include gays in their traditions. This is the height of hypocrisy. To classify gays differently is to deny them equal status as members of the community. It is degrading and humiliating. Marriage as an institution is important, not just because of the rights it affords the members of the marriage, but because of the order it bestows on society through its moral message of commitment. This is an aspect of marriage denied to civil unions by its very nature as a relationship that isn't marriage. Separate but equal is never equal for the simple reason of the stigma attached to that which is set apart. If there is a case for gay marriage, it is for gay *marriage* and nothing short of full recognition will do. Until Mr. Slave and Big Gay Al are pronounced "man and man," they are not married, regardless of whether or not they are butt buddies.

14

JUST DON'T KILL BABY COWS

Cynthia McWilliams

Tortured Baby Cows and Vaginitus

The *South Park* episode "Fun with Veal" deals with vegetarianism and the veal industry, making fun of the compassion many people are willing to extend to some animals (cute baby cows, for example) but not to others (fully grown cows, for example). On a class trip to a local ranch, Stan, Kyle, and Butters are horrified to learn what veal is "really made from." Cartman, on the other hand, far from suffering moral outrage, asks for a free sample. When they ask why veal is called *veal*, the rancher responds, "Well, if we call it *little baby cow*, people might not eat it." The boys decide to rescue the cute baby cows before they are sent to the slaughterhouse. During their extended standoff (in Stan's bedroom) – against their parents, the FBI, and Rancher Bob – the boys find that the only adults who empathize with their outrage over the plight of the cute baby cows are the "no-good, dirty, God-damned hippies," as Cartman puts it. Thanks to Cartman's slick negotiating and highly honed manipulation skills, the boys get the FDA to change the name *veal* to *tortured baby cow*, which effectively devalues the veal industry and saves the cute baby cows in question.

But despite the boys' outrage over the plight of the baby cows, only Stan decides to give up eating meat completely. Unfortunately, Stan then develops the fictional illness *vaginitus*, as anyone who completely gives up eating meat will obviously turn into a "giant pussy."

Stan is ultimately saved from this horrible fate in the nick of time, thanks to medical intervention and an IV-drip of pure beef blood. All's well that ends well, as the boys and their parents go out for burgers.

South Park revels in the absurdity of inconsistent moral beliefs. In this case, many people are outraged over the treatment of some animals while they happily eat the dead carcasses of other animals, seemingly having no problem with the pain and suffering animals endure before reaching the dinner table. And so while it's terrible to harm cute baby cows, only a giant pussy – or a no-good, dirty, God-damned hippie – would give up eating meat completely. As Stan says, "Guys, I learned something today. It's wrong to eat veal because the animals are so horribly mistreated, but if you don't eat meat at all, you break out in vaginas."

We see the same kind of irony concerning inconsistent moral beliefs in other *South Park* episodes. For example, in "Red Hot Catholic Love" Father Maxi confronts Catholicism's inconsistent beliefs, especially those arising from the combination of Roman Catholic dogma and the cover-up of the sexual molestation of young boys by Catholic priests. In "The Death Camp of Tolerance" Mr. Garrison breaks down at the end and screams at the townspeople for confusing a reasonable moral belief, that people should be tolerant to some extent of different ideas and lifestyles, with a less reasonable moral belief, that condemning or judging anyone for any behavior, even blatantly degrading and harmful behavior, is intolerant. The whole episode, including the title, is a satire of intolerance towards the perceived intolerance of others. Finally, "Starvin' Marvin" points to a possible moral contradiction in deciding to donate money to famine relief on the condition that you'll receive a free sports watch. Sounds similar to donations that are tax deductible, doesn't it?

Other chapters in this book talk about faulty reasoning and the problems that result from holding beliefs based upon errors in reasoning.[1] This chapter is about *ethics* (the branch of philosophy concerned with what we ought to do and how we ought to live) in general, and about vegetarian claims in particular.

---

[1] See, for example, chapters 4 and 5.

Kids vs. Adults and Cute Animals vs. Edible Animals

There are two story threads in "Fun with Veal" which nicely high-light two ethical issues surrounding the consumption of meat. The first issue is the difference between the ways children and adults per-ceive the killing of animals for food. The second is the implied, but unstated, *moral* difference between *cute* animals and *food* animals.

Most children get really confused about, upset over, or simply disbelieve the explanation given by adults of what their chicken nuggets or hamburgers "really are." Why does eating meat bother children, but not adults (except for the hippies, of course)? Why is it that children believe – pretty much automatically – that it's wrong to kill animals and eat them, while the overwhelming majority of adults do not?

Perhaps as adults, we are desensitized by many years of eating meat. After all, the typical person doesn't have to go out and actually hunt animals, kill them, strip them, clean them, or process them.[2] The meat that we eat is, for the most part, purchased from a grocery store and wrapped in plastic; it doesn't resemble an animal at all. Maybe children are just naïve or, perhaps, they see a kind of inconsistency most adults miss. We should be nice to others and not harm others needlessly – so we tell our children. Is there a reason this considera-tion doesn't apply to animals? Despite the claims of some opponents of vegetarianism, humans do not need to consume dead animals to survive or to live healthy lives. We could get all of our nutrition – including protein – from fruits, nuts, grains, soy products, and all kinds of vegetables.[3] Given this fact, one could argue that it's accept-able to eat meat only if it's not wrong to torture and kill animals – or unless we can draw some morally relevant distinction between the

---

[2] 2006 marked the 100th anniversary of the publication of Upton Sinclair's *The Jungle*, a story about Lithuanian immigrants who came to Chicago around the turn of the twentieth century to work in the famous stockyards. Sinclair gives a *very* des-criptive account of the slaughterhouse process. Read the book, and you may never eat meat again.

[3] For example, see the research accumulated by Peter Singer and Jim Mason in *The Way We Eat: Why Our Food Choices Matter* (Emmaus, PA: Rodale Books, 2006).

animals that are commonly eaten and the ones that aren't or shouldn't be eaten.

This brings us to the second point. Why is it that many people are outraged over the torture and killing of a "cute" animal, but have no problem with the pain, suffering, and death caused to animals like cows, pigs, and chickens that are, admittedly, considerably less cute than puppies, kittens, and baby cows? If there is indeed a *morally relevant* distinction between these kinds of animals, then such differences in treatment may be justified.

One answer might be that certain animals that we keep as pets, like dogs, are considered quite a bit smarter than animals that we eat, like turkeys. So maybe intelligence is the key. Dogs and cats surely seem to be smarter than cows, chickens, and turkeys. But that can't be it. Pigs, for example, are at least as smart as dogs, but most people in our country shudder at the thought of eating a dog, while pork is "the other white meat."[4] If intelligence is the thing to look for in deciding who or what receives our moral consideration and who or what does not, then we would need to include pigs, at least, when we draw our line. Further, why wouldn't really smart animals – like rhesus monkeys that are routinely used in neurobiological and psychological experiments – deserve more consideration than humans with impairments so severe that they are functionally less intelligent than the monkeys?[5]

Maybe the line should be drawn between animals that are "useful" for purposes other than for human consumption and animals that are not so useful. Some dogs, for example, can be trained to retrieve victims from disasters, assist handicapped people with certain daily tasks, or sniff out drugs in luggage. So, some animals have highly prized abilities that other animals do not. But the standard for line-drawing can't be physical abilities or prowess or anything like that because,

---

[4] See, for example, Donald Broom, Michael Mendl, and Adroaldo Zanella, "A Comparison of the Welfare of Sows in Different Housing Conditions," *Animal Science* 61 (1995), pp. 369–85.

[5] Rhesus monkeys, and other monkeys, have been used in experiments for years. In most cases, because of the experimenter's radical adjustments to their physiology, they are killed after the experiment. A standard paper illustrating this kind of experimentation would be Thomas Rowell, "Agonistic Noises of the Rhesus Monkey (*Macaca Mulatta*)," *Symposium of the Zoological Society of London* 8 (1962), pp. 91–6.

if it were, then Cartman would be justified in harming or killing Timmy or Jimmy, both of whom lack the physical prowess and certain physical abilities that Stan, Kyle, Butters, and even Cartman, possess.

Maybe the problem some people have with eating veal has to do with a disgust factor. Let's face it, it's gross to imagine a chained-up baby cow as your dinner. But the living conditions of other animals people commonly eat are just about as gross and disgusting, so it's hard to imagine that the disgust factor could keep someone from eating veal while they eat other animals bred in similarly disgusting conditions.[6]

Could it be the age of animals that matters? It seems worse to harm a baby animal as opposed to an adult animal, just as it seems worse to harm a child rather than an adult. Many *South Park* episodes play on the moral outrage people feel over harming children. The episodes that deal with child abuse typically face more serious and successful protest and censorship. "Jared Has Aides" is a good example. In this episode (which is also controversial for making light of AIDS), it becomes apparent that Butters is being physically abused and beaten by his parents. But when we look at crimes against people, as opposed to animals, the difference has to do with innocence and protection. A crime against a child seems worse because the child is innocent. Society has a duty to protect such individuals and watch them more closely because they are not fully equipped to protect themselves. But even if it is worse to hurt a child than it is to hurt an adult, it's still wrong to hurt an adult. It would be strange to claim that the age of an animal makes a morally relevant difference when it comes to deciding which ones deserve our moral consideration and which ones do not.

And yet we, as humans, do seem to place a high value on "cuteness." Let's say your daughter wants a puppy, kitten, or baby brother or sister for her next birthday. When you remind her of the fully grown dogs and older sibling that she already has, she admittedly finds these considerably less interesting. Or, think of all of the smiles that you see and "aws" that you hear when a cute little baby, or an

---

[6] See Peter Singer, *Animal Liberation: A New Ethics for Our Treatment of Animals* (New York: Harper Collins, 2002) for a discussion of factory farming practices in the United States. An examination of the conditions under which most animals bred for consumption are kept would result in a fairly high "disgust factor."

adorable puppy, or a fuzzy little duckling makes an appearance in a group of adults. Even a piece of poop with a Santa hat, mittens, and a happy voice is cute to people ("Mr. Hankey, the Christmas Poo"). But we can't imagine "cuteness" as being a morally relevant standard for inclusion or exclusion. If it were, then Nurse Gollum from "Conjoined Fetus Lady" would surely be afforded fewer rights than the rest of us.

So why is it that we draw a line between different kinds of animals and conclude that some of them deserve to be protected, while some of them do not? This problem is typical of a much larger issue in ethics, the issue of line-drawing or of deciding who or what deserves our moral consideration and who or what does not.

The Line Goes Here, Not There!

Ethics or *moral philosophy* is the branch of philosophy concerned with "how we ought to live," as Socrates (469–400 BCE) said.[7] A very big deal indeed! Moral philosophers explore issues surrounding how we *should* live, rather than describing how we *actually do* live – which is more the job of a sociologist or psychologist. Thus, ethics is *prescriptive* (telling us what ought to be or should be the case), rather than *descriptive* (telling us what is the case). An ethical theory should offer guidelines for acting and for treating others, and an ethical theory should tell us who should matter in our moral deliberations and who should not.

An important part of many ethical deliberations is deciding where to draw lines concerning whose interests should be considered as relevant in a moral decision. In "Fun with Veal," when Kyle and Butters happily eat beef jerky and fried chicken while refusing to eat veal, they are drawing a moral line. The cute baby cows matter, so we can't eat them. But the adult cows and chickens don't matter in the same way, and so we can eat them. Stan decides to draw his line in a different

---

[7] See Plato, *Plato's Five Dialogues: Euthyphro, Apology, Crito, Meno, Phaedo*, trans. by G.M.A. Grube (Indianapolis: Hackett Publishing, 2002). Also, for more on Socrates and Plato's ideas concerning ethics, see chapter 8 in this volume by William Devlin.

spot by claiming that all animals matter, and so he refuses to eat any of them. Cartman, on the other hand, draws his line of consideration pretty much only around himself. Cartman is an *ethical egoist* in that he would probably argue that he needn't or shouldn't worry about the wishes of others, people or animals, unless they correspond to what he, Cartman, wants.[8] Most of the adults, except for the hippies, would draw a line that excludes most animals from moral consideration, but includes most or all people and domesticated animals like dogs and cats. And so an important topic in ethics is the issue of line-drawing, or deciding who or what deserves our moral consideration, and who or what does not.

Ethical egoism is one kind of ethical theory and, although it's not particularly popular among ethicists, we've already mentioned what ethical egoists think about line-drawing – the line goes around the egoist. An ethical egoist is concerned with the interests of others only insofar as they promote or correspond with his or her own self-interests. Most other ethical theories draw the line of moral consideration differently. Ethical theories like utilitarianism, deontological ethics, and contractarian ethics, to name a few, contain some sort of principle of impartiality.[9] This means that the interests of others should count equally, unless there is some morally relevant reason to exclude them. We can't exclude some people from our moral consideration because of their gender or race, for example, because these characteristics are not *morally relevant* characteristics. But this shouldn't be surprising. After all, something very much like this can be found in our own Declaration of Independence: "We hold these truths to be self-evident, that all men[10] are created equal . . ." And

[8] Ethical egoism is a bit more complex than this. For an ethical egoist, the right action is the one that best promotes the interests of the egoist. See, for example, the treatments of ethical egoism in Louis Pojman (ed.), *Ethical Theory: Classical and Contemporary Readings* (Belmont, CA: Wadsworth Publishing, 2001); and Louis Pojman, *Ethics: Discovering Right and Wrong* (Belmont, CA: Wadsworth Publishing, 2005).

[9] For more on this, see James Sterba, *Morality in Practice* (Belmont, CA: Wadsworth Publishing, 2003); James Sterba (ed.), *Ethics: Classical Western Texts in Feminist and Multicultural Perspectives* (Oxford: Oxford University Press, 1999).

[10] Of course, the "founding fathers" probably meant *white male landowners* when they said *men*, but it is more reasonably interpreted today to mean "all *people* are created equal."

so all people, at least, matter unless we can point to some morally relevant reason to exclude them from the same consideration that is afforded to all other people. But this doesn't directly answer the question about whether some animals count and some don't.

Don't Worry, You Probably Won't Turn Into a Giant Pussy

Peter Singer, the best-known contemporary moral philosopher writing and theorizing about the way humans treat other animals, argues that humans are guilty of *speciesism*. That is, most humans draw a line of moral consideration around their own species, while excluding all others. Singer compares speciesism to racism and sexism, both of which are morally problematic because they make distinctions, or draw lines, on the basis of irrelevant characteristics.[11]

Singer claims that the interests of any creature that can feel pain or suffer significantly need to be considered in ethical decision-making. In this respect Singer subscribes to utilitarianism, an ethical theory developed by John Stuart Mill (1806–1873), which claims that the right action to choose in a given situation is the one that brings about the most happiness and the least amount of pain possible for *all* of those affected by the decision.[12] One could argue that "*all* of those affected" would have to include humans *and* animals, since they *both* can experience pleasure and pain. Given that utilitarians are concerned about the happiness of all creatures that can feel, Singer argues that animals should be included in our ethical deliberations, especially deliberations concerning the slaughter of these animals.

At this point, it should be obvious that Singer would disagree with Cartman and the majority of the *South Park* adults. We cannot *arbitrarily* draw a line that excludes some animals from our ethical consideration. Since humans don't need to eat animals to survive,

---

[11] Peter Singer, *Animal Liberation: A New Ethics for Our Treatment of Animals* (New York: Harper Collins, 2002); also, *Practical Ethics* (Cambridge: Cambridge University Press, 1993).
[12] J.S. Mill, *Utilitarianism* (Indianapolis: Hackett Publishing, 2003).

unless we can draw some *morally relevant* line that excludes them, we should not eat them.

So Singer would agree with Stan's original decision to give up eating meat completely. But before you try this at home, be on guard against turning into a giant pussy! Unless it's already too late, hippie!

15

FOUR-ASSED MONKEYS

Genetics and Gen-Ethics in Small-Town Colorado

Scott Calef

Perhaps we shouldn't be toying with God's creations. Perhaps we should just leave nature alone, to its simple one-assed schematics.

Dr. Alphonse Mephisto

Who is Mephisto?

The quiet, unassuming town of South Park has one police officer, one African American family, and one Chinese restaurant. Yet it boasts a genetic engineering ranch, a stem cell research facility, and two scientists! The first scientist, Randy Marsh, a geologist, received the Nobel Prize for his research into spontaneous human combustion. The second scientist, Dr. Alphonse Mephisto, a genetic engineer and Nobel runner-up to Marsh, does work of more questionable benefit.

Mephisto, in fact, represents Satan and evil. The name *Mephisto* is a variant of *Mephistopheles*, an alternate designation for the Devil. Some accounts assert he was the second to fall from heaven after Lucifer. According to others, Mephistopheles was originally God's partner in creation, an angel who manufactured seals, orcas, and other ocean mammals before joining Lucifer's rebellion.[1] As one who

[1] More information about Mephistopheles can be found in Jeffrey Russell, *The Devil: Perceptions of Evil from Antiquity to Primitive Christianity* (Ithaca, NY: Cornell University Press, 1977) and *Mephistopheles: The Devil in the Modern World* (Ithaca, NY: Cornell University Press, 1986).

crafts new creatures, Mephistopheles can be likened to the genetic engineer who "plays God" by designing or modifying species, utilizing science to achieve effects once thought to require omniscience. Unfortunately, the hubristic desire to assume divine prerogatives almost always spells tragedy in religious literature. Adam and Eve's sin in Genesis was motivated by the desire to "be like God" and possess divine knowledge. Their moral and spiritual fall is reenacted by Mephisto himself, who confesses after murdering Stan's mutant clone, "I tried to play God, and I failed" in the episode "An Elephant Makes Love to a Pig."[2] South Park's Mephisto is a Buddhist,[3] and Buddhism is a "non-theistic" religion stressing ethical practice and contemplation rather than worship and belief in God. Mephisto – who busily meddles in biological science without seriously questioning how or whether he should – thus embraces a "godless" philosophy (though without the ethics or reflection that characterize Buddhism's genuine adherents).

As a doctor with immense biological know-how, including knowledge of cloning, Mephisto reminds us of Dr. Evil – a graduate of evil medical school, thank you very much – of *Austin Powers* fame. Mephisto's small sidekick Kevin, who dresses like him and rarely speaks, mirrors Mini-Me, the one-eighth size clone of Dr. Evil introduced in *The Spy Who Shagged Me*. Mini-Me and Kevin, in turn, are inspired by a genetically engineered character in the 1996 film version of H.G. Wells' *The Island of Dr. Moreau*, where Dr. Moreau (Marlon Brando) also has a miniature companion who dresses like he does. Dr. Moreau uses genetic engineering to create mutant humans in the naïve hope of delivering the race from all malice. Unfortunately, he can't control his "children," whose bestial natures are difficult to eradicate, any more than Mephisto can control his mutant and murderous Thanksgiving turkeys in the episode "Starvin' Marvin." Moreau attempts to keep his unruly offspring subdued by inculcating the tendency to deify him. He thus "plays God" by creating new

---

[2] Ironically, Mephisto makes this remark after killing Stan's subhuman and mis-shapen clone. Apparently it's "playing God" to clone life, but not to take it! And if God is responsible for the likes of Streisand or conjoined fetus myslexia, maybe failing at playing God isn't so bad!

[3] In "An Elephant Makes Love to a Pig" Mephisto says "Oh thank Buddha I found you boys."

subject-species who will venerate him. Brando is the "Godfather" of the feral, half-breed inhabitants on his island. The similarities between Moreau and Mephisto are so obvious that Mephisto is a member of NAMBLA – the North American Marlon Brando Look Alikes.

South Park or Jurassic Park?

Mephisto, thus, combines elements of Satan, the mad scientist Dr. Evil, and Dr. Moreau, whose grisly and unnatural creations – like those in *Jurassic Park* – constantly threaten to lose control. Behind the ominous gates of his mysterious and sinister hilltop mansion nefarious activities transpire. But not in secret. Mephisto revels in his accomplishments and displays them enthusiastically. "Thanks to the wonders of genetic engineering," he boasts, "I have created things that will change the world for the better. For instance, here is a monkey with four asses." To which Kyle sensibly asks, "How does that make the world better?"

How indeed? Humanity has acquired the power to alter the course of evolution, but can it do so advantageously? Or is it arrogant to suppose that by deliberately selecting genetic traits we can improve on *natural* selection? Mephisto has engineered monkeys, ostriches, and mongooses – with extra asses, of course – but that's just the start. He's also spliced rats with ducks, gorillas with mosquitoes, and Swiss cheese with chalk. (His bunnyfish appears to be a scientific hoax; Cartman discovers its ears are tied on with little pieces of string.) Towlie is genetically modified for super-absorbency. Ultimately, even Stan is cloned. But to what end? How can genetic science make the world a better place, and what ethical dangers does this awesome technology unveil?

This Is Starting To Look Like Something We Shouldn't Be Any Part Of

The ethics of genetics ("gen-ethics") is a recurring theme in *South Park* and, by satirizing simplistic ways of thinking about cloning, genetic engineering, and stem cell research, Matt and Trey perform a valuable philosophical service. How can we think about these complex topics without being just silly? In the episode "Krazy Kripples" Christopher Reeve diverts attention from the accomplishments of the "truly crippled" Jimmy to plead that greater efforts be made to advance stem cell research. "Though it is controversial," he claims between frequent pauses for breath, "stem cell research is critical in the quest for helping the disabled." This is because, as he later explains to Larry King, stem cells "can form into whatever cells of the body are damaged. They are the most powerful thing on the planet."

Stem cells are "undifferentiated" cells with the unique ability to become other cell types, such as those in the retina, heart, spinal cord, or brain. Hence, many hope that injection of stem cells can successfully rejuvenate organs and replenish the damaged cells associated with chronic diseases like Alzheimer's, Parkinson's, Huntington's chorea, or diabetes. Because the most potent stem cells come from human embryos, acquiring stem cells to culture "lines" for possible transplant requires the destruction of very young, two to five-day-old embryos. Larry King thus voices the objection that "some people say stem-cell research is wrong, that taking cells from a fetus is unethical." Why think so?

The main objection focuses on the status of the embryonic tissue "donor." Pro-life advocates argue that human life begins at conception. Humans have the right to life; therefore, embryos have a right to life. Since acquisition of stem cells involves destruction of the embryo, its right to life is violated and a grave injustice done. Because stem cells are only available as a result of an immoral act, they're morally tainted, and their use is unethical. The injustice to the embryo is not made right by the fact that recipients of fetal tissue benefit. If, as German philosopher Immanuel Kant (1724–1804) argued, it's wrong to treat humanity as a means only, it's wrong to treat unconsenting embryos merely as biological material for the improvement of others.[4]

---

[4] Kant's precise formulation is this: "Act so that you treat humanity, whether in your own person or in that of another, always as an end and never as a means only." *Foundations of the Metaphysics of Morals*, trans. by Lewis White Beck (Indianapolis: Bobbs-Merrill), p. 47.

This initially plausible argument (or set of arguments) relies on several claims we should consider individually. One is that human embryos have the right to life. Philosophers, however, commonly distinguish being human from being a person. If something is genetically human, it's human. Embryos are clearly human in this sense. However, to be a bearer of rights it's not sufficient to be human; it's necessary to be a person, and this isn't a matter of mere biology. Although it's difficult to say exactly what a person is, philosophers tend to define personhood in legal or psychological terms. To be a person one must possess traits like consciousness, sentience (the capacity to experience pleasure and pain), self-awareness, rationality, the ability to communicate, desire, and the capacity to make choices. It's necessary to have at least some of these traits to be a person and have rights because rights protect our interests, and if something lacks consciousness, the capacity to suffer, preferences, and so on, it's hard to see what interests it could possibly have. Some humans are persons – you, for example, dear reader. Some humans perhaps are not – say, two-day-old embryos. If embryos aren't persons, they have no interests for rights to protect. Thus they have no rights, and no right to life specifically.

If it seems odd to separate the notion of being human from being something with rights, consider that not everything with rights is human. The corporations that produce Megaman, Beaver Dam Maxi Pads, and Snacky Cakes, for example, have rights, but that's because they're *legal* persons, not humans. In the episode "Chef's Chocolate Salty Balls" Mr. Hankey faced death, as the delicate ecosystem of his sewer was threatened by an influx of health food feces. As a being with interests, Hankey arguably has the right to inhabit an ecologically balanced sewer system uncontaminated by Indie Film Festival attendees. Hankey is a person, but a poo, not a human. If Cartman has a right not to be probed by Aliens, it seems logical that the Aliens have a right not to be probed by Cartman.

And animal rights activists will insist that the innocent species Ned and Jimbo kill in "self-defense" in the episode "Volcano" ("Look out! It's coming right for us!") have rights too. When Stan shoots Scuzzlebutt to make his uncle proud, Jimbo lectures him on the ethics of the outdoors: "Some things you do kill, and some things you don't." Jimbo thought it wrong to kill Scuzzlebutt. Did Scuzzlebutt have a right to life? The point is this: if nonhumans can have rights, then whatever it is that gives us rights, it isn't being genetically human. And that means, at least in theory, embryos can be genetically human without having whatever it is that gives us rights.

The pro-life argument claims the use of stem cells is morally tainted because they become available through an immoral act – the destruction of the human embryo. But even if destroying the embryo is wrong, that doesn't make using embryonic tissue wrong. Suppose bastards kill Kenny, but his organs are quickly transplanted into patients who need them, saving their lives. Kenny's organs only became available thanks to an immoral deed, but that doesn't mean it's wrong to use them to save lives. Nor are the doctors who transplant them tacitly endorsing murder. Similarly, even if stem cells are available through an act analogous to murder – and that's doubtful – it doesn't follow that using the cells to save other people's lives is wrong.

A third claim in the pro-life objection is that the humanity of the fetus or embryo is degraded by treating it as a means, and not as an end. According to this view, it's impossible to "respect" the embryo while simultaneously destroying it. *South Park* particularly exaggerates this last concern by the cavalier way in which Reeve, in need of a stem-cell fix, casually snaps off fetal heads, drains the cadavers of bodily fluids, and tosses aside the carcasses like empty soda cans. Such monstrous insensitivity toward the fetus and our shared humanity is abhorrent. Note, by the way, that one needn't be a person to deserve respect. Corpses too are entitled to dignified handling. Perhaps embryos deserve no less.

However, we only risk treating the embryo as a means rather than an end if it's *possible* to treat it as an end. For Kant, it's *persons* who are ends in themselves. Persons are beings capable of determining their duties and freely choosing to follow them. Persons can produce actions that have moral worth, and it's this that imbues them with dignity. Fetuses have neither rationality nor freedom, and so presumably aren't persons. Therefore, we probably don't violate them in using them to cure the afflicted, who are persons, and whose dignity may entitle them to life-saving treatment.

True, embryos can't consent to what's done to them, but neither can they refuse to consent. So the whole issue of consent seems irrelevant. Regarding corpses, we normally require that consent be obtained before bodily remains are donated for medical or scientific research. This is to spare surviving relatives the anguish or humiliation any unusual or disrespectful treatment might cause them.[5] Since embryos used in research have no relatives to speak of, however, their loved ones' potential objection isn't an issue. Embryonic remains can be used in the cause of science.

Kant's insistence that we treat humanity as an end and never as a means only is called the *categorical imperative*, a universal command of morality. An alternative version of the categorical imperative states that we should "act only according to that maxim by which you can at the same time will that it should become a universal law." This cumbersome language actually expresses a simple principle: ethical actions are those that can be "universalized." In other words, it's wrong to treat anyone in ways you wouldn't treat everyone, or in ways that you wouldn't be willing to have others treat you. There can't be a double standard in morality that permits some to be exploited, and not others.

The principle of *universalizability* – famously articulated by Kant – means a Kantian philosopher would probably oppose human cloning, at least as it occurs in the episode "An Elephant Makes Love to a Pig." There, Stan is cloned without his consent, and we wouldn't want to universalize a practice permitting experimentation on human subjects without their consent. After all, if it were universalized, *we* might be experimented on without our approval. Think about it. If we willed someone else to be experimented on without their consent, it's probably because we want the experiment to be done, realize people won't want to participate, and *don't* want to participate ourselves. That is, we want the benefits of having the experiment done without personal cost. But if we universalize use of non-consenting subjects, we place ourselves at risk since our decision to opt out won't be respected. Then we have a contradiction: attempting to avoid the hazards or inconvenience of being a research subject, we institute measures which, when carried out, will put us in the very place we sought to avoid. This contradiction arises from our attempt to allow a "double standard" into morality. Since, then, we can't "universalize" the action, it's contrary to duty: we have an obligation to respect the autonomy of others and must only employ them as scientific or

---

[5] Curiously, although Kenny's friends are always outraged at his death, no one minds when his corpse is invariably left lying around to be consumed by rats.

medical research subjects with their free and informed consent. This is Kantian moral philosophy in action.

Moreover, Stan is a child, and we'd probably be reluctant to universalize a principle permitting scientific and medical experiments on especially vulnerable populations like children or mentally retarded persons. Some have argued that people have a right to a unique identity. Although the existence of identical twins and the role of environmental factors in shaping personality weaken this argument, some feel cloning threatens not only the identity of the one cloned, but of the clone itself, whose genetic identity is deliberately determined before birth. Finally, Stan is cloned because Mephisto's son, Terrence, bet Kyle he could clone a whole person before Kyle could cross-breed his elephant with Fluffy the pot-bellied pig. Mr. Garrison suggests they submit their projects to the science expo. So, the Stan clone is not treated as an end, but as a means – to winning a childish bet and a prize at the science fair.

Of course, Kantians needn't oppose cloning in all cases. If the one cloned freely consented and did so for altruistic reasons, the practice seems unobjectionable. Some argue that, with cloning, we cross an important line and pass from reproducing humans to manufacturing them. However, it's unclear why manufacturing humans would be wrong if the clones were treated as ends in themselves and given every opportunity to develop without unrealistic expectations. For example, it would be terrible to expect the clone of a deceased son or daughter to "replace" the lost child and be just like them, or to be disappointed that the clone of a great athlete preferred philosophy to football. But these sorts of unfair expectations occur all the time in families, and no one thinks that's a reason to ban reproduction in the usual way.

Genetic Engineering Lets Us Correct God's Horrible, Horrible Mistakes – Like German People

Despite the fact that Kant was German, many ethicists think his moral theory mistaken and in need of correction. In emphasizing that we should conform to universal laws of morality, Kant held we should do our duty, regardless of the consequences. By definition, a *universal* law doesn't depend on the circumstances. Even when the right thing is painful, we must do it. For example, we should tell the truth because we can't universalize the practice of lying, and we should do so even when lying would make things easier. For Kant, universalizing lying would involve a contradiction of the will, and hence be contrary to rationality and duty. If we lie, we wish to be believed. But if lying is universalized, such that everyone lied, no one would believe anyone, and therefore no one would believe us. Thus, we irrationally will both to be believed, and to undermine the conditions under which our falsehood might be accepted. Since we cannot will both things without contradiction, lying is contrary to duty and fails the test of the categorical imperative. In the episode "Are You There God? It's Me, Jesus" Stan was ostracized for not having his period when Cartman and Kenny did. To avoid this fate, Kyle lied and pretended to be more "mature" than he was. Although Kyle got to fit in, Kant would say he failed, morally.

Consequentialists offer a different perspective. *Consequentialism* is the theory that the rightness or wrongness of an action is a function of its consequences. Kant's theory tells us never to lie, regardless of the consequences. But surely *sometimes* it's better not to tell the truth – for example, to Barbra Streisand if you have the triangle of Zinthar in your shoe and she asks where it is! Lying to Streisand under the circumstances isn't wrong, it's obligatory!

The most important consequentialist theory is *utilitarianism*. "Classical" utilitarianism maintains an act is ethical if it produces the greatest balance of pleasure over pain. Utilitarians like John Stuart Mill (1806–1873) sometimes express this by saying actions are right as they tend to promote happiness, wrong as they tend to produce the reverse of happiness. Another common utilitarian guideline says we should strive to produce the greatest good for the greatest number. Mill understands happiness and "the greatest good" in terms of pleasure. In short, the utilitarian method is to calculate as objectively as possible the pros and cons of an action, where the pros and cons are pleasures and pains, and then to act in the way that maximizes benefit.

It's easy to see utilitarianism's appeal when thinking about genetic engineering or stem-cell research. In "Krazy Kripples" Christopher Reeve argues more money should be spent to develop stem-cell cures.

Why? Because it would improve the quality of life for those who are afflicted, enhancing their enjoyment and delight in living. That is, the beneficial consequences of these therapies, if they prove viable, is such a surpassingly good result that it outweighs whatever negative consequences the opponents of stem-cell research can muster.

One reason there's so much controversy over stem-cell research is that its opponents don't think consequences are the only or most important moral considerations. Certainly, that's true of Kant. However, it's also possible for opponents of stem-cell research to make their case appealing to consequences alone. For example, one could argue that the focus on stem-cell research diverts attention from other areas that are more crucial. Jimmy complains that he's pushed to the sidelines by Reeve even though *he's* the one who's truly handicapped. And although Jimmy (and Timmy!) might benefit from stem cells too, because of Reeve's greater wealth, fame, and notoriety, he has access to experimental treatments unavailable to mere Krips. If exotic stem-cell cures will only be available to those wealthy enough to afford them, perhaps the greatest good for the greatest number would be achieved by allocating our health care dollars elsewhere (for example, on weight loss programs for obese kids and fat asses like Cartman).

Another utilitarian argument goes like this: when we consider the pleasures and pains caused by our actions, we must consider not just the immediate, or short-term, consequences, but also the more distant foreseeable effects. Whether or not having sex with chickens produces more pleasure than pain, if the practice gets Officer Barbrady to read, that good outcome must be factored into our moral appraisal. (If Barbrady is now a more effective crime fighter, that good to the community might compensate for our disgust at the chicken lover's distasteful methods and the presumed discomfort to the sorry hens he violates.) Now, concerning stem cells, what are the consequences for the embryos Reeve drains and kills? They're too immature to feel pain, so it might seem the benefit to Reeve isn't overridden by distress to the fetuses, and that the practice is therefore permissible. However, we must take into account future pains and pleasures as well as present ones. If those embryos were not destroyed, but rather allowed to grow, develop, and ultimately be born, their lifetime of joy and pleasure might override the benefit their deaths would bring Reeve. This is especially true since, being younger, they presumably have more years of life ahead to enjoy themselves. True, life isn't all a bowl of Cheesypoofs, but most people must think life worth living or there'd be more suicides.

There are at least two convincing replies to this last argument, however. First, the embryos used in research would almost certainly not be implanted and brought to term otherwise. If the intent were to implant them, they wouldn't be available for research in the first place. Second, for utilitarians, what matters isn't life, but the pleasure life makes possible. From this perspective, pleasure is the only thing good without qualification, and people are simply vessels for holding pleasure. If the death of an embryo (or embryos) restores Reeve to full function, the pleasure the embryos might have experienced isn't *lost*, it's simply transferred to a new receptacle – Reeve. And since he's rich and famous, his healthy life will probably be more fun than theirs would have been!

Of course, there are no guarantees since the future is often difficult to predict, and this is a major difficulty for classical utilitarianism. We may *think* we're doing good, but things can go awry in unforeseen ways. For example, in "Starvin' Marvin" Mephisto explains that he "was trying to genetically engineer turkeys for Thanksgiving. You know, to provide food for the needy. Well, something went wrong and the turkeys broke free. And the worst part is, they're really pissed off. We have to stop them or they could destroy everything."

In the Thanksgiving Special, Terrance and Philip arrive in America with great expectations:

Philip: Hey Terrance! Looks like this might be a good place to start a new colony.
Terrance: It sure does Philip. No one will oppress our religion here. [Farts and laughs.]

But by part two of the Special:

Terrance: I sure am cold Philip.
Philip: Yes, and hungry too. Being a pilgrim totally sucks ass.

When Mephisto and the Mayor unfreeze Gorak-Steve and discover he's still alive in the episode "Prehistoric Ice Man," an animated, utilitarian discussion ensues about what to do next:

Mephisto: Mayor, this man has not been conscious for almost three years. He won't understand what he sees! He'll be frightened and confused!
Mayor McDaniels: Well, you just can't let him die!
Mephisto: Perhaps death is better than the shock he will take trying to adapt to our time.

We just don't know. A theme in *South Park*'s treatment of genetic science is uncertainty and the pervasive possibility of disastrous mutations. Genetic engineering, cloning, and stem-cell research *may* lead to marvelous cures. They may also unwittingly be the source of our degeneration. Nobody really knows, for example, the long-term health consequences of consuming genetically modified foodstuffs. Big Stan, Stan's clone, was a freak, "a disgrace to genetic engineers everywhere." The main utilitarian argument against cloning is that it poses unacceptable risks for the potential child.

Dude, It's Hard to Stay Out of This One

Ultimately, we must reconcile Kant's respect for human dignity and emphasis on the centrality of duty with utilitarianism's sensitivity to outcomes.[6] And the show does suggest positive uses for genetic technology. In the episode "Cartman's Mom is Still a Dirty Slut," such technology enables Cartman to discover who his real father is – his mother! In "Chickenlover" genetic technology facilitates apprehension of the demented chicken lover, thus proving its worth in crime solving. In "Prehistoric Ice Man" technology accurately dates Gorak-Steve to 1996; his Eddie Bauer outfit provides valuable clues, too. And, of course, Christopher Reeve improves as a result of stem-cell applications – with a vengeance – in "Krazy Kripples." At the present time, the consequences of pressing ahead with stem-cell research, human reproductive cloning, and genetic engineering are unknown. One thing is clear, though: we don't have the luxury of saying with Stan: "Dude, I am so glad we stayed out of that one."

---

[6] One philosopher who has attempted to do just that is W.D. Ross in *The Right and the Good* (Oxford: Clarendon Press, 1930).

PART FIVE

WHO THE FUCK ARE YOU?
WHORES, ROBOTS, AND BODIES

16

RAISINS, WHORES, AND BOYS

Gender and Sexuality in *South Park*

Ellen Miller

Playground Feminism

What's a feminist to do with songs about mothers as bitches and episodes like "Cartman's Mom's a Dirty Slut," "Stupid Spoiled Whore Video Playset," and "Raisins" (a Hooters-inspired restaurant staffed by elementary school girls)? Can we laugh when the show portrays male bonding intertwined with gender stereotypes and, sometimes, even violence against women? Can we endorse feminist principles and still enjoy *South Park*?

In spite of and, oftentimes, because of its gender stereotypes and offensive language, *South Park* confronts important philosophical questions about autonomy, power, obscenity, sexual commercialization, gender roles, and sexuality. Though the show raises many red flags for feminists, some of the episodes actually endorse moral principles that feminists can support. So, yes, feminists can laugh at *South Park* . . . at least sometimes.[1]

---

[1] *Feminist philosophy* is the branch of philosophy that evaluates social, political, economic, and moral issues from the perspective, experiences, and insights of women. For more on feminism and feminist philosophy, see Chris Beasley, *What is Feminism? An Introduction to Feminist Theory* (London: Sage, 1999); Josephine Donovan, *Feminist Theory: The Intellectual Traditions* (New York: Continuum, 2003); Janet A. Kourany, James P. Sterba, and Rosemarie Tong (eds.), *Feminist Philosophies* (Upper Saddle River, NJ: Prentice-Hall, 1999).

The Detached Impartiality of Kant and Mill

Most traditional philosophical theories assume we should examine questions about morality without considering the gender, race, or class of the moral agent. Philosophical knowledge, these theories contend, involves universal truths that can be found independently of our own particular situation. For example, Immanuel Kant (1724–1804) proposed that morality involves rationally determining which moral principles can be held universally, detached from the consequences and circumstances surrounding some situation. Instead, he focuses on the reasons and motives that underpin our moral decisions. Moral actions are those that are done according to duty, which often entails overcoming inclinations, feelings, and desires. Interestingly enough, from Kant's perspective, moral principles must be *abstract enough from* circumstances so as to be *applicable to all* circumstances. In his famous work *Grounding for the Metaphysics of Morals*, Kant argues that actions have moral worth if and only if they proceed from respect for the moral law, and *not* from considerations of God's laws, love, honor, courage, or the circumstances surrounding the decision.[2] In fact, as odd as it may sound, it would be *immoral* for a rational person to act for reasons that included God's laws, love, honor, courage, or the circumstances surrounding the decision. And certainly, gender, race, or class have nothing to do with – and *should* have nothing to do with – making moral decisions.

For Kant, morality centers around, as Cartman would put it, "respecting authorita," where authority involves the bare, rational demands of moral duty solely for duty's sake, and nothing else. Thus, one needs to be wholly and completely impartial in order to make truly moral decisions. It would seem that Kyle's mom, Sheila Broflovski (who, according to Cartman, is a big fat bitch; in fact, she's the biggest bitch in the whole wide world), acts out of her own distorted sense of duty when making decisions to "blame Canada" or hurl people against Comedy Central's building in order to get producers to take *The Terrance and Philip Show* off the air. Notice, she won't take into consideration things like the harmful consequences

---

[2] Immanuel Kant, *Grounding for the Metaphysics of Morals*, trans. by James W. Ellington (Indianapolis: Hackett Publishing, 1981). See, especially, page 13.

to her family, practical concerns, or even God's laws when making a moral decision ("it's the right thing to do, Booby") and, because of this, characters on *South Park* – and those of us watching the show – shake their heads in amazement. It is as if Mrs. Broflovski is so concerned with the "principle of the matter" that she doesn't consider the potential harmful effects of her decision-making. We all know people like this; they're the ones who are on their moral high-horses judging people and situations divorced from the circumstances surrounding a situation.[3]

Another leading moral theory, *utilitarianism*, promotes a less abstract approach. Utilitarians, however, still endorse an impartial standpoint where no one individual receives special moral attention. Classic utilitarianism, advocated by John Stuart Mill (1806–1873), proposes that when confronted with an ethical dilemma, we must impartially determine which action (or set of actions) will produce the most happiness for all those impacted by a given situation, utilizing a kind of rational calculus.[4] We're to calculate the potential pros and cons of acting in a situation, and the moral decision is the one that simply promotes the most "pros" for the most people affected, even if such a decision involves using, disregarding, or harming certain people to achieve the pros. So, a utilitarian could argue that hurling people against Comedy Central's building in order to get producers to take *The Terrance and Philip Show* off the air is justified if there would be some incredibly great good or benefit for a majority of people to be gained from taking the show off the air. If this sounds silly, consider that it's primarily for utilitarian reasons that a nation will sacrifice its military forces in wartime so as to secure the greater good of security for the nation (a big pro for the nation as a whole), or a company will lay people off in a downsize so as to save the company (a big pro for the company as a whole). We might wonder whether it is always better to promote the overall good of all those affected by a given situation rather than focusing on individual rights or the personal nature of moral relationships.[5]

[3] For more on the various versions and critiques of Kant's deontological theory, see Peter Singer, *Practical Ethics* (Cambridge: Cambridge University Press, 1993).
[4] See J.S. Mill, *Utilitarianism* (Indianapolis: Hackett Publishing, 2003). Hereafter cited as (*Utilitarianism*, p. "x") in the text.
[5] For more on the various versions and critiques of utilitarianism, see William Shaw, *Contemporary Ethics: Taking Account of Utilitarianism* (Oxford: Blackwell, 1999).

Many feminists have questioned whether emphasis on impartiality distorts our special obligations and moral duties to friends and family members. For example, a utilitarian could argue that such attention to individual relationships does sometimes also promote the overall good of society; however, utilitarians are committed to maximizing overall utility and happiness through a rational calculus that weighs the potential pros and cons of a situation. Like the Kantian moral agent, a utilitarian moral agent seems unattached and self-sufficient, rationally calculating the correct thing to do. Some feminist philosophers claim that both theories present a distorted picture of the complex web of relationships that comprise our everyday lives, principally because they seem so detached from the emotions and attitudes that are significant to these relationships.[6] If we think about it, how can anyone seriously think that an important moral decision can be made by detached and impartial rational principles *without* considering the gender, race, class, perceptions, thoughts, feelings, and complex circumstances of the living and breathing persons affected by that decision?

Girl Power or Objectification: Paris Hilton in South Park

The moral dilemmas confronted in *South Park* reveal some of the inadequacies of these traditional, impartial Kantian and utilitarian ethical theories. The *South Park* boys take us inside a primarily masculine world where little boys – at times, thankfully – know much more than the adults, teachers, and school counselors. They struggle with love relationships, sexuality, gender roles, and puberty (in the episode "Are You There God? It's Me, Jesus," the boys compete over who gets their period first . . . OK, so sometimes they don't know more

---

[6] See, for example, the papers in Virginia Held (ed.), *Justice and Care: Essential Readings in Feminist Ethics* (Boulder: Westview Press, 1995); also, Sally Sedgwick, "Can Kant's Ethics Survive the Feminist's Critique?" *Pacific Philosophical Quarterly* 71 (1990), pp. 60–79; Iris Marion Young, "Impartiality and the Civic Public: Some Implications of Feminist Critiques of Moral and Political Theory," *Praxis International* 5 (1986), pp. 381–401.

than the adults). *South Park*'s highly gendered world allows viewers to see gender issues that, for many, remain invisible in daily life.

At least one episode, "Stupid Spoiled Whore Video Playset," centers on the *South Park* girls. You remember, don't you? Paris Hilton arrives in South Park and opens a whore-store named "Stupid Spoiled Whore." Soon, girls and their loving parents (who want them to be popular) embrace this store filled with revealing clothes, a perfume called "Skanque," and accessories that'll turn every elementary school girl into a certified whore. Wendy Testaburger sees a problem with this objectification of girls, but she's outnumbered by South Parkers ready to buy whatever Paris Hilton sells. In turn, Paris Hilton is interested in buying young Butters from his parents, who are willing to sell him for 200 million dollars. The town will buy and sell anything, from a young girl's innocence to buttery-haired young Butters!

The episode articulates an important critique of objectification masquerading as supposed liberating "girl power." Though non-feminists and some feminists might respond that the whore-store liberates girls from Victorian ideas about female chastity, Wendy argues that we need to promote real choices for women, not artificially created commercialized versions of female sexuality. At first, we might ask what's so wrong with girls choosing to dress in a provocative way? We could interpret this as liberating. After all, no one's physically forcing young girls in South Park to dress like Paris Hilton. They're *choosing* to do so, and isn't that what being a liberated feminist is all about – choice!?!

The Testaburger Test for Obscenity

The freedoms to choose a certain lifestyle and express oneself are basic for any person – male or female – and no one disputes these freedoms as fundamental rights. But what's really interesting and significant are the *kind* of lifestyle one leads and the *kind* of free expression one engages in. "Stupid Spoiled Whore Video Playset" questions whether some forms of free expression objectify and harm women (and men as well). The episode also raises questions about whether the boys and girls of South Park can be considered equal when the whore-store is only marketed to girls. In fact, much of the humor arises from the episode's reversal of usual stereotypes about men and women; the role reversals also reveal that we can't simply reverse current power inequities at will. Here, the girls exclaim, "I'd like to swivel his pixie stick," "gargle his marbles," and "wax his crankshaft!" They make sexual comments we're sure they don't yet understand, and the boys passively wait for the aggressive girls to invite them to their "whore parties." In a simplistic way, yes, the South Park girls can harass the boys, but it's not exactly the same as when boys harass girls.[7] Only Wendy Testaburger laments the blatant objectification of women now endorsed by the whole town. Paris Hilton has seduced them all. In a similar way, they later won't be able to resist Wall-Mart when it comes to South Park.

The key philosophical questions addressed by "Stupid Spoiled Whore Video Playset" involve free speech, equality, and how to deal with materials many people find offensive. These are central questions feminist philosophers have addressed in debates over the moral and legal status of pornographic and obscene materials. In the United States, recent court cases have protected pornographic materials viewed in one's home. In *Stanley vs. Georgia* (394 US 557, 1969), the court determined that the government can't interfere in one's private use of books and films, even if they have been deemed legally obscene. The right to distribute obscene materials for commercial purposes is not, however, guaranteed by the First Amendment.

Pornography is a multi-billion dollar global industry. Feminists have debated whether pornographic materials exist because of a sexist culture, or whether it is in fact a cause of sexual violence against women, or both. Although pornography is a lucrative and legal business, materials labeled "obscene" are not constitutionally protected. Currently, the Supreme Court uses the "Miller Test" to determine whether the materials should be labeled obscene. In *Miller vs. California* (413 US 15, 1973), the courts set out the following test for obscenity. Materials violate obscenity statutes if they appeal to "prurient interests," are offensive to the "average person," and lack "serious literary, artistic, political or scientific values." Since the

---

[7]   We'll leave aside other issues of sexual orientation that warrant further attention. For more on power, race, and class as they relate to sexual harassment, see Susan Bordo's *Twilight Zones* (Berkeley: University of California Press, 1997), especially chapter 4's "Can a Woman Harass a Man?"

majority of South Parkers support the new whore-store, the courts would not deem its merchandise obscene using the Miller Test. But in another town, such as *North* Park, the outcome could be quite different.

The Testaburger Test functions in a much more feminist manner. Unlike the Miller Test, which legally bans something if it is offensive to the average person (among other conditions), Wendy Testaburger's test would ask if something objectifies and commercializes women. If it does, then it would be banned. Oftentimes, a community cannot see obscenity when it becomes normalized. Though *South Park* often endorses libertarian ideals, "Stupid Spoiled Whore Video Playset" invites viewers to journey with Wendy in rejecting the whore-store, not just because it borders on being a form of child pornography, which is illegal, but also because there should be limits regarding the objectification and commercialization of female sexuality.

Can Raisins Cause Harm?

Feminists endorse diverse views on the subject of pornography and obscenity. Some argue that pornography ought to be limited or censored because it causes sexual violence, objectification, commercialization, and misinterpretations of women. Others think certain forms of pornography or erotic materials can be liberating.[8] These anticensorship feminists might argue that South Park's whore-store offers new pathways for female expression. An intermediary position might be that even though the store is offensive and perhaps harmful, it is still entitled to constitutional protection. To better understand whether these negative representations of women cause harm, it will be helpful to look more closely at philosophical understandings of *harm*.

---

[8] See, for example, Kathleen Barry, *The Prostitution of Sexuality* (New York: New York University Press, 1995); Susan Dwyer, *The Problems of Pornography* (Belmont, CA: Wadsworth, 1995); Wendy McElroy, "A Feminist Defense of Pornography," *Free Inquiry* 17 (1997), pp. 6–22; Andrea Dworkin, *Pornography: Men Possessing Women* (New York: Perigee Press, 1981); Sallie Tisdale, *Talk Dirty To Me* (New York: Doubleday, 1994).

Sex markets traditionally involve male consumers (and producers) and female service providers. We see this tradition represented in another *South Park* episode, "Raisins," where the entirely female wait-staff are trained to manipulate men's emotions for bigger tips. During a training session, the waitresses, who are named after luxury sports cars, all know the rules of proper Raisin development. Mercedes explains:

> First of all, there's a five-foot rule. If you come within five feet of a customer, you need to acknowledge them, even if they're not at your table. "Hey, cutie." When you're not serving food or talking with customers, you need to dance around and have fun. We use things like Hula Hoops, silly strings, and water guns to play with the other girls. Be sure to giggle a lot, and be sure to show off your raisins . . . If you want good tips, the most important thing is physical contact. Just a simple hold of the arm can mean the difference between five and twenty dollars.

Interestingly enough, the girls are not presented as innocent victims. Rather, they are shown as savvy waitresses who know how business works and use their knowledge to their benefit. Sadly, though, we know the waitresses are not profiting at anywhere near the same level as the (presumably male) owners.

In light of "Stupid Spoiled Whore Video Playset" and "Raisins," let's consider John Stuart Mill's classic formulation of the *harm principle* in his famous work, *On Liberty*. Mill reasons that happiness is the chief end towards which humanity should strive. As we have seen already, utilitarians promote the overall happiness of all those affected by a given situation. For Mill, we achieve the greatest overall happiness when the government leaves individuals free to pursue their own projects – so called *laissez-faire* government – and does not interfere with or prohibit human expression. This amounts to men and women (Mill was an early advocate of women's rights) being free to choose their own pathways to happiness, provided that no one is harmed in the process (this is the *do-no-harm* part of Mill's principle).[9] Importantly, even though people should be free to pursue their pleasures – again,

---

[9] J.S. Mill, *On Liberty*, ed. by Currin V. Shields (Indianapolis: Liberal Arts Press, 1956). Hereafter cited as (*Liberty*, p. "x") in the text.

provided they don't harm anyone – Mill didn't envision a world of egoistic pleasure-seeking Cartmans. It is better, Mill proclaimed, to be Socrates dissatisfied than a pig satisfied (*Utilitarianism*, ch. 2). For Mill, qualitative evaluations of happiness matter as much as quantitative maximization of happiness.

Government intervention might be warranted if our actions harm others. Mill acknowledged that determining what constitutes harm requires careful deliberation and wouldn't be obvious. Mill also believed the state had no place paternalistically intervening to help citizens pursue better personal choices: "The only purpose for which power can be rightfully exercised over any member of a civilized community, against his will, is to prevent harm to others. His own good is not sufficient warrant" (*Liberty*, p. 14). So, if Stan and Kyle want to watch *The Terrance and Philip Show* in Stan's house, the government shouldn't intervene and suggest they read Jane Austen novels instead. Similarly, if Butters wants to look at his new girlfriend in the most recent Raisins girl calendar in his home, Officer Barbrady shouldn't arrive on his front steps and confiscate the calendar. Although, in both cases, the boys' *parents* might want to intervene and prevent them from engaging in such activity, the state shouldn't.

We might wonder, however, whether the girls were harmed during the production of the Raisins calendar. Does their participation with this industry damage their autonomy and future decision-making abilities? And do these stereotypical images damage Butters' understanding of women and intimate relationships? Could the Raisins Restaurant, the Raisins calendar, and the whore-store cause harm? If we could demonstrate that they do, Mill's harm principle could effectively be used to argue they require government intervention and, possibly, censorship. Let's see how Butters' family responds to their son's crush on a Raisins waitress.

When Butters' parents learn he is in love with a Raisins girl, they visit the restaurant with him. Butters' mom, Linda, exclaims, "This place is horrible. To objectify girls like this" and then tries to encourage young Porsche to work where she won't be paid for how she looks; for example, in medicine or business. Porsche replies, "I could cure cancer? Omigod! That would be soooo cool! I had a cancer sore on my lip one time and it hurt sooo bad!" Butters' mom concludes that Raisins just might be the perfect place for poor Porsche. Much of the humor arises because Porsche is only in elementary school and has plenty of time to learn the difference between canker sores and cancer. Also, Butters' mom quickly changes her mind about the perils of female objectification. She moves from outraged to docile so quickly that we know it is Wendy who will be the true voice of dissent in the episode. When Butters' mom concludes that objectification might be the perfect lifestyle for certain girls, we laugh. But beneath our laughter lies the recognition that objectification like this requires our moral attention.

It's easy to understand how certain actions can be harmful to other people; there are physical harms, as well as psychological, emotional, and financial harms. For example, lighting Pip on fire causes physical harm; fining Chef two million dollars causes financial harm; and the children seem to be harmed emotionally and psychologically by stupid adults in almost every episode. Some events might not be so easy to interpret, and this is what we confront in our analysis of the whore-store and Raisins. Rather than arguing against pornography merely because it portrays sexual activity, one of the most famous anti-pornography feminists, Catherine MacKinnon, focuses on how depictions of women as dehumanized objects nourishes and supports sexism. So South Park's whore-store, Raisins Restaurant, and Raisins calendars would seem to be obvious examples of dehumanization, raising issues in debates over free speech, pornography, and obscenity.[10] Using anti-pornography arguments, we could argue that Raisins and the whore-store ought to be shut down because they perpetuate women's oppression and discrimination. As long as these establishments exist, women won't be fully appreciated as subjects and moral agents. These industries harm women, in this sense, and aren't entitled to constitutional protection. If South Park closes these stores, it would be much easier to produce more girl doctors and lawyers instead of girls posing as substitute luxury cars. Of course, these conclusions would require a complex and sophisticated understanding of harm, one that not only considers physical, psychological, emotional, and financial harms done to women, but also takes into account factors such as gender and social privilege.

---

[10] Catharine MacKinnon is a lawyer, professor, writer, activist, and expert on sex equality. Beginning in the mid-1970s, she pioneered the legal claim for sexual harassment as a form of sex discrimination. The US Supreme Court accepted her theory of sexual harassment in 1986. For more on her influential views concerning pornography's harm, see *Only Words* (Cambridge, MA: Harvard University Press, 1993).

When All Is Said And Done, Shouldn't We Allow Whores To Be Whores?

We might wonder, though, if arguments like these either turn women into victims or deprive them of their freedom to make their own well-informed decisions. Younger feminists have become critical of MacKinnon utilizing these very points.[11] The criticism is that arguments against objectification and obscene materials assume that women are passive victims of these institutions and industries, wholly unable to make decisions on their own. "Aw, poor whore . . . she doesn't know any better," one could think, "we better help her do what's good for her and not allow her to pursue such whorish ways." Think of the stereotypical idea of a woman as being more nurturing, caring and, especially, passive. We know, however, that human personalities are much more intricate and varied than what is presented in a stereotype.

So, we question if whores should be free to pursue their whorish ways. Provided that a woman freely chooses of her own accord to be a whore – fully aware of *all* of what is entailed in the lifestyle – wouldn't we be treating her like less of a person, or disrespecting her, by preventing her from being a whore? After all, as Mrs. Stevens claims in "Stupid Spoiled Whore Video Playset," being able to dress and act like a whore is "empowering" for a young, assertive woman. Here, *South Park* offers an important response. Wendy's criticism of the whore-store in the same episode does not center on her victimization. Rather, she highlights how gender inequities matter in contemporary society. Further, Wendy underscores the importance of a woman making a free and well-informed decision. It's probably safe to say that outside of South Park, prostitutes are indeed often "victims" of their circumstances – for example, they have no family support, they have few employment opportunities, they're addicts – and so, their abilities to reject objectification are severely constrained by economic and social factors. But that's not the case for the young women of South Park. For them, going to an extreme with one's sexuality by presenting oneself as a whore isn't an assertion of a woman's will to

---

[11] For example, see Sibyl Schwarzenbach, "On Owning the Body," in James Elias, Vern Bullough, Veronica Elias, and Gwen Brewer (eds.), *Prostitution: On Whores, Hustlers, and Johns* (Amherst, NY: Prometheus Books, 1998), pp. 345–51.

choose, nor is it empowering; it's simply acting like a whore! And, as Wendy Testaburger notes, "it's belittling to our gender."

So, through the mouthpiece of Wendy Testaburger, *South Park* raises the important concern that "lewdness and shallowness are being exalted, while intellectualism is looked down upon." The show confronts important philosophical questions about autonomy, power, obscenity, sexual commercialization, gender roles, and sexuality – all central issues in feminist philosophy and feminist ethics. *South Park* also explores stereotypes that are often difficult to recognize and critiques popular culture's inability to present complete, complex images of men and women. As fully rational, flourishing adults, it is probably our moral duty to delve deeper into these complexities. Do we really want to exalt lewdness and shallowness? Do we really want to be stupid spoiled whores?

17

AWESOM-O AND THE POSSIBILITY AND IMPLICATIONS OF ARTIFICIAL INTELLIGENCE

Randall M. Jensen

Can a Machine Have a Mind?

In "AWESOM-O," a classic episode from *South Park*'s eighth season, Cartman devises yet another elaborate scheme to humiliate Leopold "Butters" Stotch, whose gullibility and basic niceness make him an irresistible target. This time, Cartman's absurdly brilliant idea is to impersonate a robot so that he can gain Butters' confidence, learn his most embarrassing secrets, and then reveal himself in a tremendously satisfying moment of triumph. At first, his plan proceeds splendidly, as Butters tells his trusty robot friend about his sphincter control problem. But Cartman then learns, to his horror, that his intended victim knows one of his own deepest and darkest secrets: Butters has a videotape of Cartman dressed up like Britney Spears, singing and dancing around with a cardboard Justin Timberlake! Cartman is thus forced to remain in his AWESOM-O guise far longer than he had planned, as he tries in vain to locate the incriminating video and prevent Butters from exposing him. And, of course, much hilarity ensues.

Now, the AWESOM-O 4000 is not a real robot (although its name is a rather obvious play on the Asimo, Honda's very real humanoid robot). No, it's just a fat little boy dressed up in cardboard boxes, stickers, bits of plastic, and what look very much like oven mitts. Cartman's terribly unconvincing impersonation of a robot can be used to explore many interesting philosophical questions about the complicated and provocative issue of *artificial intelligence*, which refers to human-made robotic mechanisms and computer programs (the "artificial" part) that seem to reason and think just like natural minds (the "intelligence" part). In this chapter, we'll ponder some questions in the *philosophy of mind*, the branch of philosophy concerned with the nature and functioning of minds, as well as with the relationship of minds to physical bodies.

In wondering whether a machine might have a mind, we'll at the same time be forced to wonder what it means to say that human beings have minds. In doing so, we'll also run smack into what is traditionally known as the *problem of other minds*, a central problem in philosophy of mind that also extends into *epistemology* (the branch of philosophy concerned with knowledge). Whereas a philosopher of mind might ask, "What's the nature of mind?" an epistemologist asks, "How do we *know* what does and what doesn't have a mind?" So, with AWESOM-O as our guide, away we go!

Playing the Imitation Game

Cartman is imitating a robot, both in his appearance and in his behavior. On both counts, his imitation can't really be called a success. His costume fools only those who are easily taken in: the naïve Butters, Hollywood producers, the military establishment, and so on. As for his behavior, well, it just doesn't cut it. This cardboard robot sounds and acts just too much like Cartman. But let's imagine that we were to help Cartman to do a much better job. Suppose we were to help him build a much more realistic disguise, complete with a device to modulate his voice, so that he would look and sound enough like a robot to fool even more savvy kids like Kyle and Stan. Still, his all-too Cartman-like behavior would give him away. So we would also need to coach him on how to act and what to say in order to seem more like a robot.

What would such more authentic robotic speech and behavior look like? What should a "real" robot's appearance be, for that matter? Our first attempts to answer these questions will probably owe an awful lot to our experiences with other familiar fictional examples of artificial intelligence. When we hear the word "robot," perhaps we expect a technological tin-man that moves stiffly and rather awkwardly (as indeed Cartman does) and speaks in a flat monotone (as Cartman at least tries to do, when he can manage it). But on reflection, is there any reason to suppose that a sophisticated intelligent robot would have to look and sound like this? It doesn't seem so. Perhaps a first generation of robots would indeed be rather crude – in all kinds of ways, including their capacities to move and to speak – but it seems safe to suppose that this crudity would disappear over time as better and better robots are built. *How a robot moves, what a robot looks like*, and *what a robot sounds like* seem mere design problems, to be solved by technological progress and human ingenuity. In fact, it's rather interesting to see how our imaginary picture of a robot has changed as our own technology has improved. The clunkers of the 1950s are largely a thing of the past, even in our stories. And while the look and sound of a robot are crucial for creators of science fiction films and stories, they are not so crucial after all for thinkers who are seriously concerned with the nature and possibility of artificial intelligence. Our issues lie elsewhere.

We've been talking about how to improve Cartman's attempt to impersonate a robot, and that's led us to think about what we expect out of a robot. But at this point we need a fruitful new direction for our investigation. Here's a thought. Let's turn the tables on this robot impersonation gag. What if we were to program a robot to impersonate Cartman? For while we're not so sure what a robot should be like, we do know what Cartman is like, as we're all too well acquainted with his appearance, personality, and behavior. And speaking more generally, we are very familiar with what human beings are like. So what if we could program a machine to be like us? Is this possible? If so, what would it mean? This is more or less the direction that Alan Turing (1912–1954) explores in a classic article from way back in 1950.[1] Turing, arguably the father of the artificial intelligence movement in the twentieth century, wanted to examine the perplexing question "Can machines think?" But he quite sensibly

[1] A.M. Turing, "Computing Machinery and Intelligence," *Mind* 49 (1950), pp. 433–60. This classic article is reprinted in many places, including Margaret Boden (ed.), *The Philosophy of Artificial Intelligence* (Oxford: Oxford University Press, 1990), pp. 40–66.

found this question too unclear to take up, as it isn't obvious exactly what counts as a machine and what counts as thinking. He also worried that we'd try to answer this question simply by appealing to popular opinion, as indeed we were tempted to do ourselves a bit earlier, in spite of the fact that it doesn't seem to be a very reliable authority on this issue. Thus, he worked to develop a clear and precise question that could be addressed by a more reliable method. What he devised has become known as the *Turing test*, and it goes something like this – with a *South Park* twist.

To conduct the test, we need three rooms. Room 1 contains the tester. The tester can be any reasonable person (and, to our dismay, that pretty much disqualifies nearly every inhabitant of South Park!). In desperation, perhaps we might appeal to the scientist from the AWESOM-O episode to serve as our tester. We'll call him "Mr. Scientist," as the military personnel in the episode do, but we'll eliminate their disparaging tone. In Room 2 we'll put Cartman, who is no doubt protesting that this is totally lame and asking for some Kentucky Fried Chicken. Finally, our candidate for the test, a machine programmed to imitate Cartman, goes into Room 3. Since our goal, following Turing, is not to see whether a machine can look like or sound like Cartman, but rather to see if a machine can think like Cartman, we'll keep the inhabitants of the rooms from seeing each other, and we'll have them communicate with each other only in writing. Mr. Scientist can ask the occupants of Rooms 2 and 3 anything he wants. After a sufficient period of interaction with them, we will ask him which he believes is the machine and which is the real Cartman. Clearly, if he can identify the machine all or nearly all of the time, our machine will have failed Turing's test. But if Mr. Scientist is fooled by the machine much of the time so that he often mistakes it for the real Cartman, then our machine will have done well or "passed" the Turing test. And this, says Turing, counts as a positive answer to his particular version of the more general question "Can a machine think?"

Now Turing thought that within fifty years of writing his article, by the year 2000, advances in computing technology would permit the construction of a machine that would indeed pass his test and the issue of whether a machine can think would have been well and truly settled. We can now see that he was overly optimistic in his prediction. Although you'll find plenty of "chat-bots" on the Internet, it's fairly obvious that none of them is quite good enough to do as well on the Turing test as the creator of the test had envisioned. But that isn't a big deal. Really, the crucial issue is whether the Turing test is a legitimate test of the presence of intelligent thought – whether a machine that passes the test will, thereby, have been shown to be a thinking machine.

It may have occurred to you that a machine that's been programmed to act like a human being, even if it puts on a really good show, is still just acting like one of us: it's just a simulation. Likewise, no matter how good Cartman's impersonation of a robot is, he's not a robot. He's a boy pretending to be one. Why should we think that a computer simulation – even a very good or even perfect one – is anything more than a simulation? After all, a computer simulation of a thunderstorm doesn't get anyone wet, and a simulation of a military maneuver doesn't really get anyone killed. So why should we agree that a computer simulation of a thinking person is in fact a thinking person?

We could answer this question by noting that, while it is true that in general a *simulation* of something isn't a *duplication* of that thing, in this particular case it is. Why? Well, the idea is that you can't simulate intelligence without being intelligent, for the only way to carry off a good imitation of intelligence is to be organized, flexible, and creative in one's responses to questioning – which only an intelligent, thinking thing could do. However, this reply doesn't convince everyone. First, we might worry that the intelligence needed to pass the test resides in the programmers rather than in the machine. And second, it does seem logically possible for a machine to fool us – to pass the Turing test – without doing any real thinking at all. A holographic simulation of Mr. Hat isn't a real puppet precisely because it's missing something: the wool or cotton blend or whatever that provides the *matter* of a sock. Is it possible that a machine that's simulating intelligence is likewise missing something that's crucial to real intelligence?

The Chinese Room

John Searle, a professor at the University of California, Berkeley, and one of the most prominent philosophers of mind of the last few decades, is perhaps best known for crafting a particular thought experiment called the *Chinese room argument*.[2] A *thought experiment* is simply a detailed example that is meant to help us think about a philosophical issue. Some thought experiments, including this one, are also meant to play a key role in arguing that some claim is true or false. Among other things, this particular thought experiment is meant to be a critique of the Turing test. Let's have a look at it, once again with a *South Park* twist.

This time, we need imagine only two rooms. In the first room, we'll again call on Mr. Scientist to aid us. In the second room, we'll put Kenny, hoping he stays alive long enough to serve our purposes. All Kenny will need to do is follow some simple instructions. Oh, it's also important that he not know Chinese. Mr. Scientist, who is fluent in Chinese, will then send Kenny a question in Chinese, perhaps something like "What is South Park?" rendered into Chinese symbols. Kenny will examine this Chinese message, which is of course unintelligible to him, and make use of a complicated rulebook in composing a reply. This rulebook, with English instructions, consists of lists of Chinese symbol combinations that are correlated to other Chinese symbol combinations. Kenny finds the appropriate rule, laboriously copies the symbols that correspond to the symbols submitted to him by Mr. Scientist, and then sends the new combination of Chinese symbols out of the room. Mr. Scientist examines them and sees that they mean "a pissant white-bread mountain town."

Now, what's the point of this rather elaborate set-up? Well, won't it appear to Mr. Scientist that he has just communicated with someone in the other room who understands Chinese? After all, he sent in a message and received an accurate reply, all in Chinese. And he can do it again, over and over if he wishes. But surely it's plain as day to us that Kenny doesn't understand a bit of Chinese. With the aid of the rulebook (and how long it must be!), he is able to respond appropriately to Mr. Scientist, but it's all without him having any clue

---

[2]   This thought experiment was first presented in John Searle, "Minds, Brains, and Programs," *Behavioral and Brain Sciences* 3 (1980), pp. 417–24, also reprinted in *The Philosophy of Artificial Intelligence*, pp. 67–88. Also see the exchange between Searle and two of his critics, Paul and Patricia Churchland, in the January 1990 issue of *Scientific American*.

about what's going on. He may be able to parrot Chinese, by following a rote procedure, but he doesn't *know* or *understand* the language at all.

Searle's claim, then, is roughly that the same should be said of a digital computer that passes the Turing test. The fact that it can be programmed to provide us with output that correlates to whatever input we give it simply does not suffice to show that it *understands* anything at all. As Searle succinctly puts it, digital computers can have syntax (a programmed word order, like "if x, then y" or "either x or y"), but no semantics (an understanding or knowledge of the *meaning* of "if x, then y" or "either x or y"). And so that's what the machine is missing: understanding. According to Searle, then, that's the difference (or one of them, anyway) between a complex digital computing machine and a human mind. A clarification is in order here. Searle's claim isn't that no machines can think. Rather, he believes that only a certain kind of "machine," a human brain or something very much like it, can think. So if we can create a machine whose cognitive architecture is similar to our own in terms of all of the complex neural connections and processes, then Searle would concede it might think. But as long as we're considering the digital computers with which we're familiar, he denies this possibility.

It probably comes as no surprise to you that not everyone agrees with Searle about this. In fact, the more you learn about philosophy, the more you'll see that serious objections are raised against nearly every interesting philosophical argument. Here we'll just consider one kind of response, which Searle himself calls the *Systems Reply*. Earlier we agreed, plausibly enough, that Kenny doesn't understand Chinese simply in virtue of his ability to manipulate Chinese symbols according to the rulebook. But why should we ask whether Kenny understands Chinese? Isn't the question whether the *entire system* – consisting of Kenny, the room, the rulebook, and the communication equipment – understands Chinese? You're tempted to say no. If Kenny doesn't know any Chinese, how does the addition of these other inanimate items produce something that does? In reply, Searle's critic might point out that we really have only a very dim understanding of how it is that the human nervous system manages to give rise to understanding, so we shouldn't be too skeptical that some other system can't possibly pull it off.

Does Towelie Have a Mind?

Both Alan Turing and John Searle have been concerned with the question of whether a machine, like a computer, can have a mind. We've seen that they each have a proposed method for approaching that question. In focusing on method, we turn from the question of whether machines can have minds to the question of *how we can know* whether machines have minds. The former is a metaphysical question, as it concerns the nature of things, while the latter is an epistemological question, which means (as you may recall) that it concerns how we know things. Here we want to know if a machine has or could have a mind.

But how do we know if anything does or doesn't have a mind? This turns out to be a surprisingly tricky question, because of what's known as the *problem of other minds*. It's a complicated problem, but here's one simple version of it. Stan knows that he has a mind. How? Well, one answer is that it's because in some sense he *is* his mind. If you think about it, it's a bit odd to say he *has* a mind (in the way that he has dark hair?), for what is it that *has* his mind? If Stan knows anything at all, then, he knows that he is a thinking mind.[3] M'kay. Now, how does Stan know that Kyle has a mind? Not in the same way, right? Stan does not have immediate access to Kyle's mind in the way that he does his own, unless in some future episode he's granted bizarre telepathic powers. In fact, we might be tempted to think that Stan cannot know for sure that Kyle has a mind, since he can only infer that Kyle has a mind from observing Kyle's behavior. And Kyle's behavior can't give Stan any better evidence of his having a mind than anything a computer can do in a Turing test. But since we're all pretty sure that little boys have minds before we become stymied by philosophy, let's turn to an example of something whose mental status is more in question.

Remember Towelie, a "smart towel" who can sense how wet you are and adjust itself accordingly? Towelie wanders into the scene

---

[3] The famous French philosopher, René Descartes, makes a similar claim as a result of realizing, "I think, therefore I am." See his *Discourse on Method and Meditations on First Philosophy*, trans. by Donald Cress (Indianapolis: Hackett, 1999). Hereafter noted as (Descartes, p. "x") in the text.

whenever the boys are talking about water and, upon appearing, he invariably (and annoyingly) says, "Don't forget to bring a towel!" And notoriously, very soon after that, he asks, "Do you wanna get high?" These utterances, as well as much of Towelie's dialogue, are certainly not enough to convince us that he's a thinking towel rather than a slightly more complex (and more disturbing) version of a plush toy that's programmed with several sayings. What might convince us that Towelie is more than that? If we want to know whether Towelie has a mind, how should we proceed? What should we be looking for?

First, in order to underscore the difficulty of this task, suppose Towelie says and does nothing at all. Suppose that he behaves rather like an ordinary towel. Can we know that this more ordinary Towelie does not have a mind? One might think not. To see this point consider that, while it's controversial whether success in a Turing test shows the presence of thinking, it seems rather obvious that failure in a Turing test does not show the absence of thinking. For the inhabitant of Room 3 may be intelligent but unable to communicate with us, or may simply not care about us enough to respond. Now none of us are tempted to worry about whether our dish towels are thinking nasty thoughts about us as we vigorously dry our hands, but it is difficult to explain just how it is that we know for certain that such things lack minds. If all this talk of towels seems just silly to you, well blame it on Matt and Trey. And then imagine that we've encountered a new species, either deep under the ocean or on some other planet. If they don't communicate with us, or seem to do much of anything at all, can we be sure they aren't thinking? How?

Back to the issue of how to establish that Towelie does have a mind. To begin with, we might wonder about the range and responsiveness of Towelie's utterances. If he says nothing but "Don't forget to bring a towel!" and "Do you wanna get high?" or if he says things that don't seem to respond to what we're saying, we're less likely to think of him as a person with a mind and more likely to think of him as some sort of device. This is more or less to follow Turing's reasoning. What else might we do? What other features characterize things with minds that we might try to detect in Towelie? The list of proposed features is rather long, and contains various things that are interrelated like rationality, consciousness, free will, autonomy, emotion, creativity, and a soul. And Towelie does seem to manifest some of these things as, for example, he defies his programming by wandering off in search of weed or gets very pissed off when Kyle nabs his last joint. But the general problem here is that if I don't know how and why it is that I have one of these features, and I can't be absolutely sure that other human beings do have any of them, then it's hard to see how I can make use of any of them to settle the issue over Towelie with any certainty.

No Way! A Machine Just Can't Do That!

For nearly every feature that we might use in determining whether something has a mind, we'll find someone giving an argument that a machine simply cannot possess the feature in question. Thus, underlying any number of objections to the possibility of artificial intelligence is the longstanding brute conviction that a machine simply cannot do certain things that human beings can do. Consider, for example, the famous French philosopher René Descartes' (1596–1650) thought experiment about machines that look and act very much like us. In his *Discourse on Method*, Descartes tells us that we would have two certain ways of telling that they aren't really human beings:

> The first is that they could never use words, or put together other signs, as we do in order to declare our thoughts to others. For we can certainly conceive of a machine so constructed that it utters words, and even utters words which correspond to bodily actions causing a change in its organs (e.g., if you touch it in one spot it asks what you want of it, if you touch it in another it cries out that you are hurting it, and so on). But it is not conceivable that such a machine should produce different arrangements of words so as to give an appropriately meaningful answer to whatever is said in its presence, as the dullest of men can do. (Descartes, p. 27)

What Descartes is saying, in essence, is that a machine could never pass the Turing test. A machine just couldn't carry on a conversation with us. But while not all of Turing's hopes have been fulfilled as of yet, we have seen enough progress to make us doubt Descartes' claim here. Let's examine his second reason:

Secondly, even though such machines might do some things as well as we do them, or perhaps even better, they would inevitably fail in others, which would reveal that they were acting not through understanding but only from the disposition of their organs. For whereas reason is a universal instrument which can be used in all kinds of situations, these organs need some particular disposition for each particular action; hence it is for all practical purposes impossible for a machine to have enough different organs to make it act in all the contingencies of life in the way in which our reason makes us act. (Descartes, pp. 27–8)

So, while we might build machines that can act as we do in some limited respects, a machine cannot engage in the full range of human actions because it lacks reason, which is the "universal instrument" we use in handling "all the contingencies of life."

Notice Descartes' apparent surety that a machine that is equipped to do a job in virtue of the arrangement of its parts (organs) does not have reason. This is similar to Searle's claim that a digital computer cannot have understanding, but it is far more sweeping. Descartes insists that no material structure, including not only a constructed machine but also a biological "machine" such as a brain, can possess reason. This is an upshot of Descartes' commitment to *substance dualism*, the view that human beings consist of two distinct substances: an immaterial mind or soul and a material body (which of course includes the brain). If you are a dualist, then you're quite likely to think that no matter how meticulously you organize material parts, you can never build a mind, for a mind is simply a different kind of thing altogether. As Descartes puts it a few lines later, "the rational soul cannot be derived from the potentiality of matter, but must be specially created." Thus, Gottfried Wilhelm Leibniz (1646–1716), one of Descartes' philosophical successors, suggests that if we were to imagine a thinking machine, we could imagine going inside of it as we would go inside a mill. But we would find nothing in there but cogs, wheels, and other parts moving each other around. Where would we find anything that could produce thought or feeling or understanding? Nowhere, says Leibniz.[4] Nothing material can have a mind.

---

[4] This example is from Leibniz's *Monadology* 17, which can be found in G.W. Leibniz, *Philosophical Texts*, trans. by R.S. Woolhouse and Richard Francks (Oxford: Oxford University Press, 1998), p. 270.

But the dualism of Descartes, Leibniz, and others has fallen into disrepute. In part this is because we have learned that a material thing is capable of far more than they seem to have imagined. Computers, after all, can do a lot of things that we once thought only human beings can do. Further, we understand far better how a brain – a material thing – can do things like remember something, feel something, and so on, and we have discovered how altering the chemistry of the brain can alter the functions of the mind. If we come to recognize that we are material things with minds, it may simply seem arbitrary to deny that a machine might have a mind as well. As Mr. Scientist says, toward the end of the AWESOM-O episode, as he lies bleeding on the floor and pulling various organs out of his abdominal cavity, "Who's to judge what makes something human anyway?! Does this make me human?! Or this?! Or these?!" Clearly, he isn't talking about what makes something a member of the human species. No, he's saying that what makes something a thinking person is not just that it's made of human parts.

We might suspect that many continued attempts to deny that a material thing, such as a machine, can engage in mental activities are due more to a lack of knowledge of computer science or neuroscience or to a failure to imagine how much farther such fields might be developed. Alternatively, some people may be committed to dualism by virtue of their religious faith, believing that their sacred scriptures or some theological tenet require them to embrace dualism. Clearly, such waters are too deep for us to plumb here, but it's worth acknowledging one relevant development. In recent years, a number of Christian scholars have argued that the biblical portrait of human beings is rather more holistic than dualistic, and some of them have even argued that the Christian faith is entirely compatible with the view that human beings are physical creatures, through and through.[5] Thus, religious objections to the possibility of artificial intelligence may become less prevalent.

[5] See, for example, Warren S. Brown, Nancey C. Murphy, and H. Newton Malony (eds.), *Whatever Happened to the Soul? Scientific and Theological Portraits of Human Nature* (Minneapolis: Augsburg Fortress Publishers, 1998).

Machines Will Take Over the World!

As a way of closing our discussion – without, in any way, exhausting or fully resolving what's before us, as is inevitably the case with thorny philosophical issues – let's shift from thinking about the nature and possibility of artificial intelligence to thinking about its desirability. Would it be a good thing if there were machines that could think? Many familiar science fiction stories and films suggest not. In fact, *South Park* also plays with this theme of the evil machine. In an episode entitled "Trapper Keeper," Cartman has acquired a new *Dawson's Creek* Trapper Keeper (which is really just a glorified folder), with all the bells and whistles. As could only happen on *South Park*, a strange man calling himself Bill Cosby (but bearing no resemblance to the famous comedian) appears and becomes fixated on Cartman's new folder. Eventually, we find out that he is a cyborg sent from the future to prevent this high tech Trapper Keeper from assimilating everything around it and taking over the world. Cartman is so enamored of his new acquisition that he's reluctant to give it up, no matter what the stakes. Of course, his Trapper Keeper assimilates him and is on its way to world domination when it makes the mistake of assimilating Rosie O'Donnell. This gives the other boys the chance they need to defeat the growing monstrosity and rescue Cartman. The silliness of all this is perhaps appropriate: what reason do we have to suspect that intelligent machines would want to take over the world? Perhaps it's because we fear that a machine with a mind would be too much like us after all.

18

STAN'S FUTURE SELF AND EVIL CARTMAN

Personal Identity in *South Park*

Shai Biderman

Two Peas in a Pod, My Future Self 'n' Me

In the episode "My Future Self 'n' Me" the boys discover a joint and rolling papers on a tree stump in the woods. While they'd like to throw the joint away, no one wants to pick it up, fearing that the anti-drug commercial's claim "if you have pot, you could become a terrorist" is true. But Stan concludes that the commercial scare tactics are "just exaggerations" and, so, picks up the joint and throws it away. Days later, the Marsh family is astonished to see that "Future Stan" has stumbled upon their doorstep. It seems that, at the age of 32, Future Stan was mysteriously caught in a time matrix and returned to present day South Park. Future Stan is in miserable shape, having spent his teenage years "on a slow downward spiral experimenting with drugs and alcohol," which ultimately led him to living on the street behind a crack house, shooting heroin, and drinking heavily.

After initially believing anti-drug commercials have accurately predicted his future, Stan grows suspicious. How can his present self and future self exist at the same moment in time? How can the same human being, Stan, exist in two separate spaces at the same exact time? Ever inquisitive and doubtful, Stan tries to unmask the charade by pretending to chop off his hand. If future Stan is really the same person, his hand should vanish. But it doesn't (so Randy Marsh proactively chops it off!).

Stan's encounter with his future self raises questions and issues of *personal identity*. What makes me, *me*? Why exactly do I consider myself to be the *same person* as I was, say, in elementary school? What is it, exactly, that stays the same about me as time passes? Is it my body? Is it my mind? Is there even a continuity of identity over time? Perhaps I am just a bundle of ever changing attributes, such as physical characteristics, thoughts, or emotions? We're going to need some help with these questions. So, let's "go on down to South Park" to take a look at what they say about personal identity.

Evil Cartman, Stan's Clone, Those Darn Hats, and Cartman Possessed

What is it about me that makes me the same person over time? What are the criteria – the main qualities that must be present – in order to identify me as that same person over time? *South Park* provides us with a slew of thought experiments to help us along our investigation into personal identity. In the episode "Spooky Fish" the boys discover a second Cartman hanging around South Park. The two Cartmans look exactly alike, except that one has a detachable goatee. Strangely enough, the boys can't tell them apart from their appearances, but they do pick up on a difference in their personalities. The goateed Cartman is very thoughtful, caring, and considerate, while the non-goateed Cartman is selfish, arrogant, and rude. The boys are faced with the question: are both Cartmans the same person, Cartman?

In the episode "An Elephant Makes Love to a Pig" Stan is cloned, but the two Stans are definitely *not* physically identical. The cloned Stan is much taller and stronger, his head is twenty times the size of Stan's head, and he continuously says "Ba-Chomp. Ba-Chewy-Chomp!" Still, it is suggested that both Stans have the same memories and that they both "think alike." Recall that Mephisto tells Stan that he should be able to find his clone by thinking about where he himself would go. So are Stan and cloned-Stan the same person?

Remarkably, the boys' identities are tied directly to the kind of hat each one wears. Stan wears a "red puffball hat," Cartman sports a turquoise hat, Kyle dons a green bomber hat, and Kenny's entire body is covered by his orange parka. We, the viewers, rely on these particular items of clothing to identify the boys, and we are initially shocked when we see them without their hats, becoming confused as to who is who. Consider Stan's confusion as to who he is in the episode "Super Best Friends." There, Stan and Kyle – both with heads shaved – argue back and forth until Stan begins to argue as if he were Kyle. Stan has to put his hat back on before finishing the argument so that he knows who he is and which side he is arguing on.

Finally, recall the episode "A Ladder to Heaven" where, after drinking Kenny's ashes, Cartman becomes possessed by Kenny. The result is that Cartman begins to behave differently, saying much kinder things than he normally would. This time around, we have only one body – the body of Cartman – but this body has Kenny's soul. So how do we handle this case? Is this the same Cartman that we've seen in previous episodes? Is Cartman the same person?

Let's Get Physical . . . and Psychological

There are two broad categories of criteria for personal identity. According to *physical criteria*, identity consists of a physical thing, like your body, your brain, or other physical form (possibly your red puffball hat?). On the other hand, according to *psychological criteria*, identity consists of some psychological part, like your consciousness or memory, existing over time. Let's take a closer look at some of the specific criteria that fall under these two categories.

Since we obviously need brains in order to live, some philosophers think it's the brain that determines personal identity. In the episode "Roger Ebert Should Lay Off the Fatty Foods," the brain criterion is assumed, as certain people in South Park are brainwashed by the curator of the "Plane . . . arium." For example, Officer Barbrady is made to believe that he is Elvis. Brain scrambling with resulting changes in personhood occurs in other episodes as well. In "Good Times with Weapons" Kyle warns Stan about removing the ninja star in Butters' head, as he may scramble his brain. Meanwhile, Cartman is all for the scrambling, since it would alter Butters' personhood so that he doesn't remember the incident. Likewise, in "Super Adventure Club" Chef is brainwashed by the club and becomes both pedophile and sexual predator. In these examples, the essential ingredient in personal identity seems to be the brain. The person changes over time due to changes in the brain. You are *you* over time, if and only if you have the same brain.

Strangely, in the episode "Fat Butt and Pancake Head" Cartman's hand *is* Jennifer Lopez. She, the hand, is treated as a person with her own identity: she seems to have her own thoughts, her own voice (through Cartman), and Ben Affleck recognizes her as J-Lo. But she has no brain; she is simply a hand. Likewise, in "Die Hippie, Die" Mayor McDaniels ignores Cartman's warnings and allows her town to be overrun by hippies. Distraught, the mayor attempts to commit suicide, but survives a self-inflicted gunshot wound to the head because she has (practically) no brain at all. So, given these examples, the brain cannot serve as the *only* criterion for personal identity. If we can even imagine personal identity being preserved without the brain, then the brain is not sufficient for personal identity.

On the other hand, in the episode "The Biggest Douche in the Universe," while Cartman tries to get rid of Kenny who is still inside of him, the boys see movie trailers for Rob Schneider's upcoming films. The trailer for the first film extends Schneider's roles of alternate identities in his previous films: "Rob Schneider was an animal. Then he was a woman. And now Rob Schneider is . . . a stapler." The trailer for the second film continues this nonsensical trend as we find that Schneider is now a carrot! For each trailer the boys watch, Rob Schneider takes on another, increasingly silly, identity. Notice that he remains the same person, Rob Schneider, even though his physical form changes. This suggests psychological criteria for personal identity, or the view that personhood is determined by having a similar set of psychological states over time. One's identity as a person thus comes from psychological continuity. You are *you* over time only if you have the same mind or set of mental states. Thus, Rob Schneider retains his identity in each of his films – despite the fact that his physical form changes from human to stapler to carrot – because he has the same mind throughout the physical transformations.

Consider this challenge to the body criterion. Let's say Rob Schneider's brain is transplanted into Kenny's body. Is Rob Schneider no longer Rob Schneider? Is he now Kenny? Accepting the body criterion, we would say the person before us is Kenny. But this seems odd. With Schneider's brain, isn't the person really Schneider? He'll respond to Schneider's name, he'll recognize his lifestyle as an actor (and not as a poverty stricken child in South Park), and he'll have memories of his past experiences as a stapler and a carrot. So this thought experiment implies that it may not be the body that preserves personal identity.[1]

Now That's What I Call a Sticky Situation . . . Although, I'm Still Not Sure What "I" Refers To

In the episode "The City on the Edge of Forever" Ms. Crabtree accidentally drives the bus over the guardrail on a mountainside, so that the bus precariously rocks up and down over the cliff, seemingly ready to fall off the mountain's edge. While Crabtree goes to seek help, the children remain in the bus and spend time reminiscing, recalling previous episodes.

Here, the boys identify themselves according to one of the possible psychological criteria of personal identity, the *memory criterion*, according to which personhood is grounded in having the same memories of experiences over time. You are currently characterized by your present consciousness, and this consciousness extends back-wards towards the past with your memories. So, since Stan can recall his experiences of using Cartman and his anal probe as bait to lure the aliens to earth, the Stan who is trapped in the rocking bus is the same Stan who lured the aliens. The same goes for each boy: Kyle is the same person who encountered Skuttlebutt; Cartman is the same person who witnessed Mr. Garrison's attempt to kill Gifford; and Kenny is the same person who ran away from death.

But there is a potential problem with the memory criterion. If someone suffers from amnesia or undergoes a memory swap in which their old memories are erased and replaced with new memories, then we have a change in identity. Take Cartman's experience in the episode "Cow Days," where he practices bull riding for the Cow

[1] See Sydney Shoemaker, "Personal Identity: A Materialist's Account," in Sydney Shoemaker and Richard Swinburne (eds.), *Personal Identity* (Oxford: Blackwell, 1984), pp. 67–132.

Days Festival. Cartman takes a hard fall off a bull and ends up losing all of his memories. His old memories are replaced by a strange set of new memories of life as a Vietnamese female prostitute. He speaks Vietnamese fluently, dresses like a prostitute, and walks around the festival offering sexual favors to "soldier boys" and others. According to the memory criterion, there were two distinct persons before and after the bull riding accident. Before the accident we had "Cartman the everyday jerk," while after the accident we have "Cartman the Vietnamese prostitute." The two Cartmans each have their own personal identities due to different sets of memories.

John Locke (1632–1704) was a great supporter of the memory criterion and famously said that a person is a "thinking intelligent being, that has reason and reflection, and can consider itself as itself, the same thinking thing, in different times and places." In order to consider ourselves in this way, we must possess consciousness. It is consciousness that "makes every one to be, what he calls self; and thereby distinguishes himself from all other thinking things."[2] For Locke, then, it is our memories that allow us to be the same conscious person over time.

But the philosopher Thomas Reid (1710–96) pointed to a problem with the memory criterion.[3] Let's take three specific events in Cartman's life to explain the problem. First, Cartman had an anal probe, implanted by aliens. Second, Cartman moved to a weight gain diet as he prepared his class presentation for the public. Third, Cartman is now stranded with his classmates in the bus on the edge of a cliff. Suppose that when Cartman was on his weight gain diet, he vividly recalled the incident with the anal probe. Suppose also that now stranded on the bus, he vividly recalls his weight gain diet, but *has no memory* of the alien probe incident. We have a problem. According to the memory criterion, the Cartman who went through the anal probe and weight gain are identical; and the Cartman who went through the weight gain and was stranded on the bus are identical; *but the anal probe Cartman and the Cartman stranded on*

---

[2] See John Locke, "Of Identity and Diversity," in *An Essay Concerning Human Understanding* (Oxford: Oxford University Press, 1979).

[3] See his *Essays on the Intellectual Powers of Man: A Critical Edition*, ed. by Knud Haakonssen (University Park: Pennsylvania State University Press, 2002).

the bus are not identical. The Cartman stranded on the bus can't recall the anal probe incident and, so, according to Locke's memory criterion, they are not identical. This bizarre conclusion is a great challenge for this position. After all, common sense dictates that it really is the same Cartman who has undergone all three events. Thus, while memory may be important, it doesn't suffice as the sole criterion for personal identity.

Hella Psychological Continuity

Let's return to the thought experiment from the episode "Spooky Fish" where we encounter two different Cartmans with identical physical bodies occupying different spaces. Despite the fact that one is wearing a goatee and the other is not, Stan, Kyle, and Kenny distinguish the two by their personalities. The goateed Cartman is unusually kind and caring towards others; meanwhile, the non-goateed Cartman is his usual narcissistic self. The boys use this difference in personalities to determine that the friendly Cartman must be from "an evil, parallel universe where everything exists as its opposite."

The method the boys use to distinguish the two Cartmans follows the *psychological continuity criterion* of personal identity, where personhood is grounded in the continuity of psychological relations over time. You maintain the same identity so long as you inherit the mental features from your past being. You are *you* insofar as you have a historical relation of personality, beliefs, or memories to who you were in the past. In this sense, then, the "hella," hateful, and stubborn Cartman is the Cartman that the boys have known all those years because that Cartman has inherited the same personality and attitude over the years. Meanwhile, the angelic, good-natured Cartman *can't possibly* be the Cartman that they've known since he has, in no way whatsoever, inherited the personality and attitude of the Cartman that exists in their world.

The psychological continuity criterion develops from, among other sources, the skeptical approach of David Hume (1711–1776). In his *Treatise of Human Nature*, Hume said that each of us appears to be "a bundle or collection of different perceptions, which succeed each other with an inconceivable rapidity, and are in a perpetual flux and movement."[4] For Hume, there is no enduring self that remains the same over time. We can never be in a position to capture a "person" that is the same from one moment to the next. At best, we each are a collection of changing thoughts, feelings, and attitudes. While Hume concludes that we should reject the notion of the self or personhood, we can see how his bundle theory develops into the psychological continuity criterion. Since we are simply a bundle of perceptions – and certainly not a body or brain or anything physical – Hume's theory helps to support the idea that personality is a fictitious whole that captures the entirety of our psychological traits, actions, behavioral patterns, and reflections over time.

We Know Kenny as The Kid with The Orange Parka *and* The Dirty Little Mind

Personal identity, as we have seen, is a very tricky business. We've considered several different candidates for personal identity, but each left us with more questions. Maybe a person is actually identified using some combination of body and mind. Experience would seem to confirm this. For instance, when we judge that the friend with us now is identical to the friend we saw last week, we make this judgment because we see our friend as having a relevantly similar body and personality now as they did last week. Our friend has the same body and the same brain, our friend can recall what we did last week, and our friend has (at least some of) the same attitudes and personality. In much the same way, when Kenny comes back from the dead in the seventh season of *South Park* the other boys recognize him as the same person from a combination of his bodily appearance – arms, legs, orange parka – and his twisted little mind. But the nagging question of personal identity remains. What is it, *really*, that grounds our personal identity: some aspect of our bodily existence or something psychological like our consciousness or memories? Maybe Kenny knows. But, even if does, we wouldn't be able to understand him.

---

[4] David Hume, *Treatise of Human Nature*, ed. by L.A. Selby-Bigge (Oxford: Clarendon Press, 1888), p. 252.

PART SIX

SATAN, SUFFERING, SUPER BEST
FRIENDS, AND SONG

19

CARTMANLAND AND THE PROBLEM OF EVIL

David Kyle Johnson

There's No God, Dude!

Cartman is an ass. To put it more precisely, Cartman is a manipulative, self-centered bastard whose every action is directed either toward accomplishing his own happiness or the unhappiness of others. However you put it, Cartman is the kind of kid who deserves to be miserable. When misfortune befalls him, we think good has happened. If fortune smiles on him, we don't think he deserves it – instead, we think something evil has happened. This is precisely the conclusion Kyle draws when Cartman gets his own amusement park. In the *South Park* episode "Cartmanland" – just after he objects to being required to attend his own grandmother's funeral because it is "taking up [his] whole Saturday" and laments that her funeral is longer than the time it took her to die – Cartman learns that he is the primary benefactor of his grandmother's estate, and he inherits one million dollars from her. He immediately purchases the local amusement park, renames it "Cartmanland," and buys television commercial time to declare that the best thing about Cartmanland is, "You can't come . . . especially Stan and Kyle." Cartman then spends all day, every day, riding any ride he wants without waiting in line. In this way, Cartman attains complete happiness.

Kyle views Cartman's happiness as a horrendous evil. Cartman doesn't deserve such happiness and his attaining it just isn't right. But, according to Kyle, the problem goes much deeper. Kyle observes that these events are not just unbelievable, but given his worldview –

which includes the belief that God exists – they are impossible. God, if he exists, is an all-good and all-powerful God, who exercises a measure of control in the universe and who should not let horrendous evil occur. Thus, assuming such a God exists, it is impossible for Cartman to attain such happiness. But, since Cartman's happiness is undeniable, Kyle is forced to revise his worldview and conclude that God doesn't exist. Kyle's argument is a form of the *problem of evil*. Atheists – those who do not believe in the existence of God – have always used variations of the problem of evil. Philosophers would call Kyle's variation an example of the *logical problem of moral evil*. This problem suggests that the existence of moral evil – evil caused by human action – is logically incompatible with God's existence. If Kyle had a PhD in philosophy, he likely would have expressed the problem like this:

> Premise 1: If God exists, given that he is all-good and all-powerful, he would not allow Cartman to be completely happy (for that is a great evil).
> Premise 2: But now that Cartman has his own amusement park, Cartman is completely happy (again, a great evil).
>
> ──
>
> Conclusion: Therefore, God does not exist.[1]

This argument is valid; if its premises are true, its conclusion is true. Those who object to the argument must – if they want their objection to be successful – do so by objecting to the truth of one of its premises; they must present good reason to think that either Premise (1) or (2) is false. And that is exactly what those who object to it try to do.

In this chapter, we'll look at some solutions to the problem of evil that have been proposed by the citizens of South Park, and we will see how they parallel solutions proposed by some Western philosophers, both old and new. We'll see which proposals fail and why, and which proposal works to solve the problem. In the end, the reader should have a much better understanding of some of the arguments

---

[1] It is important to note that one could substitute any evil for "Cartman's complete happiness" and the conclusion would still follow. Often, when the argument is made, the phrase "evil exists" is substituted for "Cartman's complete happiness."

and solutions surrounding the problem of evil, as well as an understanding of the fact that debate on the issue is far from over. Belief in
God can be justified, but the problem of evil must be confronted.

And That's It?!? The Story of Job

In the "Cartmanland" episode, when Kyle's parents discover that he
has renounced his faith, they take it upon themselves to restore his
faith. They attempt to do so by telling him their *own* version of the
story of Job. The story of Job comes from the Book of Job in the Old
Testament and is about a man who suffers horrendous evils and yet
retains his faith in God. According to the Book of Job, God allows
Satan to inflict these evils upon Job to prove to Satan that Job will
remain faithful despite them. Many people use this story as an answer
to the problem of evil. Kyle's parents give their own version of the
story noting that, despite all of the horrible things that happen to him
and his family, Job "still kept his faith." Kyle's response to the story
is quite telling: "And that's it? That's the end? Then I was right. Job
has all his children killed [by God in order to prove a point to Satan],
and Michael Bay gets to keep making movies. There isn't a God."

Kyle seems to have some very good points. He observes that the
actions of God in this story seem to be inconsistent with how we view
God. Most of us would not think it morally justified to cause that
kind of suffering to "prove a point." But more importantly, Kyle
observes that the story of Job does not answer the problem of evil.
It is an example of someone continuing to believe in God despite
suffering horrendous evil, but it does not challenge a specific premise
of the argument. Yes, the "moral" of the story – what it suggests that
you do in response – seems to be "Everyone should behave like Job;
one should continue to believe in God even if one suffers horrendous
evil." But it does not show *why* one should behave like Job – why one
should not view horrendous evil as conclusive evidence against God.

Yet many people, like Kyle's parents, suggest that a full understanding of the argument of the Book of Job does solve the problem
of evil. How might we re-understand it to solve the problem of
evil? The argument could be understood this way: "The fact that
Job continued to believe in God despite 'the evidence of evil' shows

that evil is not conclusive evidence against God." However, this is a very bad argument because the fact that Job didn't find the evidence to be conclusive doesn't show that the evidence is not conclusive. Recall the episode "Chef Aid." The fact that the jury, after hearing the Chewbacca defense, finds Chef guilty does not mean that the Chewbacca defense was conclusive evidence against Chef; the jury was just easily persuaded by bad argument. Likewise, the fact that Mr. Garrison ignored all the evidence that he was gay for the first few seasons does not mean that the evidence wasn't conclusive; Mr. Garrison was simply in denial – everyone else recognized the evidence as conclusive. In the same way, the fact that Job didn't find the evidence against God to be conclusive does not mean everyone should do the same; Job simply may not have recognized the problem.

The fact that the story of Job does not answer the problem of evil is not that surprising to biblical scholars. The story was not intended for that purpose. More than likely, if Job actually existed, he would not have even considered his suffering as reason to not believe in God's existence. The belief that God was "all good" and would thus never cause suffering didn't become prevalent until after Plato's philosophical influence had worked its way through Christianity; thus, Job would not have viewed his suffering as evidence against God's existence at all. This, coupled with the fact that atheism would have been virtually unheard of by Job, makes the fact that Job continued to believe in God's existence, despite his suffering, no surprise.

In the story, what Job's suffering does is threaten his approval of God. Job never questions that God exists, in fact he admits that God is responsible for his suffering. But this divine responsibility causes Job to question whether he should continue to be faithful; he wonders what good it is to be righteous if the righteous are punished like the wicked. At the end of the story, God rebukes the answers of others and offers his own saying – in a nutshell – "I am the creator of everything; you have no right to question my actions, nor can you understand their purpose." Job agrees and once again praises God.

Even though the story is not about the problem of evil, one might think that the moral of the story of Job could be modified in order to answer the problem of evil. "You can't question God's existence when evil occurs," one might suggest, "God is the creator of the universe and is beyond our understanding. No one can understand the reason for which he allows such things to occur, nor does anyone have the right to question him." But this answer is no good because it begs the question. In other words, one giving this as an answer to the problem of evil *assumes* the truth of what they are trying to prove. Notice that the answer itself works only if God exists. God has an unknown reason to allow evil only if he exists; no one has the right to question God only if God exists. But *that God exists* is exactly what the argument is supposed to prove. You can't simply assume the truth of what you are trying to prove to prove that it is true. Not only is that bad reasoning but, also, no one who doesn't share your assumption will be convinced. So, as Kyle concluded, the story of Job does not seem to be of much help at all. What other solutions could there be?

The Sweet Milk of Our Tears

In the episode "Kenny Dies" – the only episode in which Kenny dies and "stays dead" for a while – Stan wrestles with the problem of evil. He asks Chef how God could let his friend die, and Chef responds that God "gives us life and love and health, just so that he can tear it all away and make us cry, so he can drink the sweet milk of our tears. You see, it's our tears Stan that give God his great power." Although this answer seems cruel, and clearly wrong, it actually mirrors some philosophers' answers to the problem of evil. Chef suggests that God allows evil to occur for his own benefit. This is not unlike Jonathan Edward's (1703–1758) or John Calvin's (1509–1564) solution to the problem of evil.[2] They suggest that God allows evil because he wishes to punish evildoers, an action which benefits God himself. As Edwards specifically suggests, punishing evildoers is the most perfect way for

---

[2]   See John Calvin, *Institutes of the Christian Religion*, trans. by Henry Beveridge (Grand Rapids, MI: William B. Eerdmans, 1957), Book 1, chs. 16–18; Book 3, ch. 23. Also see Jonathan Edwards, "Wicked Men Useful in Their Destruction Only," in *The Works of President Edwards, Volume* 6, ed. by Edward Parsons and Edward Williams (New York: B. Franklin, 1968). Edwards is mainly addressing the doctrine of Hell, but clearly realizes that the existence of evil is necessary for God to demonstrate his holiness.

God to demonstrate his holiness and thus bring glory to himself.[3] The idea is that a benefit to God outweighs any evil done to humans.

But not many philosophers find this solution satisfactory. God benefiting himself by demonstrating his holiness at our expense – by making us suffer through evil and punishing us for it – doesn't seem to be better than Chef's explanation; we just don't think God is that cruel. Further, it is not clear why God must punish evildoers to demonstrate his holiness. Isn't God all-powerful? Could he have not demonstrated this fact, with equal effectiveness, in some other (non-evil) way? It certainly seems so. Most do not think that Chef, Edwards, or Calvin are on the right track.

You *Are* Up There!

After Stan and Kyle try to sneak into Cartmanland, Cartman decides he needs a security guard. Since the security guard won't accept rides on his attractions as payment, Cartman is forced to let two people a day into his park to pay the security guard's salary. His problem escalates when Cartman discovers that he needs maintenance, food, drink, cotton candy, video surveillance, a box office, and janitors. Soon, Cartman has a fully functioning and successful amusement park. But since he now has to wait in line to ride his rides, he doesn't want it anymore and sells it back to the owner for the original million. Most of his money is immediately seized by the IRS (since he didn't pay any taxes when he owned the park) and the rest goes to Kenny's family (since Kenny died on the Mine Shaft ride). Cartman is now miserable. He stands outside the park, throwing rocks at it, and the security guard who once worked for him maces him in the face.

Stan brings Kyle outside to witness these events, and observes: "Look Kyle, Cartman is totally miserable, even more miserable than he was before because he had his dream and lost it." Stan, by this observation, restores Kyle's belief in God. Clearly, according to Stan and Kyle, Cartman's suffering has somehow relieved the tension

---

[3] For a wonderful rendition of Edwards' argument, see William J. Wainwright, "Jonathan Edwards and the Doctrine of Hell," in *Jonathan Edwards: Philosophical Theologian*, ed. by Paul Helm and Oliver Crisp (London: Ashgate Publishing, 2004).

between the existence of God and the horrendous evil of Cartman's perfect happiness. Their answer is this: God, being all-good, wanted to accomplish a great good: the *perfect suffering* of Cartman. But the only way to accomplish this great good was to give Cartman perfect happiness (an evil) for a brief period and then rip it away from him. Since the good of Cartman's suffering outweighs the evil of his brief happiness, an overall greater good was accomplished, making the evil of his happiness justified.

This answer mirrors a common way in which theists – those who believe in God – answer the problem of evil. They challenge a specific premise in the argument – the suggestion that God would prevent evil if he wanted to and could – by suggesting that he might have other trumping desires. In other words, they suggest that God might not guarantee the absence of all evil because there might be something he desires more than the absence of evil that requires the existence of evil. But what might that be? The presence of good! Although it is true that God doesn't like evil, it is also true that God loves (and wants to accomplish) good. If some certain goods can only be accomplished by allowing certain evils – as long as the good accomplished outweighs the evil allowed (as long as the good is more good than the evil is bad) – allowing that evil is justified. In fact, since the world is a better place if those evils are allowed and then outweighed, you would expect God to allow them because he wants the world to be as good as possible. In short, the suggestion is that the existence of evil does not stand in logical contradiction with God's existence because it is false that God would necessarily prevent all evil. God would – and in fact should – allow evil that accomplishes a greater good and, thus, the mere existence of evil is not conclusive evidence against God's existence. The mutual existence of God and evil is logically possible.

But some questions remain: What kind of goods can only be accomplished by allowing evil? Wouldn't every evil have to lead to a greater good? To answer these questions, there are different ways of understanding this answer. Stan and Kyle view the specific event of Cartman's suffering as a good that could only be accomplished at the expense of Cartman's brief happiness. Philosophers would call Cartman's happiness a "first order" evil and his suffering a "second order" good. Other examples of second order goods would be acts of compassion, like healing those who are sick or fighting for Starvin' Marvin to stay on the planet Marclar, or acts of bravery, like sacrificing oneself in battle to save others or sacrificing oneself to save Moses from the evil anti-Semitic sect of Judaism, as in the episode "Jewbilee." These acts are made possible because they are responses to evil events and their good outweighs the evil they are responses to. They are second order goods made possible by first order evils.

To solve the problem of evil, some theists suggest that for any given evil event that occurs, God allowed that event to occur to accomplish some greater (second order) good here on earth. They suggest it is logically possible for God and evil to coexist because every evil helps bring about a second order good. But this suggestion is problematic: every first order evil would have to lead to a second order good. The only way allowing a first order evil would be justified would be if it accomplished a second order good; if a first order evil ever went "unanswered" – if no greater good was accomplished as a result – God should not have allowed it, and it would be direct evidence against God's existence. Since there are clearly such unanswered evils – the rape and murder of a baby, for example – it seems that the theist still has a problem.

Another way to attempt to solve the problem is with what is known as the *free will defense*. Those who use this defense avoid the problem of "unanswered evils" by suggesting that individual evils are not answered, but must be risked by God if he is to allow good to occur. Good can only be accomplished by our free will. As Augustine (354–430) put it, only free acts are good acts;[4] if we do not have the free will to choose between good and evil, nothing we do is truly good. Unless we have the option of choosing evil (which we can only have with free will), we cannot be given moral credit for choosing good, and if we cannot be given moral credit for an action, it cannot be truly good. Thus, without free will, there is no good. But if we are to have free will – if we are to truly have the option of doing evil – we must remain unhindered. God can't stop Cartman from trying to eliminate the Jews, for example, if Cartman is to have the freedom to do so; likewise, if we are to be free, he cannot stop us if we are about to choose to do evil. Thus, "the risk of evil" is necessary if there is to be any good in the world. Since God loves good – and presumably wants to accomplish good more than he wants to avoid evil – the risk of evil is one that he

[4] See "On Free Will," in *Augustine: Earlier Writings*, trans. by John Burleigh (Philadelphia: Westminster Press, 1953).

is willing to take (even though he hates evil). Thus, the existence of evil is compatible with the existence of God and the problem of evil is solved.

One might wonder how it could be that there are goods that God can't accomplish without allowing evil. "Isn't God all-powerful?" one might wonder. "Couldn't God have created beings that always freely choose to do the good?" But the answer to this hinges upon the definition of free will. A free being is one that is not forced to act in the ways that he does. In order to ensure that everyone always did good, God would have to force everyone (in some way) to always do good. To suggest that God could create creatures that always freely choose to do good is to suggest that he could create "non-controlled creatures that are controlled" – a logical impossibility.

One might also wonder about evil not caused by human free will. After all, in the Cartmanland episode, part of the reason that Kyle lost his faith was because he developed a hemorrhoid (while Cartman was rewarded with his own theme park). I doubt there is anything that Kyle "freely chose to do" as a kid that led to that and it does seems hard to explain that evil by pointing to human free will. Such evils are called "natural evils." Other natural evils include earthquakes, tsunamis, hurricanes, tornados and Mecha-Streisand – all events that cause suffering but seem to not be caused by human free will.[5] Many philosophers think that, even though one can make sense of why God would allow moral evils, one cannot make sense of why God would allow natural evils and suggest that the existence of natural evil is conclusive evidence against God's existence. Philosophers call this the problem of natural evil. And as a solution to the problem of natural evil, the free will solution falls short.

Jesus Christ and John Hick: The Soul Making Theodicy

A solution that attempts to solve both the moral and natural evil problem is John Hick's *soul making theodicy*. The word *theodicy*

---

[5]   Given that Streisand chose to turn herself into Mecha-Streisand, Mecha-Streisand would not be a natural evil if you counted Barbra Streisand as a human. But this is something I am sure Matt and Trey are not willing to do; thus they probably view Mecha-Streisand as a natural evil.

comes from the Latin language and refers to a justification of God's existence in the face of so much evil in the world. John Hick tries to give such a justification and suggests that evil – both moral and natural – is allowed in the world so that we, individually and as a species, may develop our character.[6] Actions derived from bestowed perfect characters are not as good as actions derived from developed perfected characters. To ensure that the world contains the best kind of actions, God allows evil to exist so that we may respond to it, thus developing and eventually perfecting our characters. So, even though specific evils may go unanswered, the world as a whole is better if we develop our characters – which can only be accomplished by responding to evil – and the general presence of first order evil is justified.

Notice how John Hick's reasoning mirrors Jesus' in "Are You There God? It's Me, Jesus." In this episode, the South Park masses are ready to crucify Jesus because he promised that God would appear at the Millennium, and he has not. Stan and Jesus have a conversation where Jesus claims that "life is about problems, and overcoming those problems, and growing and learning from obstacles. If God just fixed everything for us, then there would be no point in our existence." Even though Jesus is talking about prayer, the point seems to be the same. The reason that God doesn't "fix everything for us" – the reason that he doesn't eliminate all evil – is because if he did, we would not be allowed to learn and grow from obstacles and our learning and growing is important (even more important than the elimination of evil).

Not everyone likes Hick's solution, but even if it is accepted as a solution to both the moral and natural problem, the debate is not over! There still seems to be a problem with the *amount* of evil in the world. Evil may be compatible with God's existence because it is necessary to accomplish some good, but it certainly seems that God could have accomplished just as much good with less evil than we have now. (Can't the kids of South Park learn their lessons at the end of each episode without Kenny dying so often?) One might even suggest that the amount of evil in the world seems to provide good evidence against God's existence. Even though this doesn't disprove God's existence necessarily, it may make not believing in God the more rational thing to do. This is what philosophers call the *evidential*

[6] See John Hick, *Evil and the Love of God* (San Francisco: Harper, 1978).

problem of evil. A discussion of this will have to wait, but you can do your own research on the matter.[7]

The problem of evil is not a closed issue, and the debate rages on. Since the problem is not conclusive, one could argue that belief in God is justified. But the problem has not been dismissed, so atheism seems to be justified as well. And it very well may be that, unless God appears to us like he does at the Millennium to the residents of South Park, it will always be the case that there will be a debate.

[7] See, for example, the articles in William Rowe (ed.), *God and the Problem of Evil* (Oxford: Blackwell, 2001); Marilyn Adams and Robert Adams (eds.), *The Problem of Evil* (Oxford: Oxford University Press, 1990); Louis Pojman (ed.), *Philosophy of Religion: An Anthology* (Belmont, CA: Wadsworth Publishing, 1987); Michael Tooley, "The Problem of Evil," in *The Stanford Encyclopedia of Philosophy*, ed. by Edward N. Zalta, www.plato.stanford.edu/archives/win2004/entries/evil/.

20

RELIGIOUS PLURALISM AND THE SUPER BEST FRIENDS

Jeffrey Dueck

Let's Meet The Super Best Friends

Religion is one of the key cultural and philosophical issues consistently dealt with in *South Park*. From the animated shorts *Jesus vs. Frosty* and *The Spirit of Christmas*, to recent episodes such as "Trapped in the Closet," "The Return of Chef," "Cartoon Wars Part I" and "Cartoon Wars Part II," Parker and Stone provide biting commentary on religious belief. Consider "The Super Best Friends," where the kids are seduced by illusionist David Blaine and his growing cult, and Jesus and The Super Best Friends come to the rescue. In this chapter, we'll look at a few important philosophical questions raised in that episode, including the nature of religious pluralism, miracles and the division between natural and supernatural, and, finally, the more general question of how faith relates to reason.

Let's begin by recapping the episode and addressing the most obvious issue presented there, religious pluralism. After David Blaine comes to town and wows the crowds with his masterful illusions, the South Park boys decide to participate in one of the "camps" offered by the "Blainetologists." Of course, the group turns out to be a cult, where Blaine is exalted as a powerful messianic figure and where allegiance to his cause is preached. Stan is uncomfortable with all of this and, after struggling with whether to leave his friends behind, seeks out the help of Jesus (who, if you'll remember, resides in a modest dwelling in South Park where he hosts a public access TV show). Jesus challenges David Blaine at a Denver rally, but his first-century-style miracles come across as simple party tricks compared to Blaine's illusions. Jesus calls in The Super Best Friends for help, a Justice League-like committee comprised of figures of some of the world's major religions. Each hero brings a special power to the table, including Mohammed with the power of fire, Krishna with shape-shifting powers, and Joseph Smith with ice powers. When the Blainetologists advocate a mass-suicide in an attempt to gain tax-exempt status from the US government (by all drowning in the one-foot-deep Reflecting Pool on the Mall in Washington, DC), Jesus and The Super Best Friends show up to put a stop to Blaine's evil – except for Buddha, who doesn't believe in evil. Blaine animates a giant statue of Abraham Lincoln to thwart The Super Best Friends, who use their combined powers to create a mammoth John Wilkes Booth to bring an end to the great emancipator's now destructive force. Meanwhile, Stan rescues the other boys from the Blainetologists and concludes the episode by decrying money-hungry, controlling cults and supporting the harmony and necessity of all the world's religions.

Pick Any Religion, and Picture It In Your Mind

While we laugh at Parker and Stone's portrayal of the religions and their prophets, we also might feel uncomfortable or uncertain about a number of the issues raised in the episode. For example, what are we to think about the conclusion Stan reaches at the end of the show? Should we agree with his idea that all religions are equally viable and should be held together in harmony? This seems appealing in some ways, but we might also wonder about how feasible it is to hold all religions to be equally true or interdependent. After all, different religions make different claims about what is true or best and even the episode under discussion seems to show that, while some religions should be recognized as equal, not all approaches to religion are equally good. David Blaine's religion is criticized as being like a cult, and most people find the deceptively esoteric, controlling, and brain-washing practices of a cult to not only be immoral, but also definitely *not* in line with the will of a god. Philosophers have offered three main viewpoints to deal with the diversity of religions: (a) religious pluralism, (b) religious exclusivism, and (c) religious inclusivism.

Many people believe that the best way to deal with the diversity of religions is to treat all religious beliefs as relatively equal. The viewpoint that all religions should be considered equal in terms of their truth and effectiveness is called *religious pluralism*. The *fact* of pluralism is merely the observation that there are numerous world religions that have significant adherents and that have stood the test of time. But the *philosophical* position known as pluralism goes beyond this obvious empirical fact. Importantly, it represents the view that because there are so many religions around the world and because many of them seem to do equally well in producing religious experiences and religiously minded people, we should therefore consider these religions to be roughly "on par" with one another in terms of their truth. In other words, we shouldn't claim that one religion is better than another, as long as everyone gets along like members of The Super Best Friends and each religion fosters the greater good of humankind. For instance, John Hick (a very important philosopher of religion and a card-carrying pluralist) argues that the central feature of any religion is "salvation," which he conceives of as a transformation from self-centeredness to divine-reality-centeredness. Religion is all about appreciating a higher power and the compelling message of looking beyond ourselves and reaching out to help others. For Hick, this personal transformation is evidenced by actions of love and compassion. And since all religions do about as well (or about as poorly) at producing devout, loving, and compassionate people, we should conclude that all are about on par with respect to their conceptions of salvation. Other differences about specific doctrines, historical accounts, and even overall conceptions of the divine reality should be de-emphasized, and we should focus on the truth that is expressed in all religions.[1]

It seems that, despite their implied religious affiliations, most of the boys support this viewpoint (though Cartman regularly voices condescending remarks about many religions, including Kyle's Judaism). And the fact that the combined powers of The Super Best Friends proves to be stronger than just one religious personality on his own

---

[1]   See John Hick, *God Has Many Names* (Louisville, KY: Westminster John Knox Press, 1982); *An Interpretation of Religion: Human Responses to the Present* (London: Macmillan, 1989); *A Christian Theology of Religion: A Rainbow of Faiths* (Louisville, KY: Westminster John Knox Press, 1995).

seems to further advocate pluralism. Other moments on *South Park* exemplify such pluralistic ideas. To cite one example, at the end of "All About Mormons" the Mormon kid Gary implies religious pluralism when he notes that "loving your family, being nice, and helping people" are the real essentials of any religion. It seems that as long as your religion preaches these values, then your religion is expressing "the truth" and "we all really are alike in our desire to praise the same god."

But responding to the fact of religious diversity with the pluralistic view that all religions are equal in terms of truth is not the only option. Indeed, it is poor reasoning to infer that all religions have the same truth from the simple fact of religious diversity. Are we justified in thinking that, if there is diversity in opinion about, say, the value and basic human rights of different cultures or races, that each viewpoint then must equally express the truth about the matter? Must we say that the racist, bigot, and supremacist have as much truth as someone who believes in racial equality? Or, how about Cartman's ongoing response to the hippie lifestyle? Does rationality mandate that any view, if it is held sincerely, should be respected and held as equally, or even *partially*, true? What about when Cartman tries to clear out hippies in South Park with a giant "Hippie Digger" drill? Is he justified simply because he is sincere? In general, does the mere fact that people disagree about their beliefs mean that no person is correct, or that all are equally correct? No.

Consider the "exclusive" claims of certain belief systems – those claims that set clear, uncompromising conditions for truth and thereby exclude any incompatible beliefs from being true. For example, Islam claims that there is no God but Allah, and that Mohammed is his prophet. Doesn't this imply that other conceptions of God are mistaken, and that regardless of the worth of other prophets, Mohammed is preeminent? Or take traditional Christianity, which certainly has exclusivist elements, such as Jesus claiming to be the only way to God (John 14:6). If this were true, wouldn't all other claims concerning other ways to salvation be false? Or if all religious views are equally true, shouldn't we conclude that Christianity is wrong about its exclusive claims to salvation?

So let's leave aside religious pluralism. Perhaps the most direct response to the diversity of religions around the world is *religious exclusivism*. This is the view that the claims of one religion are true, and that any claims that are incompatible with the tenets of the one religion are false. For most observations in our lives, this approach makes perfect sense. If, for example, I think South Park is located in Colorado, and you think it's located in Alaska, can both of us be right? Am I unjustified in thinking I am correct about my beliefs and that you are incorrect? This even applies to many moral questions. In response to "Cartman Joins NAMBLA," we certainly seem justified in thinking the members of the North American Man/Boy Love Association are wrong in their treatment of children, despite their leader's attempt to persuade us to tolerate them. But when it comes to religion, something causes many of us to hesitate from holding such exclusivist views. So many people feel so passionately about their religious beliefs that we feel bad about claiming someone is right and someone else is wrong. Or maybe we truly feel that there is no way of evaluating the truth-claims of a religion, and thus that we can't comment on whether or not a particular religion is true. Better to hold all religions equal if none can give clear reasons for why it is better or truer. Much more needs to be said about this, as it touches upon underlying issues about the nature of religious beliefs. For now, we can point out that while exclusivism permeates many of our beliefs, some people feel that exclusivism about *religion* is somehow disingenuous or arrogant.[2]

The third and final approach to religious diversity that we'll consider is called *religious inclusivism*. This view aims to hold one religion as superior to others with respect to truth while including other religions and their followers under the grace and salvation of that true religion. A twentieth-century Catholic theologian, Karl Rahner (1904–84), represents this view when he states that non-Christian people around the world who have honest faith in their religion should be considered "anonymous Christians" – they receive the grace and salvation of Christianity (the only *true* religion) in the midst of their religious lives without even knowing about it. Thus,

---

[2] For more on this issue, see Alvin Plantinga, "Pluralism: A Defense of Religious Exclusivism," in *The Philosophical Challenge of Religious Diversity*, ed. by Kevin Meeker and Philip Quinn (New York: Oxford University Press, 2000), pp. 172–92; also Philip Quinn, "Toward Thinner Theologies: Hick and Alston on Religious Diversity," in *The Philosophical Challenge of Religious Diversity*, pp. 226–43.

in this case, Christian salvation is the only genuine kind, but God is gracious enough to extend that salvation to honest adherents of other faiths. Inclusivism represents a "middle-of-the-road" approach, where a person believes his particular views are true but includes others under that truth in the grand scheme of things.

Evaluating Underlying Reasons

All this is fine and good, but we don't want to just *list* responses to the fact of pluralism. And as philosophers, we shouldn't stop here with asking questions. We don't just want to formulate possible responses to the fact of religious diversity; we also want to understand and evaluate the underlying motivations and reasons for the positions one can hold concerning the issue. It's pretty clear why religious exclusivism has some appeal – people want to do justice to the truth claims of their religion. But we also want to do justice to the kinds of reason and evidence that exist for people's religious beliefs, and oftentimes those reasons seem similar to each other. The branch of philosophy that examines how beliefs can be justified by reasons is called *epistemology*, and so oftentimes we refer to the apparent equality between different reasons as *epistemic parity*.

For example, it seems that how and where we were raised from childhood has a deep impact on our beliefs and upon what reasons are available to us for why we believe. The *South Park* boys learned this early on in their adventures with Starvin' Marvin, and we have a lot of fun watching them interact with people of different cultures and religions throughout the series. If culture and upbringing provide many of the major reasons for holding our religious beliefs, perhaps we should be pluralists about religion because of the epistemic parity among these different belief systems. But as we saw earlier, culture and upbringing can't be the only kinds of reasons; otherwise, anyone would be justified in their beliefs just because they were raised that way. Mr. Mackey's believing that 2 + 2 = 5 (while smoking mar-e-joo-on-e, m'kay?) or Cartman thinking that a certain race of humans is inferior is not justified based on upbringing. And even if one were justified in holding a belief because of culture and upbringing, this certainly does not mean the belief is *true*.

Another place to look for good reasons is by investigating internal, logical kinds of standards. For instance, we might reject a religion because it is incoherent – it makes claims that are self-defeating, or it has some doctrines that clearly contradict other doctrines it maintains. For example, if one claimed to be a Christian Muslim, then that person would be saying that they believed Jesus was God (Christianity) and a mere human (Islam) *at the same time*, an obvious contradiction that cannot be tolerated by any rational person. Although there are incoherencies and contradictions to be found in the world's religions, people either ignore them, rationalize them through a leap of faith, or use philosophical discussions and distinctions to make the incoherencies and inconsistencies go away. Perhaps most of the world religions do not suffer from such radical inconsistencies, as it would be difficult to imagine their persistence over time if they advocated blatant contradictions.

The final kind of reason we could look for in evaluating world religions and our response to their diversity is *empirical* kinds of evidence. In other words, what can the observations of our senses reveal to us about the diversity of religions and an appropriate response? As mentioned earlier, Hick thinks that we can see parity about the results of religion (selfless, loving, compassionate people) and, thus, that we should judge all religions to be on par with each other. One might wonder if this is truly the case, and it's hard to imagine how a clear empirical test could measure how loving and compassionate all the various adherents of religion are. So perhaps we could also observe the history of a religion and judge whether it involved suspicious developments, or we could even examine the lives of the great prophets of religions, aiming to see whether or not there was consistency and plausibility among their teachings and lifestyles. A further kind of empirical evidence might be testimonial. While it seemingly couldn't *prove* that a religion was true or not, if vast numbers of people testified that a set of religious beliefs and practices was life-changing, compelling, and purpose-giving, or if a significant group claimed a religion failed at these things, we might consider such testimony as a kind of evidence for or against a religion. But are these kinds of measurable evidence the only empirical standards for the truth of religion and for a philosophical response to diversity?

David Blaine Will Now Eat His Own Head

"The Super Best Friends" episode focuses on another kind of empirical evidence: miracles. David Blaine is portrayed as a powerful miracle-worker, magician, or illusionist. Jesus is portrayed as an outdated miracle-worker, whose "tricks" depend far more on the audience's gullibility than on authentic power. It would seem that miracles are mocked throughout the episode and, yet, in the end we see each of The Super Best Friends demonstrating fantastic abilities. And this leads us to consider one of the most important underlying questions about the justification of religious belief: is there a way of understanding and evaluating religion that relates to the apparently central role of *supernatural* elements of religion, or can we only reference things in terms of the *natural* world we are most familiar with?

The philosopher David Hume (1711–1776) famously examined this question with respect to miracles. His argument against believing in miracles runs something like this. A miracle is defined as a violation of a law of nature, which itself has been clearly established by human experience. The only kind of evidence one could give for a miracle is testimonial. But the limited amount and quality of testimonial evidence for supernatural events could never outweigh the overwhelming experience and testimony for natural events (by definition of what is natural), and thus rational belief in a miracle could never be justified.[3]

While this argument focuses on miracles (as does the battle between David Blaine and The Super Best Friends) the underlying issue is natural and supernatural empirical evidence. Since our standards of rationality are largely, if not entirely, based on the common experiences of day-to-day "natural" life, it seems difficult to fit supernatural kinds of experience into our epistemic framework. Even John Hick, for example, frames the discussion of pluralism in what can be experienced in the natural world: the empirically verifiable actions of people. Oftentimes it seems that evaluating underlying reasons

---

[3] See David Hume, *An Enquiry Concerning Human Understanding*, ed. by Tom Beauchamp (Oxford: Oxford University Press, 2006), pp. 83–99; also, *The Natural History of Religion*, ed. by H.E. Root (Stanford: Stanford University Press, 1967).

for religious belief must involve a translation or *reduction* of the supernatural realm into the natural realm of observation. But this might make us wonder why the supernatural elements of religion are needed at all. If, under Hick's scheme, the only thing that matters is a transformation from self-centeredness to divine-reality-centeredness resulting in love and compassion, as opposed to specific religious beliefs, why not get rid of the supernatural divine reality aspect altogether and just focus on loving and compassionate behavior? Why focus on divine incarnation and a virgin birth when the same amount of Christmas Spirit can be promoted by Mr. Hankey, the Christmas Poo? Why is Kyle's Judaism or Stan's Christianity any different from honest, compassionate atheism?

The answer, of course, is that the *content* of their beliefs is different, even if the actions stemming from those beliefs appear to be the same. And this has parallels with both miracles and the issue of pluralism. When a religious person and a non-religious person confront a supposed miracle, we have a common observable event but a difference in explanation – the religious person sees a supernatural cause, while the non-religious person sees a merely yet-to-be-known natural cause. And with pluralism, in many cases we may have similar observable results with respect to the actions and character of people, but different claims about reality serving as the motivating force behind such actions and character. But the question remains: if all religions are practically the same in terms of observable results, how should we deal with their unobservable spiritual claims?

You Gotta Have Faith

The common answer that even David Hume agrees with is *faith*. Seeing an event as a miracle as opposed to a strange natural event depends on faith. What separates religion from science and other domains of empirical justification is that it requires a kind of belief that transcends the standard limits of reason. To some this seems like a copout, a crutch for people who can't deal with life in terms of the natural world. But beyond such condescending remarks there are important philosophical considerations. The standards of reason and our dealings with the natural world are not cold, hard rules and facts.

Life does not always fit into our preconceived notions. And it is entirely possible that the risk-taking, transcendent nature of faith might be required to discover some kinds of truth. William James (1842–1910), an American Pragmatist, argues precisely this in his famous essay "The Will to Believe."[4] Establishing a friendship, for example, requires us to take risks and initiate interactions that don't have clearly predictable results. But certainly we are justified in those risks because of the good that can be achieved and the confirmation of our resulting experiences. Or imagine a situation where you are lost while hiking and you have to choose which way you will proceed to find the way home. Is it rational to just stay put, to avoid making *any* decision because the evidence isn't clear? Shouldn't you make your best educated guess, commit to your plan, and hope for the best?

Parker and Stone mock much of what religious faith is about. But even with episodes including "The Super Best Friends" and "All About Mormons" they wish to maintain the importance of religious belief in people's lives and the separation of cults from genuine religious expressions. While practices of love and compassion can be developed without religious faith, it may be justifiable to develop a transcending faith to honestly deal with the claims of a religion that strike a person as genuinely compelling. It's very possible that when it comes to our sense of the divine, whether we have none, whether it is ingrained from childhood or discovered in a heightened moment of transcendence, faith is a justifiable response in light of the limits of strict rules of logical, empirical reasoning.

The overarching point is that while standards of empirical evidence should be maintained in our search for religious truth, they may not be the only relevant concerns. Judging an event to be a miracle based on testimony and observation is important and desirable. Stan has every right to be suspicious of South Park Jesus telling him to look away while he turns water into wine. But, of course, questions about the miracles of the historical person Jesus cannot be confronted so directly. And for most religiously minded people, beliefs in miracles don't develop in an empirical vacuum. Rather, a whole religious way of life is usually in place, where interactions with God, other people in communities of faith, and life experiences that shape and confirm

---

[4] William James, *The Will to Believe and Other Essays in Popular Philosophy* (New York: Dover Publications, 1956).

233

belief direct the religious person with respect to beliefs about doctrines, historical events, and miracles.

None of this advocates rejecting commonly held rational or empirical standards, but rather presents an enlarged scope within which a person can operate. And within ethical and empirical constraints that are rationally and socially justifiable, it seems that we should advocate not only the societal right, but also the rational right of people to find meaning and purpose in religious ways of life that stand up to those constraints.

The Hope of Finding Supernatural Confirmation

But all of this brings us full circle. If it is possible that God exists, and possible that a prerequisite for experiencing such a supernatural force is faith, then perhaps one is rationally justified in moving past standard empirical evidence in hopes of finding supernatural confirmation. And if this is true for religious belief in general, then why can't a person who feels compelled by the claims and evidence of a particular religion be within their rational rights in believing their religion's exclusive claims? Certainly, tolerance should be advocated, to the extent that anyone who lives by general ethical and social standards in practicing their beliefs should be allowed to do so. But this doesn't imply everyone is equally right anymore than it implies all things should be tolerated. As Mr. Garrison found out in "The Death Camp of Tolerance," there are limits to what can and should be tolerated. And of course, as the camp master says, "Intolerance will not be tolerated." Even religious pluralists must hold that some views about religion are better than others (namely, pluralistic views are better than exclusivist or inclusivist views), and as philosopher Alvin Plantinga has argued, the person who holds their beliefs to be exclusively correct is not necessarily guilty of any moral or epistemic wrongdoings.[5] If we are compelled by evidence, doctrines, and by experiences deemed

---

[5] See Alvin Plantinga, *Warranted Christian Belief* (Oxford: Oxford University Press, 2000).

234

supernatural while being morally and rationally considerate of others, we are within our rights to believe as we will.[6]

"The Super Best Friends" raises important questions about religious diversity and how religious belief relates to evidence. And while the messages of tolerance and careful consideration of religious claims seem clearly defensible, the notion that all religions have truth in them or that supernatural truth pales in comparison to standard empirical evidence is philosophically suspect. It certainly is *one* view of the situation, but holding certain beliefs to be better than others – be they religious beliefs or any other kind – is not only allowable but, in many cases, is really unavoidable. The fact that we are limited in our natural, empirical knowledge concerning religious claims may mean that judgments about such claims also have limitations. But *some* standards of judgment remain, as do the rights of people to believe at their own risk any hypothesis that meets such standards and makes sense of the human experience. It is good to beware of the Blainetologists in our world, but we should also be careful about surrendering justifiable ways of life that may define us as the people we really are.

[6] Besides Alvin Plantinga, other thinkers have advocated this position. See, for example, Robert Merrihew Adams, *The Virtue of Faith and Other Essays in Philosophical Theology* (Oxford: Oxford University Press, 1987).

21

AESTHETIC VALUE, ETHOS, AND PHIL COLLINS

The Power of Music in *South Park*

Per F. Broman

> Now, if they say we accept philosophy since it gives discretion to human life and restrains the spiritual passions, by much more do we accept music because it enjoins us not too violently, but with a certain enchanting persuasiveness prevails over the same effects as does philosophy.
>
> Sextus Empiricus[1]

Maybe I Can Put It Best in the Words of a Timeless Song

In the episode "Kenny Dies" Cartman gives a passionate and sentimental speech to the House of Representatives as he argues for the legalization of stem-cell research in order to save his dying friend, Kenny. Unable to get the lawmakers' full attention, Cartman begins to sing Asia's "Heat of the Moment." It turns into a sing-along with tight clapping fill-ins from the audience, as, surprisingly enough, every member of Congress knows this rather rhythmically complicated song. The shared musical experience makes the legislation move along, despite the fact that the love lyrics have nothing to do with the issue. So, from this example, it would seem that music itself has greater

---

[1] Sextus Empiricus, *Against the Musicians*, trans. by Denise Davidson Greaves (Lincoln: University of Nebraska Press, 1986), p. 129. Hereafter noted as (Sextus, p. "x") in the text.

value than the lyrics according to *South Park* aesthetics. This should not surprise us since effective music doesn't necessarily need words. Think of the commanding opening of Beethoven's "Fifth Symphony," the tear-jerking melody of *Love Story*, or the repetitive power-chord progression found throughout Deep Purple's "Smoke on the Water."

Music has abilities to influence people's thoughts and emotions, a topic discussed from the outset of Western philosophy. Philosophers, rulers, and parents have known this and tried – often in vain – to control and censor music. People have critiqued the structure of music as if music had a content that could easily be tweaked. The following account from Sextus Empiricus' (ca. 3 CE) *Against the Musicians* recounts the power of music in poetic words: "Pythagoras (582–507 BCE), when he once observed how lads who had been filled with Bacchic frenzy by alcoholic drink differed not at all from madmen, exhorted the aulete who was joining them in the carousal to play his aulos for them in the spondaic melos. When he thus did what was ordered, they suddenly changed and were given discretion as if they had been sober even at the beginning" (Sextus, p. 131). The Greek term *melos* (meaning "song"), in combination with *spondaic*, denotes a solemn piece dominated by long note values. The aulos was the ancient double piped reed instrument often used as a Dionysian instrument of exaltation. It could perhaps be considered the distorted electric guitar of ancient Greece. It was a controversial instrument and some commentators, including Plato (ca. 427–347 BCE), argued that it should be banned.

In his *Republic*, Plato echoes the lesson of this Pythagoras story, as he describes which of the seven *Harmoniai* – a term somewhat corresponding to today's "modes," or scales, though the Greek modes differed from contemporary modal scales – were appropriate for performing music.[2] The Ionian and the Lydian modes were "utterly unbecoming" as they are "relaxed" and "soft or drinking harmonies." Such modes had to be avoided, even "banished," according to Plato. The acceptable *Harmoniai* were the Dorian and Phrygian, both useful for military activities in defense of the republic. Plato seems to indicate

---

[2] For Plato's discussion of the tonal modes, see *Republic*, trans. by G.M.A. Grube (Indianapolis: Hackett Publishing, 1992), Books 2 and 7. Hereafter cited as (*Republic*, Book "x") in the text. For historical discussions of the various tonal modes of music, see Cristle Collins Judd (ed.), *Tonal Structures of Early Music* (New York: Garland Publishing, 1998).

that just altering the pitch would completely change the impression of the song. German musicologist Hans Joachim Moser has suggested that today this kind of alteration would be equivalent to changing a minor-mode tango to a major-mode, thus de-eroticizing it.[3]

Although the authenticity of the Pythagoras story is suspect at best (for one thing, Sextus Empiricus lived several hundred years after Pythagoras), the purpose of Empiricus' discussion is to make the power of music problematic so as to argue with the Stoic tradition of philosophy. Plato's characterization of the modes was disputed even during his time, and his account does not provide us with more details about the character of the modes or the musical context, only the well-documented scalar content. But they both make the point that changes to music can alter its entire effect on the listener. For both Plato and Pythagoras, it was music's mathematical properties, the relationship between different pitches, and the correspondence of pitches with the movements of the planets that made an impact on one's soul. This occurred more or less automatically: Aristoxenus' (ca. 3 BCE) objection that "if a man notes down the Phrygian scale, it does not follow that he must know the essence of the Phrygian scale"[4] has less importance for music's impact in Plato or Pythagoras' view. The direct effect of music was subconscious.

Despite their flaws, these accounts are excellent examples of the matters that occupied Greek thinkers, which included music's impact (what is often referred to as *ethos*), its mathematical properties in relation to the universe, and how these two aspects interact with one another. The stories are amazing in their simplicity: music's powers make it a crucial part of society.

Diegesis in *South Park*

My favorite musical? It changes all the time. I'm just a diehard, I'm totally old school, like I'll sit and watch, if they are redoing *Oklahoma* in New York, I will be the first one there.

Trey Parker

---

[3] Hans Joachim Moser, *Musikästhetik* (Berlin: Walter de Gruyter, 1953), p. 151.
[4] See Louis Harap, "Some Hellenic Ideas on Music and Character," *Musical Quarterly* 24 (1938), pp. 153–68.

Music is of immense importance to Trey Parker and Matt Stone. Parker started out at Berklee College of Music in Boston before transferring to the University of Colorado, and Stone is also an accomplished musician. Many of the songs on the show were composed by Parker ("Blame Canada" from *South Park: Bigger, Longer & Uncut*, for example). Both the diegetic (or source music – music for which there is a source of sound in the narrative) and non-diegetic music (the background music that is not perceived by the characters on screen) play a crucial role in the series.

The non-diegetic music is frequently used to set the mood. Examples include (a) the laid-back chord accompaniment of the hyper-ironic moral at the end of many episodes, the "You know, I learned something today," and traditional suspense or love music; and (b) the allusions to existing music, such as the rhythmic pulse from *Jaws* accompanying the man fishing on the lake before getting hit by an elderly driver in a car in the episode "Grey Dawn," or the use of Barber's *Adagio* in "Up the Down Steroid" after Jimmy's violent rampage, harkening to *Platoon*.

Like non-diegetic music, diegetic music also serves as a source of cultural reference. The range of musical allusions is astonishing, including references to the musical *Oklahoma* in *South Park: Bigger, Longer & Uncut*, appearances of rock bands and musicians (including Korn, Ronnie James Dio, Radiohead, Rancid, Ozzy Osbourne, Meat Loaf, Blink 182, Metallica, Britney Spears, Missy Elliot, Alanis Morissette, and The Lords of the Underworld, although some of them never perform), allusions to nineteenth-century Italian opera (as in the Dreidl-Song quintet in "Mr. Hankey's Christmas Classics") and the musical genre, in general, as characters burst into song in many of the series' episodes. The narrating Joseph Smith song from the episode "All About the Mormons," Chef's erotic musical storytelling, and the Canada song alluding to *The Wizard of Oz* (from the episode "It's Christmas in Canada") are just a few examples. There are even musicals within a musical, as in the performance of *Lease* in *Team America: World Police* (though the film as a whole is hardly a musical except for Kim Jong Il's "I'm so lonely") and the Terrance and Philip film in *South Park: Bigger, Longer & Uncut*.

This chapter will focus on diegetic music in *South Park*, how the characters interact with it, as well as which ideas this diegetic music conveys and how its use corresponds to historic Western philosophical

239

accounts. The aim is not to provide a single philosophy of music of *South Park*; it wouldn't be possible, as the series is too eclectic and self-contradictory. But the series raises a number of questions about music that philosophers – particularly Plato – have dealt with again and again.

Musical Spraying

The *Toronto Star* reported that classical music has been used successfully to "clear out undesirables" in Canadian parks, Australian railway stations, and London subway stations. Robberies in the subway went down by 33 percent, assaults on staff by 25 percent, and vandalism of trains and stations by 37 percent. "London authorities now plan to expand the playing of Mozart, Vivaldi, Handel and opera (sung by Pavarotti) from three tube stations to an additional 35."[5] Musicologist Robert Fink argued that music used in this fashion resembles "bug spray." "Bug spray" terminology is what a company named Compound Security uses to describe its own brand of teenager deterrent, a device that emits an annoying mosquito-like sound *clearly* audible to younger people: "Acclaimed by the Police forces of many areas of the United Kingdom, the Mosquito ultrasonic teenage deterrent has been described as 'the most effective tool in our fight against anti-social behaviour.' Shopkeepers around the world have purchased the device to move along unwanted gatherings of teenagers and anti-social youths. Railway companies have placed the device to discourage youths from spraying graffiti on their trains and the walls of stations."[6]

These findings resonate with the Pythagoras story, and several *South Park* episodes draw on the power of music to change people's behavior. In the episode "Die Hippie, Die," when South Park is infested by thousands of hippies holding a music festival, the only way to break up the crowd is by changing the music. "We use the

[5] Scott Timberg, "Halt . . . or I'll play Vivaldi," *Toronto Star*, February 20, 2005, p. C05.
[6] See the company's website: www.compoundsecurity.co.uk/teenage_control_products.html.

power of rock 'n' roll to change the world," announces one hippie. But Cartman's response is to use even more powerful music – Death Metal. After having convinced the town that the hippies are bad, a group of town people builds a machine to drill through the masses of hippies to reach the center stage. Once they reach the core, they play Slayer's "Raining Blood."[7] The hippies disappear quickly, and the town is saved. Strangely enough, the episode begins with a more literal allusion to bug spraying, as Cartman searches through a house, like an exterminator, looking for hippies hidden in the attic and inside the walls.

Another instance of musical spraying occurs in the episode "Two Guys Naked in a Hot Tub." During a wild party, the adults attract the attention of ATF agents, who believe that the party guests are members of a suicide sect. To break up the party, a version of Cher's "Do You Believe in Love" is blasted through gigantic speakers. As one officer puts it: "Nobody can stand this much Cher. This is her new album. If this doesn't drive them out, nothing will." Surprisingly enough, the intoxicated party guests appreciate the music.

South Park shows that music has different effects on different people. The difference between music and noise is not as clear-cut as it might seem. Cher's music is in a mode, or style, for drinking (like Plato's Ionian mode), while Slayer's music is in a mode for war (like Plato's Dorian mode). But in South Park there is no one-to-one mapping of effects. For Plato, music's effect was universal: the Lydian mode, for example, has the same impact on everybody. This is an unfeasible stance today and a position not represented in *South Park*: Cher and Slayer work differently in different contexts and with different audiences.

Music has direct physiological effects as well. In the episode "World Wide Recorder Concert" Cartman discovers the Brown Noise, a sound that causes the bowel to loosen, located "92 cent below the lowest octave of E-flat." On a school-sanctioned trip to perform "My Country 'Tis of Thee," Cartman alters the score to make the note heard. When the entire four-million-child orchestra plays this note,

---

[7] Cartman is not completely correct here: Slayer's music is typically not categorized as Death Metal, but as another somewhat gentler subcategory of Heavy Metal, Thrash Metal.

the consequences are global.[8] Unfortunately, such a low pitch could never be performed on recorders, not even bass recorders. But the story points to a connection between the magic in music and the physics in physiology. There is something believable in the notion of sound waves resonating and interfering with the electrical waves of the autonomous part of the nervous system.

Music to Move Plato's Soul

Plato divides the soul into three parts: (a) the appetitive part, where we can find our most base, irrational emotions and inclinations; (b) the spiritual part, which gives us our vim and vigor, and is supposed to respond to situations where we need to be courageous, moral, or rational; and (c) the rational part, where we find our most complex reasoning capacities, and which is supposed to direct the spiritual part while controlling the appetitive part – much like a charioteer directs and has control over a two-horsed chariot (*Republic*, Book 4). The bug-spray music and the Brown Noise both "resonate with" (pun intended) the appetitive part of Plato's human soul. In these cases, music directly affects the body, in a guttural fashion.

Music also works directly on the spiritual part of the soul. In "Prehistoric Ice Man," the group Ace of Base's hit "All That She Wants" is played for the "Ice Man" Steve, who was frozen in ice for two years and has been placed in a habitat with familiar cultural elements. Like a lullaby soothing a baby, Steve needed the familiar music from his own time, 1996, in order to function. In the episode "The Succubus," Chef has fallen in love with Veronica, a woman who draws him to her by singing "The Morning After," an Academy Award-winning song made famous in the 1972 movie *The Poseidon Adventure*. The boys believe that Veronica is taking Chef away from them, and Mr. Garrison tells them that she is a *succubus*, a female

---

[8]   On the commentary track on the DVD, Stone and Parker claim that there were real attempts to find this frequency to be used in WWII as a weapon. That may or may not be true, but the topic resembles one episode of *Monty Python's Flying Circus*, a series of which Parker and Stone were long-time fans, in a sketch about the world's funniest joke. The joke was so funny that anyone who heard it laughed to death. It, too, was used as a weapon during WWII.

demon that seduces men. They find a definition in an old dictionary: "Succubus: enchants its victim with eerie [*sic*] melody. This is succubus power. Only playing this melody backwards can vanquish the succubus power." During Chef and Veronica's wedding, the boys perform the song backwards, and she reveals her true diabolical self, before being destroyed by the music. Music alone can create a spell, and the only way to break it is to reverse the order of the notes.[9] This seems logical enough; a literal reversal would also reverse the spell.

For Plato, though, it was the third part of the soul, the rational, that was most important. "Then, when any one says that music is to be judged of by pleasure, his doctrine cannot be admitted," Plato argued, "and if there be any music of which pleasure is the criterion, such music is not to be sought out or deemed to have any real excellence, but only that other kind of music which is an imitation of the good."[10] To make judgments of what is good, we need to consider aesthetic value rationally.

Some music is simply bad, by any account. Plato believed that there must be a way of separating good music from bad through consideration of the consistency of individual parts of a musical performance.

> The poets are artists very inferior in character to the Muses themselves, who would never fall into the monstrous error of assigning to the words of men the gestures and songs of women; nor after combining the melodies with the gestures of freemen would they add on the rhythms of slaves and men of the baser sort; nor, beginning with the rhythms and gestures of freemen, would they assign to them a melody or words which are of an opposite character; nor would they mix up the voices and sounds of animals and of men and instruments, and every other sort of noise, as if they were all one. (*Laws*, Book 2)

In *Symposium* he adds, "you cannot harmonize that which disagrees."[11] Although we cannot say what good music sounded like in

---

[9] The technique, referred to as retrograde, was considered the most esoteric of the contrapuntal techniques during the medieval period, as the original melody becomes completely incomprehensible. See, for example, Virginia Newes, "Writing, Reading, and Memorizing: The Transmission and Resolution of Retrograde Canons from the 14th and 15th Centuries," *Early Music* 18 (1990), pp. 218–32.

[10] See Plato, *The Laws of Plato*, trans. by Thomas Pangle (Chicago: University of Chicago Press, 1988), Book 2. Hereafter cited as (*Laws*, Book "x") in the text.

[11] Plato, *Symposium*, trans. by Christopher Gill (New York: Penguin, 2003), Part 1.

Plato's time, his argument makes lots of sense today. Although we may not be able to pinpoint the problem with a particular piece of music exactly, we all have a strong feeling when something is not right.

In their 1997 project titled "The People's Choice Music," Soldier and Komar & Melamid demonstrated what a flawed musical work would sound like. They placed a poll on the Internet where some 500 visitors responded to questions regarding musical genres, instruments, and structures. They used the survey results to write music and lyrics for the "Most Wanted" and "Most Unwanted" songs. The "Most Unwanted Music" is a 25-minute composition that alternates between a number of moods, styles, and dynamics: an opera soprano raps and children sing commercial jingles out of tune.[12] Few, if any, listeners will find anything to appreciate in this music. The problem is its blend of incompatible elements, just as Plato described. The instruments are also important, as the work features the least popular instruments based on the poll result: accordion and bagpipe. Indeed, it's easier to make bad music than good.

There are no such horrendous pieces performed in *South Park*, but still the dichotomy between bad and good music is expressed clearly. In *South Park*, good music serves the same functions it did for the ancient Greeks: it educates, boosts morals, and sometimes is used to indoctrinate the people – add to this that good music must be authentic. The series takes strong stands against several artists who seem to have no redeeming qualities. Bad music has no value in *South Park*. Good music has to be coherent and has to follow certain aesthetic criteria set by the *Art World*.[13]

As for the Greeks, music is part of education; but music is always a chore in the officially sanctioned educational system, South Park Elementary School. Consider the school orchestra during the Fourth of July celebration in the episode "Summer Sucks." The assignment is forced upon the students and is not artistically rewarding. On the other hand, music is creative and joyous outside of schoolwork, and is greatly beneficial to the children. The true spirit of music does

[12] See the Dia Art Foundation, www.diacenter.org/km/musiccd.html.
[13] The Art World is a term developed by George Dickie; it denotes the network of artists and audience that create the framework for what is art. George Dickie, *Art and the Aesthetic: An Institutional Analysis* (Ithaca: NY: Cornell University Press, 1974), and *Art Circle: A Theory of Art* (Chicago: Spectrum Press, 1997).

not come through scholarly activities. A true artist works for him or herself, and true artistry cannot be taught. Consequently, a true artist is considered a genius, a persistent notion in aesthetics since the Romantic era. A garage band, such as "Timmy and the Lords of the Underworld," is superior to a school-sanctioned recorder orchestra (even one consisting of four million players).

Phil Collins and Aesthetic Value

South Park features many instances of strong reactions against musical performances. In the episode "Mr. Hankey, the Christmas Poo," during the big controversy over the display of religion in the school holiday celebration, the compromise that is supposed to appease those who want a non-sectarian holiday show is Philip Glass's performance during "the happy non-offensive, non-denominational Christmas play." His minimalist composition "Happy, happy, happy, everybody happy" upsets the audience, however. As a stark contrast, Barbara Streisand's piercing voice makes the boys cover their ears in the episode "Mecha-Streisand." She even uses her voice in the torture chamber to make the boys reveal the location of the Triangle of Zinthar. During the Lalapalalapaza 2000 festival, the children can only appreciate Phil Collins in concert after taking Ritalin. As Kyle says with a blank expression, "His flowing melodies are really enjoyable to us."

It is clear why low-keyed repetitive music – like that of Glass – is problematic for a Christmas celebration and that loud piercing singing is unbearable (with an effect similar to the Mosquito ultrasonic teenage deterrent). But what's wrong with Phil Collins (except for the fact that he won the Academy Award in 2000 for best song instead of "Blame Canada" and is holding on to his Oscar statuette in the show)? Answer: he lacks authenticity and integrity, and fails to inspire artistic devotion. His low-keyed music does not ignite the boys, and he appears unfocused on stage.

Phil Collins would not have been a particularly big problem for Plato, who was not concerned with detailed discussions about real music making, only philosophical and mathematical considerations, departing from music's all-encompassing properties. Music is much more than just the notes; it involves interactions with other art forms. In fact, the Greek word for music, *mousiké*, included more elements than just the pitches and metric organization; it was the art of the Muses, the nine daughters of the titan Mnemosyne.[14] In *South Park* too, music should be more than notes. It should relate to society, and a musician should express an artistic persona.

Having taken Ritalout, the anti-Ritalin prepared by Chef, the kids realize, to their horror, that they have become Phil Collins fans and boo him off the stage. Their intellects have started to work again. They notice now that he sings out of tune, and that it is not cool for a nine-year-old to like Phil Collins. In the hopelessly collectivistic South Park, there is not much room for revolting against peers. As one Goth kid expressed it in a later episode: "To be a non-conformist, you have to dress in black, and listen to the same music we do." Their notion of what is good and bad resembles Plato's rather harsh and uncompromising judgments of some of the *Harmonai* and of the Aulos instrument. But there is something else, namely, a general aversion against low-keyed expressionless music as defying the very foundation of rock 'n' roll aesthetics and life itself. Kyle's description of Collins' melodies as "flowing" is crucial here. An active, focused intellect is necessary for appreciating music. Mr. Mackey was right, "Drugs are bad, m'kay," and here Plato agrees: "Thus far I too should agree with the many, that the excellence of music is to be measured by pleasure. But the pleasure must not be that of chance persons; the fairest music is that which delights the best and best educated, and especially that which delights the one man who is preeminent in virtue and education" (*Laws*, Book 2). Although an elitist statement, it highlights the fact that passive enjoyment of music, with or without drugs, is problematic. This may appear as a contradiction. On the one hand music functions subconsciously, but on the other it needs to be appreciated with the intellect. There is no either/or, however. For both Plato and *South Park*, music works on a subconscious level as well as on an intellectual one.

---

[14] Cleo protects the stories of heroes, Urania astronomy, Calliope elegies, Melpomene the tragedies, Euterpe flute playing, Erato love poems, Tepsicore choir lyrics, Thalia the comedies, and Polyhymnia dance and music. Music was like a servant or medium for the greater good.

Remember the episode "Fat Butt and Pancake Head" in which Cartman, without any effort, writes taco-themed songs for his hand puppet Jennifer Lopez? Although he claims that the "style of music is so easy; it doesn't require any thought at all," his intellect has grasped the technicalities of this kind of artistic creation, and his skills even impressed the real Jennifer Lopez's record company. Cartman displays similar skills but with a more scornful twist when he starts a Christian rock group, "Faith + 1," with Token and Butters to win a bet against Kyle. He takes an existing love song, "I need you in my life, baby," changes "baby" to "Jesus" and voilà – he has created a hit song. It is, of course, a cynical approach so typical of Cartman, as he acknowledges after being told that he doesn't know anything about Christianity: "I know enough to exploit it." The songs of this Myrrh record-winning group (the Christian Rock equivalent of Platinum) make a deep impact on the audience. But putting new words to old songs to make money is an absolute no-no for an authentic musician.[15] And if any genre should be based on authenticity and sincerity, it would be rock with "Christian" as the prefix. The downfall of the band is rapid and hard, when the audience realizes the insincerity.

Schopenhauer and Death

At the very end of *The Republic*, Plato recounts the legend of Er, a soldier killed in battle who returned to life telling about the hereafter. The story he tells is one of reckoning, punishment, and accountability for the actions taken in life. But there is also an absolutely stunning description of how music relates to the workings of the universe. At the universe's very center is a spindle turned on the knees of Necessity. The eight Sirens, one for each known body of the solar system, are "hymning" a single tone and forming one harmony at equal intervals. The three daughters of Necessity accompany the harmony. Needless

---

[15] As popular-music scholar Simon Frith argued: "Rock, in contrast to pop, carries intimations of sincerity, authenticity, art – noncommercial concerns. These intimations have been muffled since rock became the record industry, but it is the possibilities, the promises, that matter." Simon Frith, *Sound Effects – Youth, Leisure and the Politics of Rock 'n' Roll* (Suffolk: St. Edmundsbury Press, 1983), p. 11.

to say, it's impossible to figure how this would sound, but the combination of the circular motion of the rotating spindle and the single chord gives a supernatural sense of a slow, never-ending repetitive music (Philip Glass's music comes to my mind).

The episode "Death" provides a musical image of dying. Stan's grandpa wants the boys to assist him in euthanasia, and so he illustrates how it is to grow too old by bringing Stan into a dark room where he plays an Enya song on the CD player. Stan is appalled: "It's cheesy, but lame and eerily soothing at the same time." Like Philip Glass's music, the emotionless music proves quite upsetting after a while. It's so terrible that Stan agrees to assist Grandpa. Enya, of course, is far from the depictions of Hell in later episodes. The music is a representation of despair prior to death or, in Plato's words, a *mimesis* of dying. The story also brings to mind the pessimistic philosopher Arthur Schopenhauer's (1788–1860) central concept, *Will*.

For Schopenhauer, Will is the dominating force in humans, and in the universe, above intellect. By itself, Will is neither good nor bad, but its representation to us in reality is destructive, as it is the central source of suffering in the form of desire and will to life. Satisfied desires are meaningless, leaving us bored and leading only to other desires. Schopenhauer described this perpetual striving quite strikingly as "constantly lying on the revolving wheel of Ixion, is always drawing water in the sieve of the Danaids, and is the eternally thirsting Tantalus."[16] The Greek mythical references are not coincidences, as Schopenhauer was strongly influenced by Plato. But for Plato, music was just another imitative art, an imitation of the World of Senses, which in turn was an imitation of the World of Ideas: "The imitative art is an inferior who marries an inferior, and has inferior offspring" (*Republic*, Book X).

Schopenhauer, however, had a completely different conception of music, and maintained that there were striking differences between the arts. "Music answers [the question, 'What is life?'] more profoundly indeed than do all the other [art forms], since in a language intelligible with absolute directness, yet not capable of translation into that of our faculty of reason, it expresses the innermost nature

---

[16] Arthur Schopenhauer, *The World as Will and Representation*, trans. by E.F.J. Payne (New York: Dover, 1966), Vol. I, p. 196. Hereafter noted as (*Will* Vol., p. "x") in the text.

of all life and existence" (*Will* II, p. 406). Schopenhauer saw two distinct categories of art: music on one side and every other art form on the other. Music is distinctive since it does not copy anything from the world of appearances, an opinion in complete disagreement with Plato. In fact, music is a copy of Will itself. Schopenhauer meant that music was the key to suspending Will for a moment through an aesthetic respite from everyday pain. But this is, of course, not what Enya is doing. Enya is aggravating the existential anxiety. Music is not a therapy against anxiety. In accordance with Schopenhauer's pessimism, Enya provided a suspension of the will to live and could communicate this to Stan in a most direct way.

The Only Way It Works Is Through Music

The discussions of musical forms, instruments, and structures in philosophical writings often appear bound by time, as can be witnessed in the description of the ancient modes. The time-bounded discussion of music is true for *South Park* as well, a series that is famous for producing episodes dealing with issues from a very recent past, some of which may appear quite dated in a not-too-distant future. Strangely enough, Pythagoras, the Enya episode, and Cartman's encounter with the House of Representatives are very similar, despite their differences in musical context and ethos. Enya and Asia may not survive history's merciless aesthetic filter, just as the Aulos vanished long ago. But where the underlying philosophy is concerned, the issues are timeless. Neither Grandpa, nor Cartman, nor Pythagoras was able to communicate his vision verbally; interestingly enough, the only way it worked was through music.

22

SATAN LORD OF DARKNESS IN *SOUTH PARK* COSMOLOGY

Dale Jacquette

But who prays for Satan? Who, in eighteen centuries, has had the common humanity to pray for the one sinner that needed it most?

> Mark Twain, *Autobiography*

Get me behind thee, Satan, m'kay?

> Mr. Mackey, *Uncollected Future Possible Philosophical Remarks*

Evil Incartoonate

Satan, the scarlet Lord of Darkness with the remarkably over-developed upper torso and skull codpiece, plays a diabolical role in *South Park* episodes. He welcomes Kenny to hell after some of the luckless lad's more spectacular fatalities. He is depicted as Saddam Hussein's manipulative prison bitch in the underworld. He plots havoc for those of us living above the cartoon inferno. He even composes his own twisted Christmas carol that he moonfully sings to celebrate the holidays down below.

What is intriguing about *South Park* cosmology is in part its simultaneous reflection of the beliefs, doubts, aspirations, hopes, and fears of the resolute imaginary Colorado third-graders – Stan, Kyle, (Eric)

Cartman, and Kenny – as they cope with the problems of growing up absurd in contemporary America against a background of bizarre incidents and bewildering adult expectations. Satan features prominently in this worldview as a chief cause of mayhem and as Hades' master of demonic ceremonies. There he presides over an astonishing collection of dead celebrities. The damned include Adolf Hitler, as one might expect, but also Mahatma Gandhi, Ho Chi Minh, John F. Kennedy, and Michael Landon (the poor schmuck, how does he wind up down there?), among many others. Satan, himself, in the inferno below the crust of earth on which the town of South Park precipitously perches, is nevertheless a sympathetic figure. He is portrayed in the series as just a regular guy stuck with a shit deal like most of us, who seems to have drawn the wrong straw and has to play his part, ending up as reluctant gatekeeper to the lake of eternal fire.

South Park's Satan wallows comically in reflective moments of self-doubt. After his initial bluster, he usually displays remarkably human qualities in an emotional sensitivity that is hard to reconcile with his day job as torture master in the bottomless abyss. The fun for Parker and Stone seems in part to consist in being able to consign to eternal perdition dead persons that for one reason or another they do not like. In the movie-length feature, *South Park: Bigger, Longer & Uncut*, there are only 1,656 people who make it into heaven when Kenny seeks admittance. The counter registering the number of souls entering hell by comparison spins too quickly to read. Perhaps it reflects a universal third grade mentality that dreads damnation for any slip or misstep in life, while at the same time lacking any clear guidelines as to the rules or what is likely to be judged as misconduct. The uncertainty and shocking hypocrisy of moral injunctions in religion and conventional ethics in the adult world are thereby held up to smirking ridicule, as they no doubt deserve.

The figure of Satan in *South Park* compares favorably with some of the most dramatic depictions in Western literature. Beginning with Genesis and the Book of Job, and proceeding through Dante, John Milton, Goethe, and Flaubert, *South Park*'s Satan stands in stark opposition to prevailing religious assumptions. His vicious but human (all too human) machinations complete the picture of the cosmos seen through the eyes of iconic post-industrial American youngsters.

Sympathy for the Devil

The traditional account of Satan's origin and his place in the world is adopted and interwoven without much modification into the events of the maddening world. Satan is a fallen angel and, as such, a rather big-time screw-up.

Were he not such a colossal doofus, created by God as an intermediary between the human and divine, Satan would still be an angel living in heaven and sharing in the glory reflected from God's shining countenance. Whatever Satan did wrong, leading a mutiny of rebellious angels against God the Father, or opposing God's will in some other unforgivable way, it did not look good on his résumé. Still, he couldn't have performed so badly that, despite being driven from heaven, he was not the natural choice to head up the netherworld's diabolical administration.

The fact that he'd been an angel among the blessed and showed good conduct up to a certain point was possibly taken into account. Or his special talents and management skills were recognized and he was transferred to a branch office despite being demoted. We can scarcely believe that an omniscient and omnipotent God could have been hoodwinked by a mere angel, no matter how clever and powerful, to depart the celestial shores on his own hook and take up residence elsewhere to practice evil without God somehow being complicit in the act. These are questions we must ask ourselves – provided we don't expect any logically satisfying answers. For it is said with a weary sigh by many a catechism instructor when these challenges arise that God "moves in mysterious ways." Satan was not just sent to hell, after all, but reassigned to wreak havoc especially on the lives of third graders who in their own imaginations, at least, are always just tottering at the brink of eternal damnation.

All of which could go on their permanent record to follow them throughout the rest of their miserable lives, as they are sometimes reminded by their mentors at South Park Elementary. The *South Park* creators seem to take hell more seriously than any hazard from outer space, the rainforest, nuclear waste, the PTA, Sexual Harassment Panda, or the do-gooders that threaten to disturb the cruel but natural harmony that prevails throughout the universe. Parker and Stone follow the adventures of the intrepid gang of four together with certain of their associates at school, parents, teachers and townsfolk, as they cope with the deepest mysteries and worst disappointments life has to offer. Satan is no different, in his own way; it's just his bad luck to be Lord of Darkness and have the onetime dictator of Iraq driving him home to Santa Fe in his broiling subterranean love-nest.

Little Boy, You're Going to Hell

A foreshadowing of Kenny's journey to meet Satan is given near the beginning of *South Park: Bigger, Longer & Uncut*. Stan and Kyle hook up with Kenny (and eventually with Cartman) on their way to see the Terrance and Philip movie, *Asses of Fire*. Sweet. A foreign (Canadian) film, Kyle tells his mother in begging permission to attend; and on a Sunday, no less. Kenny's white trash mom screeches at Kenny: "You go ahead and miss church, and then when you die and go to hell you can answer to Satan." Kenny pauses, reflecting on his choices before mumbling through his orange parka hood a barely audible: "Okay."

Off to the movies they all go (sing along), where they learn everything that they know. And they do indeed learn some interesting new modes of verbal expression. On the sidewalk, after the show, practicing their new obscenities and inspired by Terrance and Philip's incendiary example, a scientific dispute arises concerning the possibility of setting one's farts ablaze. Cartman denies that it can be done. Kenny, apparently on empirical grounds, insists that it can, and volunteers to demonstrate. Of course, we know in advance where this is going to go. Like Terrance (or is it Philip?) in the movie they have just seen, Kenny goes up like a marshmallow held too long over the campfire, while Cartman tries frantically to beat the flames out with a stick. An ambulance arrives almost immediately, bringing the hope of the sort of speedy rescue on which all of us in a civilized but potentially hazardous society depend. The accident and chance that also govern human affairs, together with the cartoonists' cynical humor, nevertheless quickly reassert themselves, when the ambulance is knocked out of the way by a salt truck that promptly dumps its load, completely burying the flaming torch to which Kenny has been reduced. Next, in the emergency ward, Kenny receives (almost) the best care modern emergency medicine can provide. As often happens in South

Park, however, there is an unfortunate discrepancy between promise and delivery. Kenny rises to consciousness from the surgical anesthetic surrounded by green and white masked doctors and nurses just in time to hear some bad news. His heart, previously jump-started in a microwave oven, has been mistakenly replaced by a baked potato, and he has only seven seconds to live.

He rockets then through a jazzy-looking cosmos of colored spiraling nebulas to heaven's gate, surrounded by gigantic naked voluptuous and enticing cartoon women. He approaches and touches the entrance panel at an evidently exclusive address. The panel flashes ACCESS DENIED! for the happy-go-lucky but incurably underprivileged lad, and he plunges into a fiery demonic hell. There are creatures of flame, decomposing human harpies, guest appearances by Gandhi, Hitler, and George Burns complete with cigar, all swimming about like eels through the sulfurous depths, and finally Satan himself delivering medieval punishments in the molten inferno. Their best friend not only toasted to a crisp but lying dead with a spud and sour cream in his exploded chest cavity, Cartman expresses his concern: "Oh shit, dude. Now our parents are gonna find out we went to the Terrance and Philip movie again!" Kenny is exterminated for the umpteenth time (you bastards!) and, true to form, Kyle's mom's piercing accusation is merely: "You've seen that movie again!"[1]

Down in hell, Satan addresses Kenny on a lakeshore of fire. "Fallen one," he tells the doomed boy, "I am Satan. I am your god now. There is no escape. Now feel the delightful pain." He's got Kenny stretched out over a flaming brazier, and he's ratcheting down a skull-topped lever that seems to be making things incrementally more agonizing. Kenny's already been pinched and pulled apart and had his face caught in a tug-of-war with the fiery creatures he first encounters when he is cast down.

Enter, to everyone's surprise at this precise moment, the then President of Iraq: "Meet Saddam Hussein, my new partner in evil." Saddam grabs the lever away and starts lowering it with all his might.

---

[1] Why the exclamation, "You bastards!"? I know of no authoritative explanation, so here are some conjectures. Who is being blamed when Kenny buys the farm in those episodes in which he is killed? It could be the gods, or the cartoonists. Or it could be the audience, we ourselves, for enjoying the spectacle and encouraging its repetition in each new installment.

Makes his nipples hard, he says, sounding like he has just taken a couple of hits from a helium balloon. Kenny is now at his mercy. "Move over, Satan," he demands, "you're hoggin all the fun!" Satan is exasperated. "Saddam," he replies, "would you let me do my job, please?" But Saddam can't help himself. He wants power in any form and under any circumstances it may be available, and Satan as an irritated lover resorts to a familiar tactic. "Saddam," he begins, "could I talk to you over here for a second?" They stand out of Kenny's earshot. "I don't see why you have to belittle me in front of people like that." Satan is naturally concerned about sustaining his reputation. "Sometimes I don't think you have any respect for me." Saddam, for his part, assumes he can sweet-talk his way out of anything with the promise of sex, but Satan is reading in bed: *Saddam is From Mars; Satan is from Venus.* "Who's my creampuff?" Saddam asks his bud. And Satan wistfully concedes: "I am."

After the United States, led by Kyle's crusading mom, declares war on Canada for Terrance and Philip teaching all their kids some highly inventive vulgarities (and for bombing the American movie industry clan, the Baldwins), the execution of the two Canadian entertainers is announced. Satan realizes that his time to rule the earth has arrived. "It has come to be," he tells his dictator pillow-mate. "The four horsemen are drawing nigh. The time of prophecy is upon us." Saddam, unimpressed, just wants to "get busy" in bed. "No, I'm being serious," Satan continues. "It is the seventh sign. The fall of an empire, the coming of a comet," and now the shedding of innocent blood as Terrance and Philip are sentenced to death for abusing free speech. "Do you always think about sex?" Satan demands. "I'm talking about very important stuff here." He continues: "Is sex the only thing that matters to you?" "I love you," Saddam counters. "I want to believe that." "So what do you say we shut off the light and get close?" The screen goes black. "Uhhh . . ." "Yeah," we hear Saddam say, "you like *that*, don't you, bitch?"

Respect My Authorita!

Satan chortles: "Soon Saddam and I will rule the world! Har har har har har!" Saddam returns from shopping with suitcases for the trip up to earth. "Let's fuck to celebrate!" he proposes. "Do you remember when you first got here?" Satan asks in reply, disillusioned. "We used to talk all night long until the sun came up. We would just sit in bed and talk." And Saddam in his squeaky voice replies: "Well, yeah, cause I was still waiting to get you in bed, dummy!" Satan, wounded, wants to know: "How come you always want to make love to me from behind? Is it because you want to pretend I'm somebody else?" To which Saddam answers, reasonably enough: "Satan, your ass is gigantic and red. Who am I gonna pretend you are, Liza Minnelli?" Satan is in no mood, and withdraws to mope about his hopelessly one-sided relationship. "Oh, don't get all pissy!" Saddam challenges.

Satan now sings his theme song, "Up There." He pours out his soul, crooning like Lohengrin on a craggy mountaintop in this cartoon operetta. All he longs for is a normal life in the sun and some genuine human affection. "I want to live above!" he pleads. Instead, of course, he is eternally damned. He waxes philosophical when he asks the musical question: "But what is evil anyway? Is there reason to the rhyme? Without evil there can't be good. So it must be good to be evil sometime." The argument is that without the existence of evil there can be no contrasting good. Many people seem to believe something like this. But is it true? There can be no right without a left, no up without a down. No strong without a weak. So why not no good without evil?

Truth to tell, there are many concepts whose opposites may be possible but never come to exist out there in the world. Everything is identical to itself, for example; nothing fails to exemplify the property of being self-identical. Yet no one complains that nothing could be self-identical unless something were not self-identical. Perhaps all we need is the *concept* of a property's opposite, rather than its *instantiation* or *exemplification* in the real world. Why shouldn't it be the same, then, where goodness and the contrasting concept of evil are concerned?

That evil exists we already know. This fact by itself requires some explaining if there is an all-knowing, all-powerful, and perfectly good creator of the universe. When we speak about the *concept* of good, on the other hand, it's not immediately clear why there must actually be some evil in order for good also to obtain. Anyway, why should there be so much evil? Why wouldn't it be sufficient for just a little evil to exist for the sake of whatever complementary good might be found? Why should there be a fallen angel like Satan presiding over a dungeon of fire and tongs? And why, for that matter, if God is so powerful and so smart, does he choose to create human beings with combustible flatulence?

Finally, what are we to think of the qualification that it must be good (for the sake of good) to be evil sometime? If it is good to be evil, isn't evil simply good? Presumably not, for then there could be no distinction between good and evil. It is evil, generally speaking, to be evil; but it's good to be so at least sometime or in some measure for the sake of the existence of good. Questionable assumptions, to say the least. That there is some good in some evil only suggests that the evil in question is impure. Can pure evil ever be good? Then, of course, it wouldn't be pure. It appears as a consequence that what good requires is not the existence of pure evil. In vouchsafing the existence of good, evil itself partakes to a certain extent in the good, which disqualifies it automatically as pure. What seems instead to be presupposed by the existence of a greater good is for there to be a lesser good, and this might generally be enough to guarantee the logical-conceptual contrast whereby good, real good or *the* good, the GOOD in capital letters, can also exist. Such a condition nevertheless rules out evil, or at least pure evil. It seems that if Satan's argument is to hold any brimstone, it can only do so by acknowledging at most the existence of various degrees and shades of good.

Conceptually, we require only the tiniest amount of less good in the world in order for a greater good universally to prevail. While Satan with all his self-doubt and longing for love is a sympathetic character in *South Park* cosmology, he is not an especially competent logician or philosopher. More importantly, *South Park*'s Satan himself is not *purely* evil. We see this at the movie's end when he relents in his monstrous bid to rule on earth and casts Saddam back into the fiery pit where he gets impaled on a giant stalagmite (not so severely, however, as to miss taking part in the movie's musical grand finale). "That's it!" Satan declares, Saddam having finally crossed the last line. "I've had enough of you!"

Satan's Soft Spot and *South Park*'s Saint Michael

Satan, on the other hand, develops a soft spot for Kenny. At one point, when Satan thinks he's alone and breaks from his spell of weeping over Saddam's relentlessly selfish love, Kenny sneaks up. "Oh!" Satan is surprised, momentarily off-balance. He amps up his demonic laugh: "Ha ha ha har! Soon the world will belong to me!" Kenny is not fooled. To his muted question about what is bothering him, Satan answers: "It's Saddam. He doesn't nurture my emotions. He just wants sex and he can't learn to communicate." Kenny again mumbles something barely audible that sounds like "Why don't you leave him?" spoken through a shirtsleeve into a cocked elbow. "You're right," Satan acknowledges. "I should leave him. I'm just going to tell Saddam: I'm going to earth to rule alone. I'm strong, and I don't need him."

"Must be strong. Must be strong." He stokes his courage. He confronts the Iraqi: "Saddam, I need to talk to you." There follows a well-rehearsed breakup speech. "Saddam, sometimes you can love a person very much but still know that they're not right for you." Saddam, predictably, answers: "What the *fuck* are you talking about?" "You treat me like shit, Saddam. I'm leaving. I'm going up to earth to rule *alone*!" This pushes Saddam's button. Satan – and how could he otherwise be Satan? – fastens on to the one pleasure Saddam cannot stand to be deprived. He wants to go back to earth to perpetrate misdeeds. Like Satan, he also wants to return "up there," to create even more terror and suffering than Satan himself. The point in portraying Satan as a sensitive new-age kind of Lucifer is to show just how evil the cartoonists think Saddam is in contrast. Satan is a pussycat compared to Saddam, who inflicts wickedness wherever he sets foot. For Satan, this is just a job for which he has only minimal natural enthusiasm and has to muster up an occasional depraved laugh. Saddam launches into an astonishing song and belly dance. He acknowledges his wrongdoing, but claims that he can change his life in order to win his way back into Satan's good graces and avoid being cut from the field trip to the earth's surface. Even now Satan would like to believe Saddam as capable of repentance and reform, but he wonders introspectively to himself concerning his eternally damned Mesopotamian heinie-pirate, as we must also wonder philosophically: "What if you remain a sandy little butt-hole?"

"Saddam," Satan reminds him, "I'm the dark ruler, not you." When he has finally had enough and flings Saddam back to hell, he is grateful to Kenny. "I have you to thank, little one," he tells the miniature *South Park* hero. "Just make any wish and I shall grant it." What Kenny wishes is that everything could go back to the way things were before he went to hell. He is asked if he understands that this means he will still be dead, and he nods and makes that little noise that passes for speech emitted through several layers of clothing surrounding his virtually hidden face. What remains unclear is why if Kenny can have anything he wants he doesn't ask for the world to be restored to the point *before* he lights the fart. If he's gained any wisdom about the ill-advised sphincter pyrotechnics in the meantime, then, setting back the clock, he wouldn't even have to go to the hospital.

Manicheanism is the theological worldview that there exists a tenuous balance between good and evil forces in the universe personified by God and Satan. The two powers are locked in a temporal struggle for the souls of human beings. On Judgment Day, the armies of Satan, consisting in part of his minions brought down from heaven with him from the time of his revolt against the Creator, but mostly recruited from the earth through temptation and the damnation without salvation that are the wages of sin, are prophesied to do battle with God's good angels, led by Saint Michael. This superhero angel-saint is favored especially in the Baroque religious art of the Austrian, Southern German, and French Church Militant. Michael comes down to earth to destroy Satan with a flaming sword following a spectacular battle scene. As described in Catholic lore, it is not unlike the combat in which Kenny saves Satan through kindness and understanding, and thereby prevents Satan's evil from succeeding. In this regard, Kenny is *South Park*'s Saint Michael. With a flaming anus more potent than Michael's flaming sword, he defeats Satan's wicked hold over the earth with two introverted passive-aggressive weapons that no medieval monk or canvas tent revivalist could ever have foreseen: a little irreverent humor and a little sincere sympathy.

Despite going back to his death, Kenny may have chosen most fortunately. For he is propelled through outer space once again to heaven's door, and this time as the South Park Saint Michael he is welcomed in by eager boobs and other carnal delights of the rapturous strumpets that apparently await only the very selectively chosen few. "I guess I'm destined to live in hell alone," Satan reflects sorrowfully. At the last moment, strange to say, he is joined by Mr. Hat. This, I think, is possibly a little too peculiar, even for *South Park*. First, what will Mr. Garrison do without his alter ego? During the battle between Americans, Canadians, and the forces of evil from the underworld, we hear Garrison cry aloud as the hand-puppet is tossed out of the foxhole: "Mr. Hat, nooooo . . . !" We must also ask, if there is to be any metaphysical integrity to the storyline, how does Satan get to carry Mr. Hat down to hell if *everything* as Kenny wishes is to be restored to its state *prior* to the fatal ignition of his alimentary propulsion? Can there be two or more Mr. Hats existing in parallel universes? What will happen if they meet?

It's Aboot Not Censoring Our Art!

Parker and Stone have much of Mark Twain in their humor. When they nail something, they truly nail it *down*. They want above all to use the forum of their animated adventures to engage in provocative dialogue about politics, religion, sex, violence, death, the meaning of life, and other controversies of growing up in America. The illustrated stories they tell stand as a refreshing challenge to conventional standards of propriety, civility, and good taste. The Canadian ambassador who complains as the US and Canada come to war seems to speak directly for the cartoonists when he declares in the lovable Scotch-derived accent that is ridiculed throughout the movie: "It's *aboot* not censoring our art!"

Whether Terrance and Philip are in any sense *art* is perhaps the crux of the matter.[2] What is clear, even beyond dispute, I would say, is that we need artists like Parker and Stone to push the envelope and repeatedly test the limits of public discourse. It's often juvenile, and the humor doesn't always work. But they have a reasonable built-in defense: what do you expect from a pack of confused soul-searching third graders who are only imitating the adult behavior around them? Against a backdrop that mixes dizzy bathroom humor with frontal politics and brazen irreverence, they make worthwhile points about the hypocrisy of contemporary society and its effects on children, where they may be most deeply felt and readily diagnosed.

---

[2] That Terrance and Philip are (more) crudely drafted and "the animation is all crappy" is beside the point. Parker and Stone have explained their creation of the scatalogical Canadian comedy duo as a response to criticisms of the regular *South Park* cast and episodes as badly drawn with nothing but fart jokes. Their reaction was to say, in effect: we'll show you really badly drawn characters spewing nothing but fart jokes – and thus were Terrance and Philip born.

Near the end of the movie, Terrance and Philip are about to be executed. Cartman's implanted electronic chip that is supposed to prevent him from using profanities by giving him a painful shock has been turned into a potent weapon. He discovers its capabilities quite by accident, and then deliberately curses in order to short-circuit the electric chair into which the pair have been strapped. He is at once empowered by the very same technological controls to which he had previously been subjected. Kyle's mom calls for a military firing squad, and the South Park gang counters by coming forward to block the bullets or shame the soldiers into holding fire. Kyle now confronts his activist mother, who with zero answerability has started a bloody war between two of the world's most cordial neighbors, and, as the firing squad breaks up, discharges two pistol rounds into Terrance and Philip's foreheads. "I don't want a fighter," Kyle whines at this predictable denouement. "I want my mom." Weak, I know. But Parker and Stone indulge in this sappy kind of moralizing near the end of almost all the *South Park* episodes.

"Stand down, children," the gruff Patton-like helmeted general orders the assembled members of the youthful La Resistance. "You can still see fart jokes on Nickelodeon." The principle, as the gang immediately reply, has nothing in particular to do with this or that style of entertainment, but with the importance of not tolerating government interference in artistic production of any kind. Thus, we have throughout the *South Park* series, and even more poignantly in the movie, a contrast between a little vulgar but otherwise harmless foul language on the one hand, and the worst acts of bloody violence perpetrated in the name of unexamined values.

Don't Take the Devil Seriously

No religion is exempt from *South Park* mockery, but Christianity for obvious cultural reasons comes in for especially frequent derision. There is not a lot of humor in Christianity. Jesus weeps exactly once in the Gospels (John 11:35), but nowhere does he laugh or even give up a chuckle. Is this credible? Whether Christ was in fact the Son of God in the sense intended by the doctrine of the Trinity, or just a mortal misunderstood spiritual reformer and insurgent against the

Roman occupation of Judea, I imagine him enjoying an innocent and maybe even occasional belly-busting earthy joke. If we thought that Satan was real and we wanted to defeat him, what better method could we use than a little dismissive good-hearted laughter and ridicule? Does the Devil not need us to take him seriously in order to accomplish his dirty work? Why not then join *South Park*'s creators in depriving him of the malicious pleasure?[3]

---

[3] Here are titles for additional sections I'd like to add to an expanded version of this chapter, based on some of my favorite quotations from the movie: *Fucking Windows '98!*, *Die, Canadians, M'Kay?*, *Dude, What is Wrong With German People?*, *The Clitoris Has Spoken*.

SPECIAL SURPRISE BONUS!

An Interview with Trey Parker and Matt Stone (not really . . . it's made up)

ALL CHARACTERS AND EVENTS IN
THIS INTERVIEW – EVEN THOSE BASED
ON REAL PEOPLE – ARE ENTIRELY
FICTIONAL. ALL CELEBRITY QUOTATIONS
ARE IMPERSONATED . . . POORLY.
THE FOLLOWING INTERVIEW
CONTAINS COARSE LANGUAGE
AND DUE TO ITS CONTENT IT
SHOULD NOT BE READ BY
ANYONE.

I had the chance (not actually) to sit down with the creators of *South Park* and ask them a few questions about the show, the book, and philosophy in general (this is all made-up bullshit). It was stimulating and enlightening (about as stimulating and enlightening as Sexual Harassment Panda Bear's theme song).

Rob Arp (RA): What do you think of the book?

Trey Parker (TP): We love it and, really, it's like a dream come true. Ever since the publication of *The Simpsons and Philosophy* we've been hoping for *South Park and Philosophy*.

Matt Stone (MS): Yeah, we just hope that there won't be a *Family Guy and Philosophy*. That show really sucks ass.

RA: What does philosophy mean to you?

TP: Philosophy has to do with constantly questioning the status quo.

MS: For me, philosophy is all about a bunch of dead Greek guys who, while they were living, went around and talked a lot of bullshit so they could give young boys a sweet beef injection in their dumpers.

TP: Well put.

RA: Do you read any philosophy?

TP and MS (in unison): Are you fucking kidding?

RA: What stands out as one of the finer points of the book?

TP: I think the authors really got the point that *South Park* is a philosophical show that deals with all kinds of important issues.

MS: Right. I was impressed with the depth and breadth of the chapters, especially "Vote or Die, Bitch" which sounds strikingly similar to Patrick Henry's "Give me liberty or give me death" . . . but with a west-side backbeat feel, mother-fucker.

RA: What would you say sucks about the book?

MS (looking at Trey): Who was the guy who wrote that shit piece that just droned on and on and on about friggin' fallacies and crap like that?

TP: Oh yeah . . . something about Chewbacca and bullshit logic lessons.

RA: That was my chapter.

(Silence)

TP: Best shit piece in the book, no doubt.

MS: No doubt.

RA: This is a book in the Blackwell Philosophy and Pop Culture series, and one of the points of these books is to use a fad, event, or phenomenon in pop culture as a way to introduce people to philosophy. Do you think that's a good idea?

MS: Absolutely. Anything that can get the masses to start thinking.

TP: I think they should do one called "Assaholics and Philosophy." An assaholic is just like an alcoholic, except he's addicted to being an asshole . . . like Dick Cheney.

RA: Who are "those bastards" that are referred to in the show after Kenny gets killed?

TP: George Bush and the entire GOP.

RA: You mean to tell me that George Bush and the GOP are responsible for Kenny's death every episode?

MS: Well, actually it's George Bush, the GOP, and everyone who votes republican.

TP: And it's not just Kenny's death they're responsible for . . . you remember that thing called freedom of speech?

RA: You guys don't seem to have any problem making fun of religion. Do you think that's a good message to send out to people?

MS: Look, what's the difference between believing in god and believing in Santa Claus or the Tooth Fairy? The answer is . . . nothing. So, like Freud says, it's about time people grew up and got rid of the "big daddy in the sky" nonsense idea.

TP: Wait . . . there's no such thing as the Tooth Fairy!?

RA: Why the sappy moralizing endings?

TP: We want to make a point and, sometimes, the point is just to make a point. Or, other times the point is to make a point about some point that someone made, but they didn't know they made it because they missed the entire point about making points.

RA: Will you purchase the book?

MS: Not on your mother's fucking life . . .

TP: I may . . . just so I can photocopy the entire thing and return it for a refund. Rob, I actually put together a "Top-Ten Things to do with *South Park and Philosophy* Other than Read It." Would you like to hear it?

RA: Sure.

TP: Number 10: Tear out pages and wrap Christmas ornaments for storage. Number 9: Use as platform on bathroom sink for grandma's dentures. Number 8: Paste *South Park and Philosophy* cover over *The Atkins Diet and Philosophy* cover at Border's so as to bring total sale of the *Atkins Diet* book to a whopping ten. Number 7:

Buy 10,000 copies just so you can tear off the cover and wallpaper your bedroom. Number 6: Send copies to friends commemorating the 250th anniversary of the publication of Kant's *Critique of Pure Reason*. Number 5: On drumset, tape on inside of kick drum as dead ringer. Number 4: Submerge in vat of Elmer's glue, let dry, and use as boomerang. Number 3: Carve out hole, stash dope, and place on shelf alongside other classics such as *Hip Hop and Philosophy* and *Buffy the Vampire Slayer and Philosophy*. Number 2: Buy ten, cut into tiny pieces, and eat so you secure that "Most *South Park and Philosophy* Books Eaten" record in the Guinness Book of World Records. And the Number 1 thing to do with *South Park and Philosophy* other than read it: place on coffee table just before chick comes over so you can appear smart in order to get laid.

RA: Well, thanks guys.

TP: You bet.

MS: Hope it sells . . .

SCREW YOU GUYS ... I'M GOING HOME

Acknowledgments

First, I want to thank my wife's brother and his wife, Rob and Melinda, who turned me onto *South Park* in the winter of 1997 by telling me something to the effect of, "You *gotta* see this show." The first episode I saw was "Mr. Hankey, the Christmas Poo" and, at that time, I thought it was the funniest thing I had ever seen in my life. Every once in a while, I still tell my wife, "Gosh . . . you sure do smell all nice and flowery!"

Bill Irwin has been incredibly patient with my somewhat obsessive compulsive personality; he's a solid guy – sharp, reasonable, and down to earth. Jeff Dean, at Blackwell, is a great support and a person who is willing to listen to creative ideas. I thank the two of them for believing in the project, along with Kevin Decker, who has been helpful from the very beginning and took a look through my chapter for this volume.

A Mr. Hankey "hidy-ho" goes out to the authors of this volume for all of their hard work. Because of their insights, I have become convinced of the importance of a show like *South Park* for free-thinking adults in a democratic, pluralistic society. This volume would not exist if it were not for the creativity of Matt Stone and Trey Parker, so much thanks goes to them as well.

In a large way, my own humor derives from my family growing up. So much love – but not the Chef kind of hot, sweet, love – goes out to my mom and dad, LaVerne and Jerry Arp, and my sister and her husband, Laura and Jim McDonald. Also, Wally DeRoeck is a lifelong friend and confidant. Finally, I thank my wife, Susan, for her continued insights, unconditional love, and support. The Chef kind of hot, sweet, love could go out to her, no problem.

CHEF'S SALTY BALL-LESS INDEX